The Permaculture Student 2
The Workbook

Matt Powers

Thank you to all the experts, crowdfunders, and collaborators who contributed to this work directly and indirectly - we are in this together. Thank you for making this true.

ISBN: 978-0-9977043-9-6
Copyright © 2018 by Matt Powers. All Rights Reserved.
Published by PowersPermaculture123, WA, USA.

All rights reserved, including the right to reproduce this book or portions thereof in any form whatsoever without author permission.

Contact: PowersPermaculture123, 28419 SE 67th St, Issaquah, WA, 98027

This publication contains the opinions and ideas of the author and the resources used to create this work. It is intended to provide helpful and informative material on the varied subjects addressed in the work. It is sold with the understanding that the author and publisher are not engaged in rendering medical, health, or any kind personal professional services in this book. The reader should consult their medical care providers before adopting any of the suggestions in this book or drawing inferences from it. This work is informational based on empirical and research data. What can work in one case study can fail in another for a variety of reasons. The author and publisher are not responsible for anything that may go wrong or for any negative consequences in relation to applying or attempting to apply the ideas, concepts, or recipes in this book. In addition we are required by law to say that there are no financial guarantees in this book, but the intent is to provide materials that will aid in success in all areas of life and business in harmony with the biodiversity and people systems of all areas.

Table of Contents

Introduction to Change p. 1

Observation p. 2

MapMaking: Your Site p. 5

Planning: Your Dream p. 22

Research: The Possible p. 27

Action: The Reality p. 33

Water p. 34

Soil p. 53

Fungi p. 67

Earthworks p. 78

Trees & Food Forests p. 85

Gardening p. 97

Regenerative Ranching p. 113

Regenerative Agriculture p. 118

Aquaculture p. 122

Water & Ocean Restoration p. 130

Land Restoration p. 133

Alternative Energy p. 139

Permatecture p. 148

Social Permaculture p. 151

Your Next Step: The Future p. 165

About the Author p. 166

References p. 167

Index p. 172

Introduction to Change

Are you ready for change?

Change always comes and will keep coming. "The ineluctable modality of the visible" as Joyce describes extends through all the holons contained within and without our world and ourselves. If we are ready to make changes, we must be ready to change and be changed.

This book is designed to spread change. This is not just a workbook for your yard, your ranch, and your bioregion - this is a book for life on earth. It includes social, economic, horticultural, agricultural, and more methods and strategies for partnering harmoniously with nature. Acquiring a notebook dedicated to writing in your answers to the questions in this book is highly recommended - your answers will change every time you design something new, reflect, and throughout the seasons of your life. You can go paperless and type it on a computer, but there's something unique to using pencil or pen and paper to work out ideas.

This book was written as a companion to **The Permaculture Student 2**, but it is also designed to be used independently, so here and there sections from the textbook are adapted, copied, condensed, reframed, and combined with new content in new frameworks and patterns. I hope you enjoy it, use it wisely, and explore beyond these pages in further research and your own experience.

Thank you for choosing to live regeneratively,

Matt Powers

Observation

The World is your Oyster

Everything waits to be recognized, and much of the amazing possibilities open to us are left untouched in our daily lives. We can see this throughout history as well. Wheels were used on toys in PreColumbian America, but they weren't used for anything else. A plow with a fulcrum wasn't employed in Europe until it was observed in China. We often blame ourselves, our luck, our lack of creativity, or our attitude for missing something ubiquitous or easily available, but it is our observation that determines it, and though a positive attitude will allow us to observe more of our world, we don't even have to have a negative outlook on life to miss powerful insights - we could just be living in an area or spending time in a space not exposed yet to those ideas. We must explore, interact, and encounter new ideas and insights to improve our ability to observe - observation is active learning in real-time with our senses. In this sense, all education is observing new ideas and trying to incorporate them into our understanding - the ultimate learning comes from nature itself. Sharing nature's point of view is ultimately the most empowering, effective, creative, and influential, so observe with an eye to the possible using natural patterns even as you examine for faults and flaws.

Though there is some evidence to synchronistic inventions and discoveries happening across the globe in near simultaneity, we all instead tend to learn by observation, experimentation, and adaptation. As adults we learn much the way we did as babies: we observe, test things out, reflect on that, and try again. This is what we call the Scientific Method, but it's also basic to all wise observation, learning, and application. One of the advantages we have over our younger selves is we can think about thinking and grow in leaps and bounds with our minds well organized. We can in a sense observe ourselves as much as we can observe others and the world around us. This objectivity and reflection are keys to success in interacting with any system. If we are to know how to appropriately apply ethics, principles, techniques, and strategies, we first invest time in observation to know what we are working with and how it all should be done. It all begins with observation.

Keys to Observation

Slow Down. Turn Off. Tune In.
Slow your breathing, quiet your mind, and connect with the space, people, the life, and your body in the moment. Turn off your cell phone, computer, or anything that can interrupt. Empty your pockets and take off your shoes if you can. Feel your feet pressing into the ground. Feel your breathing. Listen. Wait. Let silence build for a few moments "too long", and then begin to observe.

Look Near. Look Far. Look Within. Look to Others.
Sometimes we can get stuck in a pattern of looking at distant views and landscapes, awed by their vastness and beauty, or we look up at the trees and mountains while neglecting what is close and right beneath our feet. Always looks for the connections between what is near and far to tie your understanding of that place together. Asking ourselves questions and seeking our own answers is how we find our own truth and confidence, but to progress, we also need to see the same or similar observations through others eyes and reflect on the similarities and differences. Through this we grow, adapt, and enrich our own perspective.

Don't Impose. Harmonize.
There's an orchestration of life already in motion or implied by the landscape and climate on any given site - if we try to impose an idea, we may cause damage or endanger others. Some areas are just too dry and hot for open water duck ponds; some areas are too cold for chickens in winter outside. If we impose our assumptions with people too, we find conflict quickly. If we instead are keen observers, we can find the "notes" to play that will harmonize with the local symphony of life.

Don't Rush. All Things in their Season.
Observing a landscape for a day or an afternoon is not enough to know that landscape completely, but the more experience observing the landscape the more it tells you and some areas can speak volumes, especially to an experienced eye. That being said, it often takes multiple seasons observing an area to know what is fully possible and what all the guiding patterns are at play. Some design choices are also easier than others, and some seasonal observations can be made anytime of year using GoogleEarth and public data like annual precipitation and county records. It's also important to recognize that these things can

change and can be changed too. You can make that tree line lower to let in more light. We can give local policymakers more autonomy in the regenerative space. We can make more precipitation possible with more trees. Meditate on what you are designing, the objectives, and the observations you've made, and open yourself to the possibilities. Give yourself the time to realize what you wouldn't have thought of if you'd rushed.

Write It Down.

You can film it or type it out, but writing is somehow unique in its ability to connect us to what we are writing down. Write down your observations and experiences to get an entirely new level of understanding and insight. If we regularly write observations of the same site or subject, we remember it and connect those observations to our own understanding more fluently which leads to deeper insight. Keep a garden journal, a gratitude journal, a life statement, a financial record - write it all down and see how your vision begins to take shape.

Don't Stop Observing.

Observation doesn't end when we conceive the design - it manages how the design progresses and adapts over time. The feedback we get from continued observation is invaluable, and the process becomes more valuable every time we do it with new eyes and greater experience.

How to Improve Your Observation Skills

Practice makes perfect. Take the time to immerse yourself in the greatest educational spaces available: thriving natural wilderness. Do your best to leave no trace of your presence in these sacred spaces. Spend your time there observing natural processes. Follow a stream up to its source. Visit old growth forest. Take wilderness, survivalist, or tracking courses to help develop your pattern recognition for native plants, animals, and natural cycles. If permissible take small samples of fungi and healthy soil to bring home from these incredible spaces to scale up their unique and vital microbiology and to observe their activities on your own site. Read accounts of the wild spaces you visit. Read about the history of the geology and indigenous peoples in that area. Try to see the long term changes in the site as they are now. Go bird watching. Go hunting or tracking. The more you immerse yourself with intention with experienced perspectives in wild settings, the more you will improve your observation skills.

MapMaking: Your Site

When we make a map, we are making a visual representation of our understanding. Mapmaking helps us see what we are seeing or considering even if it isn't meant to change or adapt an area or an idea. Though mapmaking might sound linear or purely visual, it often takes some clear understanding through site analysis to make wise decisions on placement and mainframe design.

What's your Climate?

Where do you live in the world? What's your climate? Are you coastal mediterranean? Tropical inland? By a river in cold temperate? Are you landlocked in a desert climate? What's your broad climatic zone? Use the temperature ranges below to guide you. What's your lowest and highest annual temperatures on average? What are the recorded biggest rains, hottest and coldest days, strongest winds, the average soils like? Dive deep into your area: the more you explore, the deeper your insights will go.

In the social setting, knowing our social climate can determine much if not all of our longterm success in our communities. We all can use support from our local communities, and in some cases, it is vital to implement lasting changes. Know your climate, so you plant the right seeds at the right times.

Tropics - At and close to the equator with temps above 18°C/64°F year round
SubTropics - Extends away from the equator to the Tropics of Cancer and Capricorn with temps never below 0°C/32°F
Temperate *(Mediterranean-Warm-Cool-Cold)* - With temps below 0°C/32°F in winter and above 10°C/50°F in summer—this zone extends from the Tropics to the Arctic and Antarctic circles.
Polar - Below 10°C/50°F year round, dominated by ice and snow
Arid - 50cm/19.5 inches or less of rain a year
Desert - 25cm/10 inches or less of rain a year

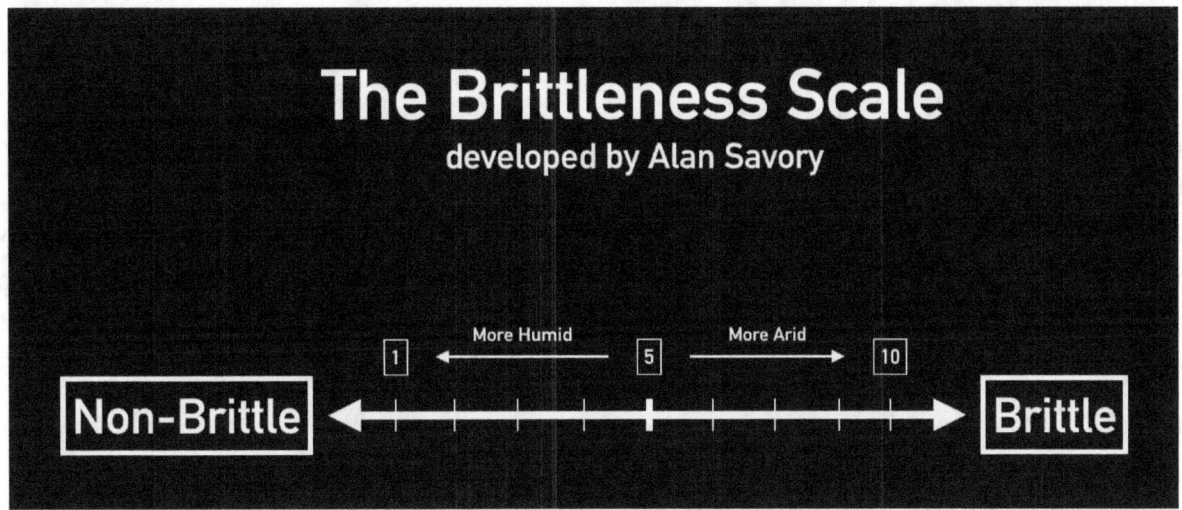

How Brittle is your Climate?

If you disturb your soil, does it quickly get covered and occupied by new vegetation or does the disturbance spread? If it spreads, it is a brittle climate. If it heals quickly, it's a non-brittle climate. Knowing which we are in will guide when and how we use disturbance.

What are your Climate Analogs?

Using the Köppen-Geiger climate classification map online (on Wikipedia.org) we can quickly find the highly specific climate that we belong to - it serves as a climate analog identification map in this way. We can see all the regions in the world that share our relative climate. While every site has microclimates that shift the climate warmer or cooler, drier or wetter, the overall climate is within a common range. This allows us to know what is possible in the global seed pool for that area. We have to be careful to not displace native species by introducing non-natives, but we can at the same time improve ecologies and bring in stability where there is desertification by bringing in new plants and animals. It takes careful experimentation, management, and application, but it can revive gene pools by rewilding genetics with new crosses of all sorts.

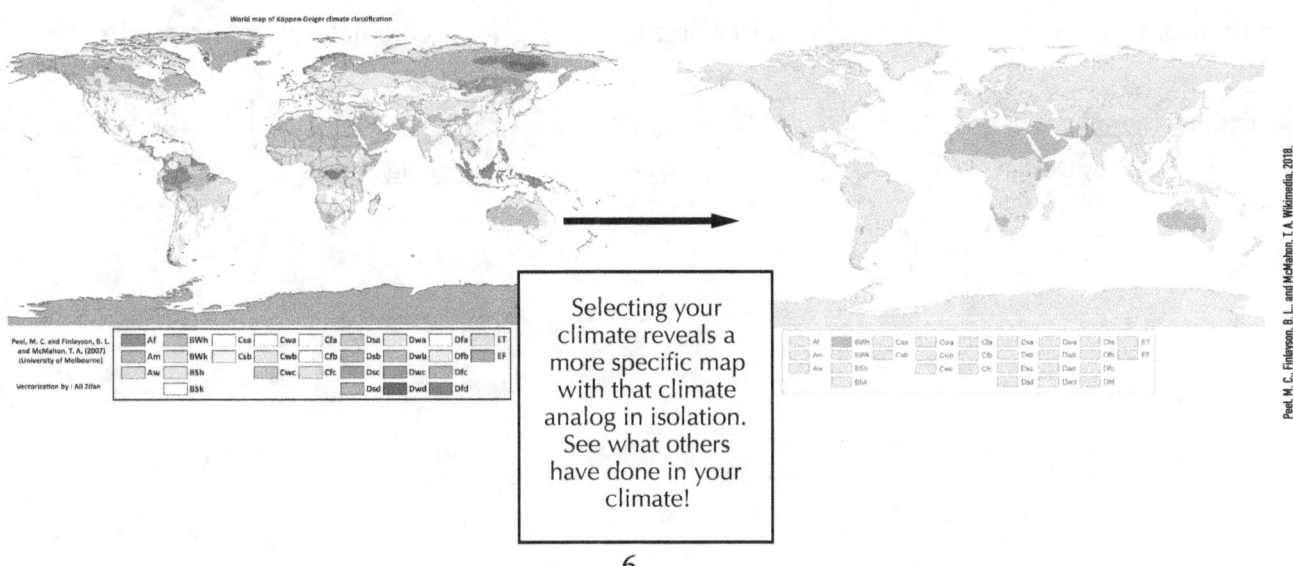

Selecting your climate reveals a more specific map with that climate analog in isolation. See what others have done in your climate!

Visit the Köppen-Geiger climate classification map online and create a list of your climate analogs. Research these areas: what did they eat, what did they grow, what were their medicines, what were their homes like, what diseases did they get, what cooking methods did they use, and what did they wear? Find some recipes online or a recipe book at a local library focused on your region(s). Make a list of desirable plants and animals and research them further, but don't allow yourself to get too set on any one element: just gather and examine each as if it were a piece in a game yet to be played. Understanding our analogs is the only way to wisely apply the elements sourced from them, so keep researching and sharing your ideas with others.

Continue Learning
- Wikipedia's Köppen-Geiger climate classification interactive map: https://en.wikipedia.org/wiki/Köppen_climate_classification

How much Sun? When & Where?

What's your sunpath? What's your sun angle? How does it change throughout the year? There are online sun angle calculators. They can tell you the angle of the sun in the sky throughout the year. At Winter Solstice it is at its lowest, and at Summer Solstice it is at its highest in the sky. At the equator, the path doesn't change much, but at the poles, it is dramatic: some areas are dark for weeks at a time each year. Knowing these things precisely might not matter to your garden because you already can visualize where the light comes in and how it will be throughout the year (either from experience or using GoogleEarth to view the site over the course of the year at both solstices), but for designing a home, food forest, or a homestead, knowing the light angle at different times a year is critical. Where the windows will be placed, the orientation of the house, and how long and low to make the eaves - these are just common considerations and do not encompass the many other times knowing your sun path and angle will help you. Refer to the table on the next page to calculate your sun angle.

Continue Learning
- Sustainable by Design's Sun Angle Calculator http://susdesign.com/sunangle/

Calculating the Sun Angle

Using just a meter long stick on flat ground, we can measure the sun angle at any time. Just hold the stick perfectly upright (you can use a level to do this) and then mark and measure the shadow length. Use the Inverse Tangent function or simply divide height from length and use the tangent chart to find the Sun Angle.

$$\text{Vertical Height} \div \text{Shadow Length} = \text{Tangent}$$
$$2m \div 3m = 0.67 \text{ Tangent}$$

$$\text{Tan}^{-1}(\text{Tangent}) = \text{Sun Angle}$$
$$\text{Tan}^{-1}(0.67) = 34°$$

Tangent	Angle
0.088	5
0.176	10
0.268	15
0.364	20
0.466	25
0.577	30
0.7	35
0.84	40
1	45

Tangent	Angle
1.19	50
1.43	55
1.73	60
2.14	65
2.75	70
3.73	75
5.67	80
11.43	85

Based on information sourced at DesignCoalition.org, 2016.

How much Precipitation, When, & in What Forms?

How much precipitation does your site get? Is your water harder to calculate: does your area rely upon fog condensation for moisture? When does that moisture arrive? Is it relatively uniform throughout the growing season, during distinct time frames, or once a year in a huge storm? Has rainfall been increasing in your area in recent years or decreasing? Has it been stabilizing or destabilizing? Have the events been becoming fewer but heavier or lighter? Considering these questions will help us see the broader and longer term relationships

Calculating Total Precipitation

"Every square meter of land receiving 1mm of water gets 1 liter of water"
Neal Spackman, Sustainable Design Masterclass, 2016.

1m² of land x 1mm of rain = 1 liter of water

1 acre = 4047m²

4" of rain = 102mm of rain

4047m² x 102mm = 412,794 liters
(conversions here are rounded off to avoid decimal places)

In hectares: 1 hectare = 10,000m²

---

between the climate, precipitation, and your site. Those connections can help us plan for the future, foresee changes ahead, create an abundance, and even prevent or avert disaster. Calculate your total precipitation by letting all your precipitation melt to liquid form - track both monthly and annual levels to get a clear picture of your precipitation distribution.

Continue Learning
- *Rainwater Harvesting for Drylands and Beyond* by Brad Lancaster (2013). Paperback.

How much Water is On-site?

Do you have ponds or a lake on your site? How much water do they contain? Are you planning on making any dams? How big? How much water does your land currently hold, and what is the potential carrying capacity for open water?

How to Approximate Dam, Pond, or Lake Volume

average depth x average width ft x average length
= the approximate water volume

2m depth x 4m width x 7m length x 1000*
= 56,000 liters
*needed to convert to liters

To convert liters into US gallons:
liters ÷ 3.785411784 = US gallons

How to Approximate Stream or River Volume

stream length x average width x average depth
= approximate volume
100m x 2m x 0.5m = ~100 m³

How to Calculate Stream Flow Rate

Knowing how fast the water is moving can help us figure out how much water is passing through our site on a daily or even annual basis, but it takes a few steps.

The Cross Sectional Method (or Float Method) for Stream Flow Rate

Mark off a section of stream to measure flow rate within. Calculate the area of a cross section of the stream by first measuring the stream depth at equal intervals across the stream (measuring every half meter or foot). Average the depths and multiply that average by the width of the pond to get the area of cross section.

width x the average depth = cross sectional area
6m x 2m = 12m²

Repeat this process 2 or 3 times in the section of the stream you are using to calculate the flow rate. Average the areas to get a more accurate representation of the stream bed. Next, float a buoyant object down the stream and use a stopwatch to time it. Repeat the process and average your results. Now, calculate the stream's velocity:

distance ÷ average time = velocity
6m ÷ 4 sec = 1.5 m/sec

Velocity Correction is needed to account for the drag created by the bottom of the stream. Smooth stream bed velocities are multiplied by 0.9 while rough stream beds are multiplied by 0.85.

velocity x 0.9 = corrected velocity
1.5 m/sec x 0.9 = 1.35 m/sec

the corrected velocity x the average cross section area
= the stream flow rate
1.35 m/sec x 12m² x 1000* = 16.2L/sec

*to convert from cubic meters into liters

Sources: sciencing.com & appropedia.org

Calculating Annual Runoff
sourced from Brad Lancaster's *Rainwater Harvesting for Drylands and Beyond* (2013)

Catchment area in square meters x Rainfall in Millimeters x Runoff Coefficient
= Net Runoff in Liters

Catchment Area in square feet x Rainfall in feet x 7.48 gal/ft^3* x Runoff Coefficient
= Net Runoff in Gallons

*7.48 is needed to convert the answer into gallons.

100m^2 bare earth x 400mm of rain x Runoff Coefficient

600ft^2 bare earth x 1 ft of rain x 7.48/gal/ft^3 x 0.2 = 897.6 gallons of runoff a year

Runoff Coefficient - This represents the amount of water that does not get caught or is evaporated. Loss can range from 5-20%. Hard surfaces like roofs and pavement would have a 0.95-0.8 runoff coefficient range (i.e. 95% - 80% runoff). 5% loss (0.05) to runoff would mean 95% of the rainfall that fell on the roof stayed, flowed down the gutter, and was stored in the roof rainwater tank. Vegetated areas may be able to have zero runoff in some light rains.

How much Runoff is Flowing into your Pond, Swale, or Rain Barrel?

How much roof runoff or hill runoff are you receiving a year? How much are you receiving in your biggest storm events? This is incredibly valuable information because it begs the question: What happens when your ponds and swales overflow? We must be prepared by running all the approximations and maximums through our designs to see if it is viable. Swales can easily create erosion if used in the wrong climate or soils - or if placed inappropriately.

How much water will you be harvesting?

Calculating Catchment

Using a contour map and starting from the pond site or the furthest edges of your catchment area, trace at a right angle (90°) to contour until the ridge is met on both sides. The outlined area is the water catchment. How much rain do you get in your largest storm events? Your local county records or town or city library will have the maximum rainfall historically recorded. To know what will be coming into your pond or swale during that event you have to calculate the total area you've outlined. On GoogleEarth, it is easy. You can point and click to create something similar to the lower picture and, with added contour lines, gain even greater accuracy. You can then easily multiply the area by the annual rainfall to get precipitation per square meter (or foot) per year.

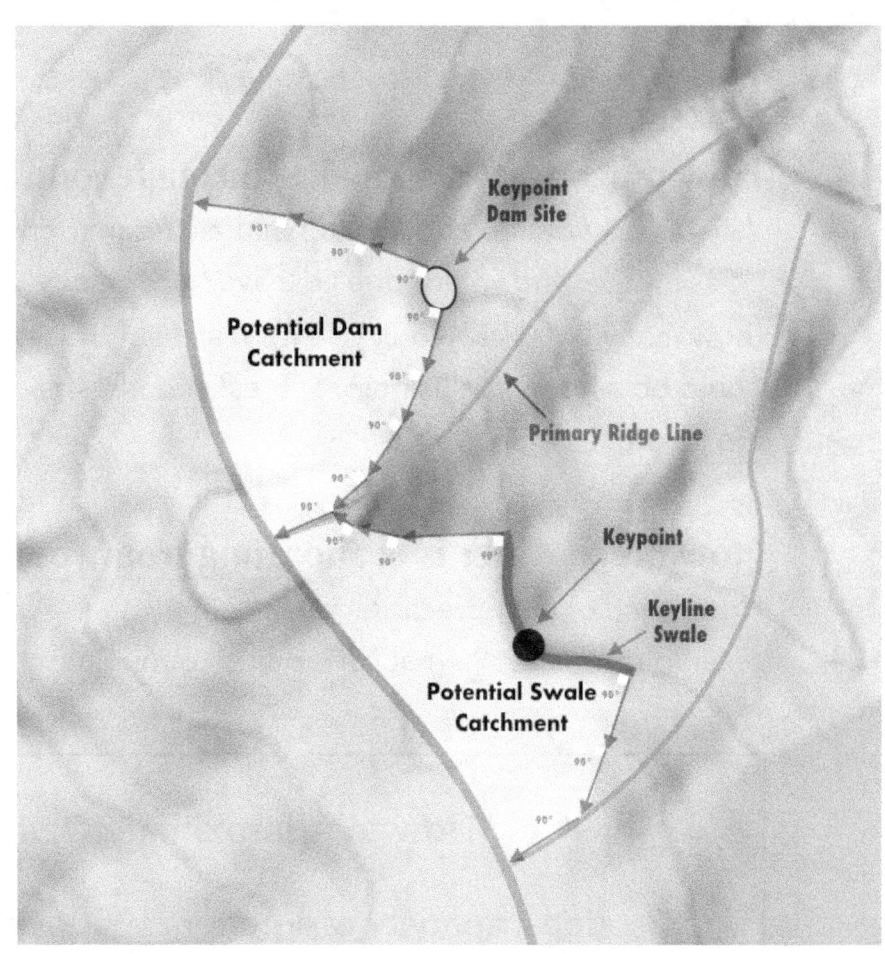

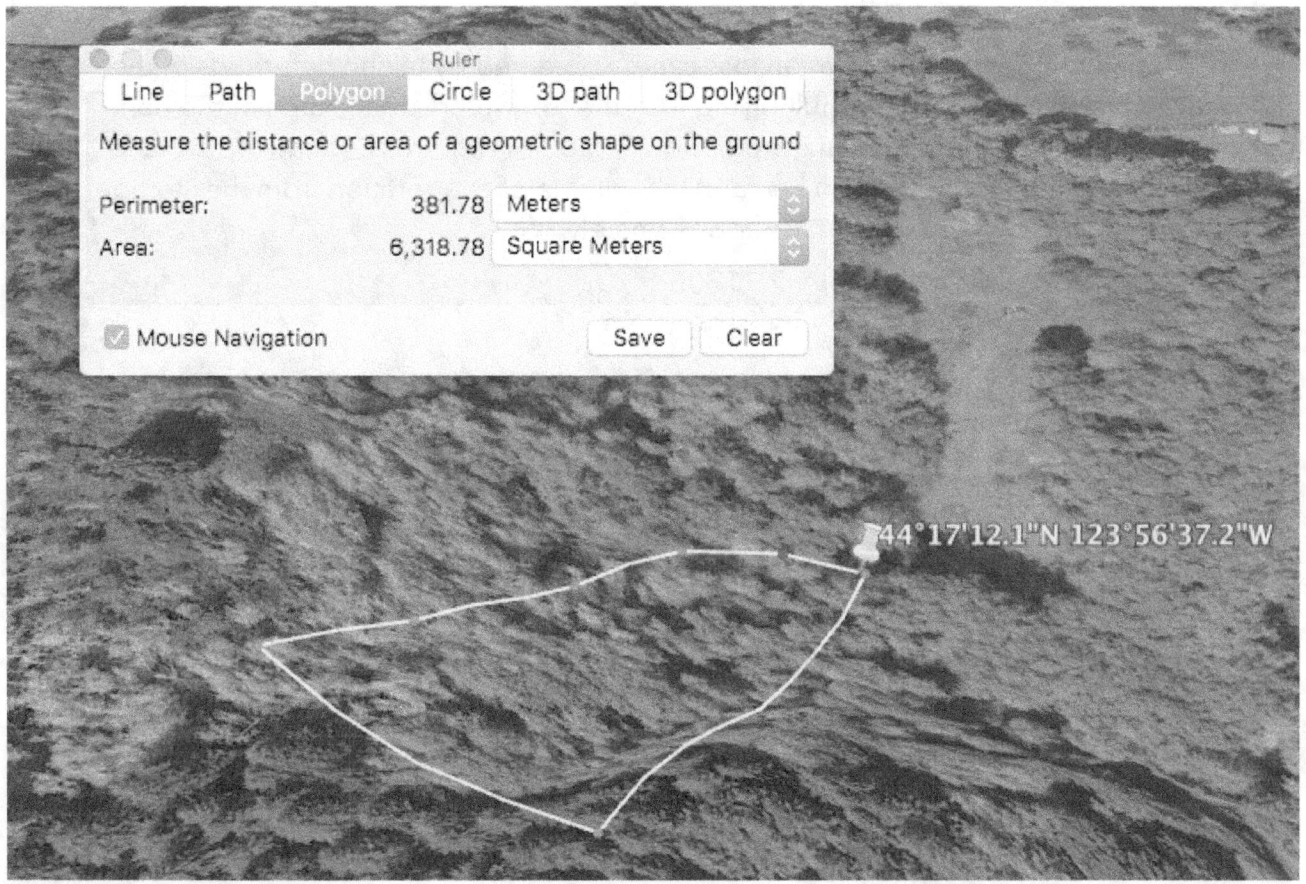

How much water is moving through your Land?

What is the volume of the water in that stream or river? How fast is it moving? Where does it enter and where does it leave? How many uses can you get out of that water (how many times can you cycle it) before it is released out of your system? The site could be a home, a business, a forest, a homestead, an orchard, or a yard. *Refer to the previous pages.*

How much water is evaporating from your ponds each year?

How much of your precipitation is being lost as evaporation from your ponds, pools, reservoirs, or lakes? What can you do to mitigate that or offset it?

How to Approximate Dam Evaporation

2/3 x (local annual evaporation/1000) x surface area of the dam
= approximate annual dam evaporation

"A rough figure for the evaporation loss can be obtained by taking two-thirds of the local annual evaporation and multiplying it by the top water surface area of the dam. For example, if the local annual evaporation is 1200 millimetres and the top surface area 5000 square metres (half an hectare) the volume of evaporation from the storage is approximately

$$\frac{2}{3} \times \frac{1200}{1000} \times 5000$$

which is equal to 4000 cubic metres or 4 megalitres"
Nelson, K.D. <u>Design and Construction of Small Earth Dams</u>. 1985.

How much Wind & from Where?

From which direction(s) do the prevailing winds come from in your area? The trees flag or lean away from the constant wind, but we can just as easily find wind patterns that change seasonally or present complex behaviors. Knowing the wind direction(s) will help you create effective windbreaks, animal shelters, homes, and food forests as well as provide locations for wind power generation.

How much wind? Build or buy an anemometer. You can build one by having 4 cups connected horizontally on a cardboard cross that is pinned to a pencil eraser but loose enough to spin. Make sure to have all the cups facing the same direction, so wind can catch them and spin them all the right way - they should be sideways and identical in the way they are attached to each arm of the cross. Spin the anemometer over your head and count the rotations in a 30 second span of time.

Calculate Your Wind Speed

(# Rotations in 30 sec x the rotation's diameter in cm) ÷ 265 = Windspeed in kph
(# Rotations in 30 sec x the rotation's diameter in inches) ÷ 168 = Windspeed in mph

(160 rotations x 30 cm) ÷ 265 = 18 kph
(150 rotations x 18 inches) ÷ 168 = 16 mph

Source: eHow.com

What Other Larger Cycles & Patterns Exist?

Are there 50 or 100 year cycles or patterns in your area? Do you have something like El Nino or extended droughts that can sometimes last hundreds of years? A prime example, California, has had a long history of both. Maybe it's the opposite in your area, and it floods instead every century washing out unsuspecting establishments of all kinds. You might even face seasonal fire in a pyrophytic mediterranean landscape, or you might have a volcano or regular earthquakes. You might have spikes of heat or cold that even kills indigenous species of plant and animal. While our climate instability may increasingly become the norm, we can do a lot to mitigate and start to reverse the trend. Keep in mind the outliers as you design - nature throughout history has humbled us with new surprises, and the future will be no different. Design with an eye to resilience even in the throes of major stressors.

Calculating Record Rain Events

total area x heaviest rainfall event x runoff coefficient
= approximate runoff in a record 24 hr rain event

Knowing this information effects the size and design of the pond, freeboard, dam wall, spillway, and level sill.

What About Snowmelt?

Snowfall can be melted and measured just like rain. We can see how much water awaits to be runoff. Knowing how long the annual snow melt lasts can reveal the average rate for that snow to turn into liquid water again, but it is trickier as seasons are not fixed and uniform with their changes year to year and some soils absorb water more than others - it makes for a broad generalization that can sometimes fail us in our design considerations if we do not use it carefully.

total precipitation in snow ÷ days of average snowmelt
= average rate of snowmelt

20cm of melted snow ÷ 2 days = ~10 cm per day

Now you can use your daily snowmelt rate to calculate the runoff for that area:

total area x daily snowmelt rate x runoff coefficient
=
approximate rate of runoff during snowmelt over a 24 hr period

$1000 m^2$ x ~10 cm/day x 0.9 x 0.001* = 9 L of water in 24 hrs

*to convert to liters

How Distant from the Ocean or Large Bodies of Water?

While it's nice to know how far you have to go to harvest some sea water or sea salt, it's vital to recognize the mitigating power of water on the climate. British Columbia's coast enjoys a beautiful climate. San Diego's cool breezy climate turns into dry desert soon after leaving the coastal region. Michigan's ability to grow a wide range of food has a lot to do with the great lakes creating a coastal effect. The deeper our winters and summers can be the further we are from water as well. We can use water in our designs to create microclimates and protect areas from frost.

What's Your Elevation?

Changing your elevation changes a lot of factors. Just go and try to bake a cake at sea level and then at 5,000 ft with the same recipe, heat, and timing: it won't turn out the same! Elevation seems like we are moving away from the equator because it gets colder, but it doesn't change the sunpath, aspect, and intensity. As we go up in elevation, the air thins and air pressure changes which affects all sorts of things like the way corn regulates growth. In Peru, Pisscorunto corn grown at 2,700-3,000m (8,000-9,000ft) elevation can grow to be a polite 2 - 4 m (7-12ft) tall, but take the corn out of the highlands, and it can grow freakishly tall, 6-8m (18-21ft). I was able to adapt this corn by mimicking its light patterns from Peru and growing it at 670m (2,000ft) elevation. The light also gets more intense as you go up in elevation. The higher you go, the less life and diversity there is because of the intensity of the light, thinness of the air, the changes in the water behaves, and overall harshness of the climate.

What's Your Orientation?

Are you facing the sun or are you on the dark side of a hill? I used the dark side of a hill to mimic Peru's light patterns to adapt Pisscorunto corn, so it's not a "bad" thing to be in the shade as long as you design with it in mind. In contrast, full sun in Central Valley California can easily scorch many plants labeled full sun in the seed catalog. While it can be intense, the sun is the source of energy for all life. Create multiple canopies to handle excessive sun. Trap the sun's energy in plant life and soil carbon. If you don't get enough light, design ways to magnify the light.

What's Your Slope?

Knowing how steep your site is can guide your zone planning: 20-40+% slope areas are typically too steep for anything but perennial-based systems unless terraces are used. Proper soils, creative placement and selection of plants to hold the terraces together, and proper construction can create stable structures that can last millennia. In contrast, many areas that look flat are not and catchment using even a subtle slope can be dramatic. Calculate all your major slopes and add the results to your maps.

$$(\text{Rise} \div \text{Run}) \times 100 = \text{Slope \%}$$
$$(1 \div 3) \times 100 = 33.3\%$$

What's Your Aspect?

How is your slope angle in relation to the sun path - is that area absorbing the solar radiation? The more perpendicular the slope aspect to the sunpath - the more it faces the sunpath directly, the more energy gets absorbed. Receiving light indirectly lessens its absorption. Where is the area of the most direct light for the longest period of time during the growing season? Is the house shaded in summer? Will that hill get the sunlight it needs for the forage to be sufficient for my grazing animals with a 7m high windbreak in this position or will that windbreak cast a shadow, shrinking the number of frost-free days for that area? Figure out what are the questions you need to ask to utilize your solar radiation wisely.

Make a Topographic Map

A topographic map is excellent at displaying a landscape profile. Topographic maps can be found online for almost anywhere in the world now, though you may find that those surveys don't account for recent changes to the land. This is why GPS devices which indicate latitude, longitude, and elevation are used to map site coordinates to generate a topographic map. Drones can be used as well - both to take up-to-date photos and to map the topography. For designs that require precision like a house, large commercial orchard, large fence installation, or city planning, using the most accurate and professional mapping services available is one of the best ways to insure a safe and accurate installation.

Make a Multilayered Map

Just having one layer won't help you make the design decisions needed - just making a topographic map won't convey a complete story though they are incredibly powerful. Maps can also show prevailing winds, sun paths, areas that are in permanent shade, proposed planting arrangements, changes throughout the season, areas of flooding, earthworks, underground hazards, and more. They can also be used to calculate areas, distances, and catchment. Maps can be arranged stacked on top of each other on the computer or printed out as transparencies.

Making a Topographic Map with SketchUp Pro

There is a quick and easy way to generate a contour map using SketchUp Pro, a graphic design program that architects and landscapers use to articulate and communicate their ideas. There are thousands of videos and webpages dedicated to describing how to make a map with this professional program. The program can grab a section of terrain from GoogleEarth using the GeoLocation: Add Location function under the File tab - Show Terrain under GeoLocation must be turned on to see the terrain. Adding the lines gets a little trickier: you have to place a level and flat shape at the lowest point in the terrain, and make sure it is bigger than the section you are adding contour lines to. From there you, copy and paste that same shape vertically (along the blue axis) a hundred or more times equidistantly at intervals like 1m, 1 ft, or 10 ft, so it covers the entire height of the terrain to be contour mapped. You can then highlight the entire group and right click and choose Explode. Then right click and choose Intersect Faces. Then you can erase the shapes intersecting your terrain. You will have a terrain now with contour lines. You can even now erase the original terrain map and have only the contour lines remain! To account for the multiplicity of SketchUp versions out there and to make this easier, you can watch a few videos on youtube - it's quicker and simpler than you think!

Making a Topographic Map with MyTopo.com

There are topographic maps for almost everywhere on earth now, and many are free and online - some like MyTopo.com allow you to create maps to order. If you can screenshot, overlay images, and change the opacity of images, you will be able to create a quick and generalized topographic map using MyTopo.com's free features. The contour lines below are at every 20 ft, and the 2 acre site's growing area is almost 20% slope on average. These generalized maps show the watersheds superbly and give our smaller sites a larger context. For larger sites, this can be a superb map to start out with. You can take this concept to another level using GoogleEarth to do the same thing.

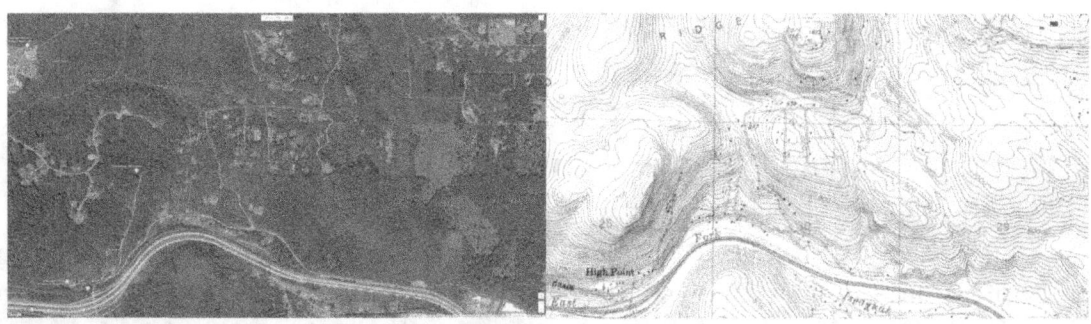

A 2 acre site

In GoogleEarth, Layers are a primary function of the program. You can create layers, hide and remove them, zoom in as close or far as you like, and share them in various arrangements and opacities. This makes GoogleEarth an incredibly powerful tool for communicating and analyzing landscape and design.

Making a Topographic Map with GoogleEarth

GoogleEarth allows you to import images just like we did manually by taking a screenshot in the MyTopo.com example above. The only problem with that was it was a macro point of view - we couldn't zoom in! By importing that same topographic image into GoogleEarth, we can overlay it until it matches using the Image Overly function under the Add tab in navigation bar at the top of the screen.

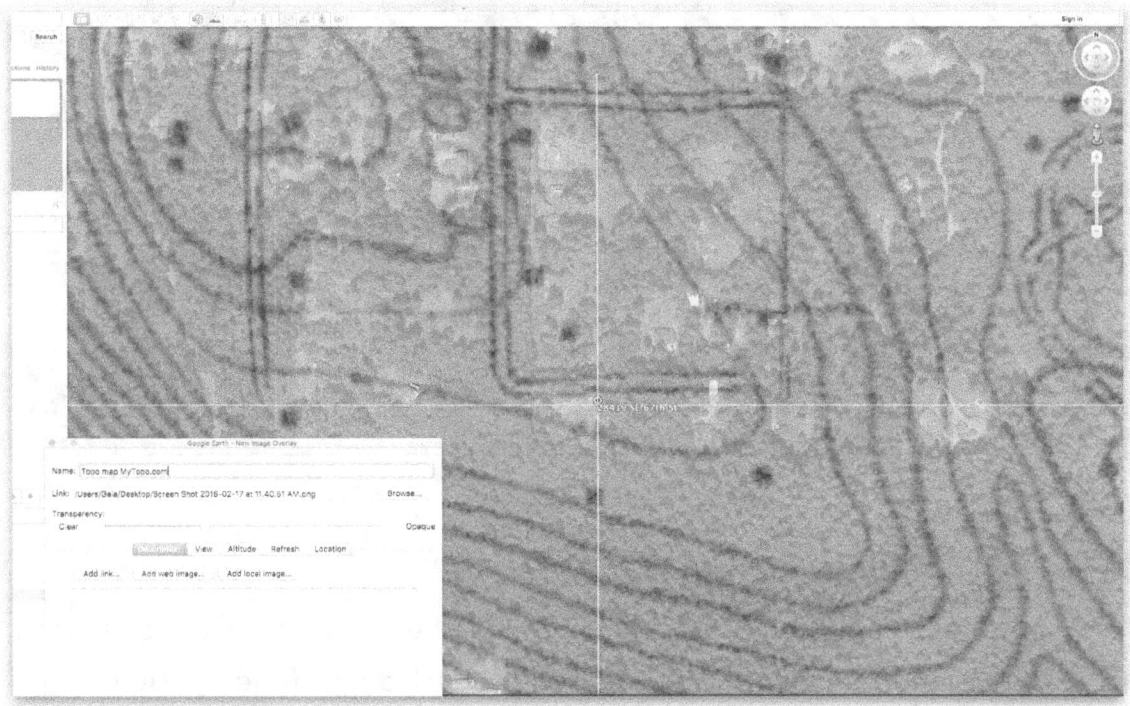

Then we can choose the Add Path function from the top toolbar and trace the contour - you can even name it for its elevation.

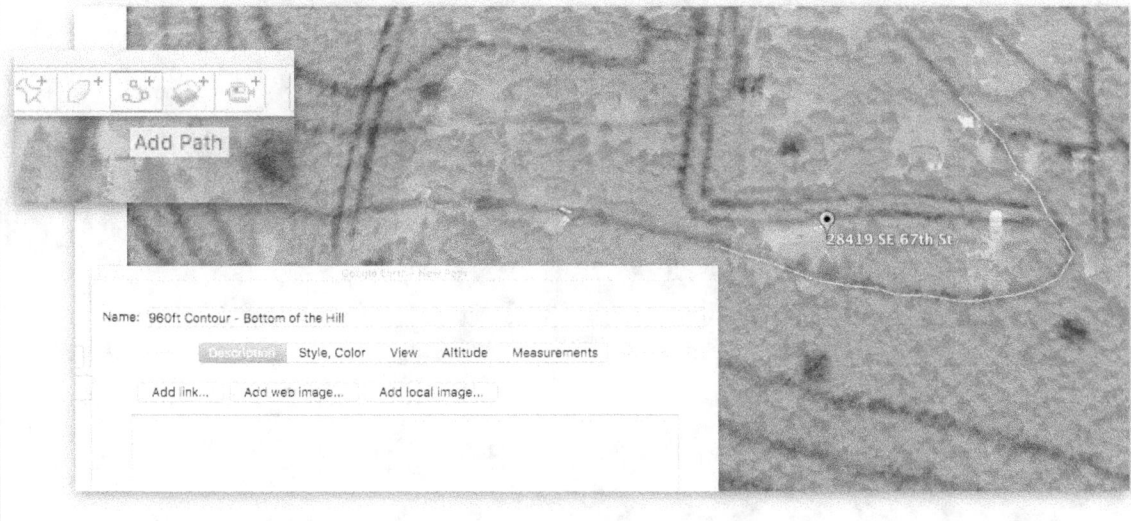

Now you can remove the guidelines and see your site at any distance with your clear contours - notice how my lower garden is on contour with many homes and how we are below other homes? That means we need to be very careful about the runoff and groundwater we receive because we are potentially taking on biocides, heavy metals, and more toxins that need to be addressed before they can enter the garden, orchard, or our bodies. Though the contours are set to 20ft - topographic maps can be generated that are set to any distance.

If All Else Fails, Still Make a Map

If you can only make a map on paper with a pencil, then start there, but start mapping out the site, your ideas, and deepening your understanding of the possible.

Planning: Your Dream

Every great accomplishment starts with a goal and a plan. Consistent accomplishment is no accident. Using these questions and frameworks we can get different perspectives on our design: we may change our mind as we inspect the design from different perspectives. It may no longer fit our goals because of the landscape profile, a neighbor's proximity, or any given reason, but the process of analysis is similar to creating and using map layers.

List your Available Resources

What does your site already have? Do you have a garden? Do you have pasture? Do you have a tractor? Do you have friendly and experienced neighbors? Do you have family or friends in the area? What local organizations could help? Does the site have ample water? Water rights? Electricity? What resources do you have? Do you have seeds or trees ready to plant? Do you have goats to help clear the land? What tools do you have? Do you have a budget for this project?

Decide to Manifest What You Lack

Become determined to acquire all you need to accomplish your goals, no matter what it takes (within the boundaries of the 3 ethics). When we are determined, we allow failure to become our teacher, and by doing this, our performance will immediately begin to improve at an exponential rate. It's this confidence, determination, and focus that guides those of us who accomplish audacious dreams and goals, so as you set your goals, do so with conviction and faith. What education or skills do you need to accomplish these goals? How will you have to change to make these new goals possible? Who will you have to become?

Define your Holistic Goal(s)

What are you trying to accomplish? Why are you trying to accomplish it? Why are you trying to accomplish that? Play this game enough and you will arrive at your deepest seated reason for being and desiring. From here we can explore and complex our goals into a holistic goal that takes the full context of our situation into consideration - this does imply that we are limited by our current understanding. This is exactly why further study, reflection, and revision are always needed with all goals both longterm and short term.

The Framework of Holistic Management

Using the holistic management framework, we can help shape, refine, and generate our holistic goals.

- *Define the Whole* - Define what it is in its entirety that you are working on.
- *Set Ethical Short-term and Long-term Goals* - Set goals for what you want and need based on how things will be in the future, not as they are now.
- *Observe and Document* - Careful observation for signs of degeneration or regeneration gives managers early indicators for course correction. Documentation helps locate patterns, extend retention, and deepen comprehension.
- *Use your Toolkit* - These are in no way limited to Savory's list for cattle management; your toolkit will likely have specific tools addressing your situation, but his list includes: financial capital, human ingenuity, herbivores, wildlife, soil biology, fire, rest, and technology. The concept can be adapted to any situation: you might add carnivores or seasonal flooding.
- *Test your Decisions* - For economic, financial, and social success over both the long-term and short-term, choices must be tested and reflected upon from different angles and through different lenses.
- *Feedback Loop* - Without regular monitoring, reflection, and adaptation, productivity and the regenerative progress will inevitably decrease. Apply your insights.

The Regrarians Platform

The Regrarians Platform is a superb design framework that captures the full holistic picture in its scope and guides designers logically through foundational design decisions. It builds off PA Yeomans Scale of Permanence with two additional yet equally critical aspects to consider: Economy and Energy. The amazing logic of this platform is each section works in succession and informs the ones after it. Your climate determines your geography while your geography and climate determine your water on site. Whatever you do, you will want to access that water,

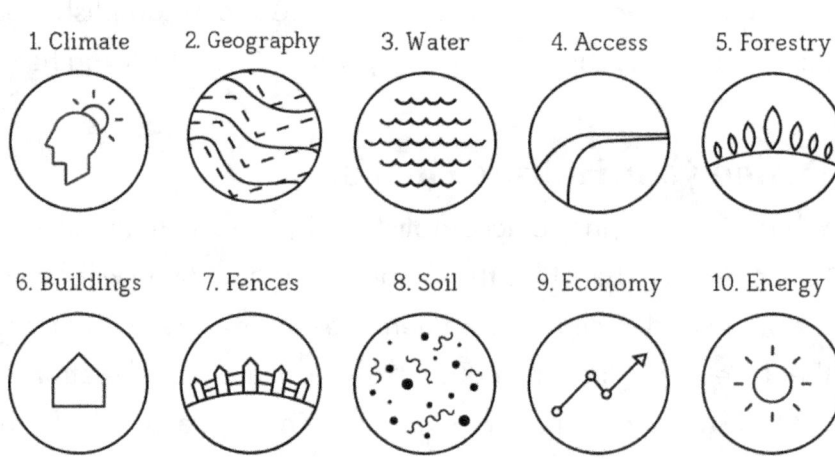

Regrarians Platform® www.Regrarians.org, Regrarians Ltd 2018.

and the water access and the geography will determine the road placements. Those roads will cut up the landscape which will divide up the landscape to a degree. The access, geography, water, and climate will determine where the forest and windbreaks will be planted - slopes, ridges, watersheds, etc. Once those sites are clearly defined, sheltered areas for the buildings will become obvious especially when examined through the lenses of the climate, geography, the access, and the water access. Once the buildings are up - fences can be considered (though Joel Salatin says use a temporary fence for 3 years before installing an expensive permanent one - in all likelihood you will move the fence!) Once those fences are up or active and mobile, we can begin to improve the soil with a focus on the goals for the site. The size of the area fenced off can often determines the soil improvement method, and you want your soils, the foundation for all operations on the site, to be deep and robust. The next section to consider is economy: how is the farm or ranch going to produce a return on investment - the previous sections should define the possible in many ways, making it easier to determine what could be grown or raised on that landscape. Lastly, how is it all going to be powered - is it rendered lard biodiesel in that tractor? Is it all solar power? How will it get off the grid? The Regrarians Platform is elegantly simple but endless complex as you begin to apply it.

Continue Learning
- Learn the Regrarians Platform in-depth with the creator of the platform, Darren Doherty, in REX, his online course and online global community of Regrarians: Rex.farm

Zone Planning & Analysis

Zone planning helps us arrange the elements of our system to limit the distance we travel to tasks by having high maintenance elements closer to home and elements we rarely access or are easy to manage from a distance further from the home. The exact layout of the zones will differ with each design based on the elements included, the geography, the people involved, the economics involved, and the designer's own style of designing.

- **Zone 0** - The home or house which can include an attached greenhouse, shadehouse, trellis, passive solar, etc. Seeds can be saved indoors, fungi can be prepared and grown, and numerous other regenerative plans and actions occur in the home. (Sometimes zone zero refers to the self as well).
- **Zone 1** - The immediate area around the home is ideal for elements that need continuous observation like tree nurseries, greenhouses, vermicompost, kitchen and herb gardens, edible and medicinal mushroom patches and logs, and quiet animals like rabbits. Other common elements: rainwater catchment, trellis, graywater systems, and greenhouses. This is an area you pass or visit

daily and can spend time daily working in. This is also the area that usually has the longest growing season, being warmed by the house and closely attended.

- **Zone 2** - This area is less intensive and less visited than Z1. It includes small domestic stock, orchards, food forests, small pastures, broadacre crops, and animals shelters that connect to Z1 ideally. This area is visited every other day or just briefly once a day though it can occupy longer periods of time routinely as well.
- **Zone 3** - This is often a place of seasonal, annual, or monthly work, and it usually requires animals or machines to manage. It includes broadacre crops, larger animals, larger pastures, natural or low maintenance trees, large water storages, barns, feed-storage, windbreak, and hedgerow.
- **Zone 4** - This the wildest of the managed areas in the system; it borders the wilderness. It includes: timber, the largest pastures, firewood, native and non-native hardy trees, and large water storages. This is an area that is visited seasonally for specific tasks and lightly interacted with.
- **Zone 5** - The unmanaged or least-managed zone, Z5 is wilderness for hunting, timber, foraging, wild fungi, restoration, water catchment, and observation.

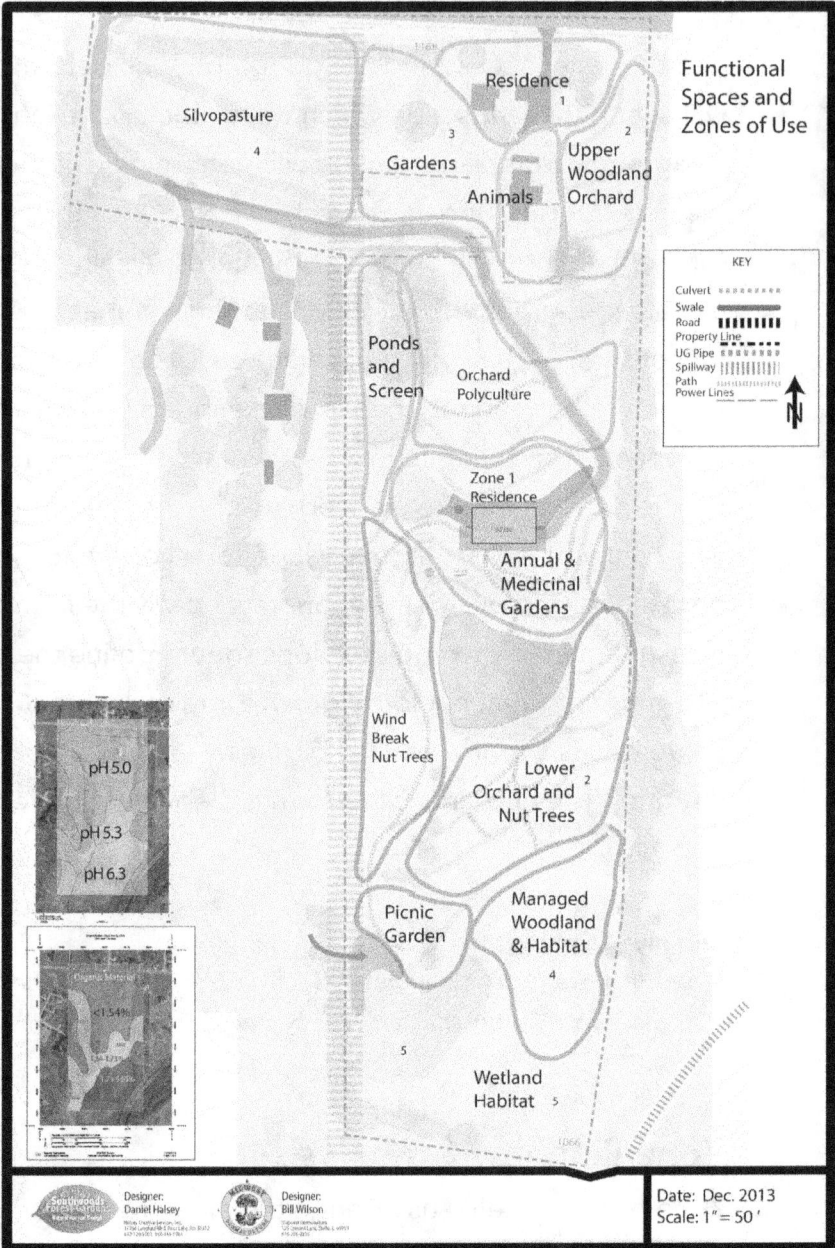

How can you Reuse, Repurpose, Share, Recycle, Connect, or Stack the Components?

Looking back at your design, at your resources, at your goals, and all the elements that can shift (if you've done the Regrarians Platform, you might discover you have a well-defined space to work within with implicit possibilities inherent in that area). Shuffle things around in your head or on paper. What can connect? What can stack? For instance, having the duck pond above the garden allows the pond water to drain directly into the garden, routinely delivering liquified, aerated, and diluted duck manure to the garden soil. Maybe your bunnies are above the garden, so their manure rolls down the hill? Maybe your garden and chicken yard trade places each season in the classic victory garden style? You never know what might come to you if you give yourself the time to consider what you wouldn't have.

Get Feedback, Reflect, & Adapt

Share your ideas and designs with others. Reflect on their feedback, create a new plan, and adapt. Always make room in your mind and in your plans as much as possible for change - your plans will change as you consider the details and as time goes on. Over your lifetime, the landscape may not change, but your goals and perspective will.

Research: The Possible

Make Lists

Making lists can show us the possible even as it demonstrates the limits. When we make lists, we can select the best of the best in each area as well as problem solve complex or problem areas by searching through the elements on the lists. Making lists gives us a mental break and allows our working memory to reset, making space for new epiphanies and recollections to bubble up.

Scour your climate analogs for plants, animals, methods, techniques, and strategies, and add them to the lists you've accumulated from your local region and national hardiness zone. It's not about selection yet - it's about accumulation. Let your curiosity guide you: what new tastes and textures are out there waiting for you? What new fruits? Nuts? Perennial vegetables? Building designs? Alternative energy sources? Recipes? Water harvesting designs?

List the Possible Plants & Animals

- *Annual and Biennial Plants* – grouped around season
- *Perennial Plants* – grouped around season
- *All Plants* – grouped by forest layer
- *Mulch Plants* – grouped around season
- *Animal Feed and Forage Plants* – grouped around season and animal
- *Animals* - list the animals and their behaviors, needs, products, characteristics, and functions

Test your Soil

Testing is the only way to know for certain if you have heavy metals contaminating your soils or stubborn carcinogenic pesticide residues present. It's also a great way to prove to yourself how critical life can be for dirt to transform into soil. You can also predict the outcome of planting a field of corn before you even plant a seed if you know the average NPK levels of your soil. Soil tests can reveal advantages and disadvantages as well as successes and failures. In many areas there are soil profiles for the entire region described in county records, online, and freely available, and you can get a better understanding of what to expect and plan for when using them. Try out all the soil tests you can (geotechnical, NPK, soil food web, etc.) using samples from 5-10 locations on the site. Send soil samples in to the Soil Food Web Inc. certified laboratories to get a detailed report on the soil life - certified laboratories are listed online here: http://soilfoodweb.com/Labs.html Local universities and state universities are excellent resources for mineral and chemical soil testing.

The Jar Soil Test

Using only a jar, a soil sample, some water, and some observation, we can see the composition of our soils. Fill a jar halfway with soil and the rest of the way with water, leaving room (air) in the jar for shaking. The sand, silt, clay, and organic matter settle out individually when you shake soil up in water and give it time. The heavier particles settle out first and the lightest settle out last. We can measure the individual thicknesses of each layer, note them individually, and then add them together. If we divide each individual section's thicknesses against the full soil's height in the jar and multiply by 100, we can calculate each section's percentage. Organic matter is the most critical component, the top layer, and it can be very small, hard to calculate, and often float. We should aim for at least 10% if not 20% as the minimum organic matter levels for our soils. Most tillage-based agricultural soils have 1-3% organic matter.

(Total Soil Height ÷ Height of a Layer) x 100 = % of that Layer
(10cm of total Soil ÷ 6cm of Sand) x 100 = 60% Sand

Mixed → Separated

Reading Your Jar Soil Results

Once you know your percentages you can mark them on a soil chart. Find the intersection between all three percentages—each percentage has only two lines extending away from it. For dam building, knowing your soil types and placement on the site is critical to knowing what is possible using only on-site materials.

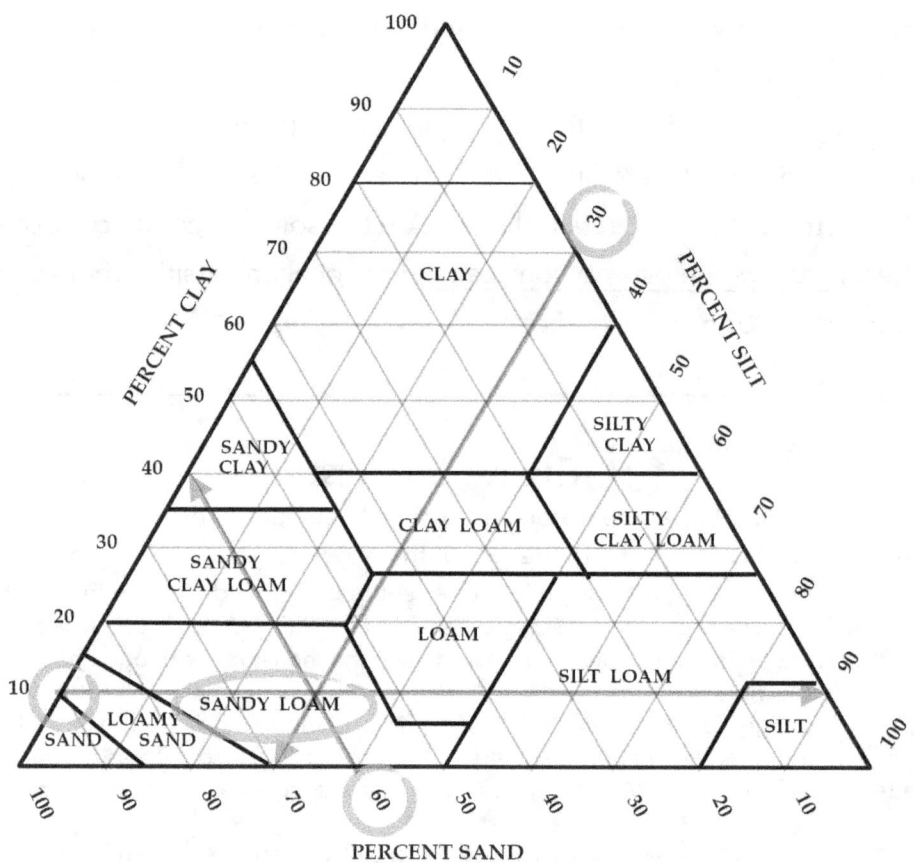

By intersecting the percentages of clay, silt, and sand, the soil type can be categorized which makes planning for earthworks, gardens, dams, and more considerations easier. If you have access to the internet, you can find blank versions of this chart to print out for free in seconds using Google Images and searching for "Soil Chart". You can map out your soils and their percentages without a chart, and you can guess what types of soil it is by looking at the top two most dominant soil elements and name it that way without a chart. If it's a lot of clay, half as much sand, and only a bit of silt, it's sandy clay.

Determining Soil Texture by Hand
1. Wet the soil until it is like workable putty.
2. Rub the soil between your forefinger and thumb to ascertain its feel
3. Squish the putty between your forefinger and thumb to create a smooth length of soil, or ribbon.
4. Measure the length of the ribbon

What did it feel like when you rubbed it?
- Gritty soils are sandy.
- Sticky soils have a lot of clay.
- Smooth soils have plenty of silt.

How long was the soil ribbon?
- Good Ribbon - 2"(5cm) or longer is correlated with 40% clay content or higher.
- Fair Ribbon - 1-2"(2.5-5cm) lengths of ribbon are correlated with 27-40% clay content.
- No Ribbon - less than 1"(2.5cm) is correlated with less than 27% clay content.

Test for Soil Life
Soil life is the key to a healthy garden, orchard, and ecosystem just as beneficial gut biome microbes are the key to healthy digestion and well-being for all animals. Testing to soil life is likely the most important test we can do. We can turn to the professionals for detailed reports, but we can also examine our soils as well with these simple yet scientific tests.

By Hand
Get a shovel full of dirt and sort through it; look for arthropods, earthworms, and nematodes. The last will be visible only if you can see down to a mm. If you sample on a warm, damp night you may get a better sampling of the current population.

Pitfall Trap
Pitfall traps catch large soil organisms, allowing us to count them to get an idea of the populations present in your soil. Dig out a hollow in the soil for a small dish or cup to be level with the soil surface (yogurt cup to a soup bowl size), and pour non-hazardous antifreeze or ethyl alcohol up to 1 cm deep in the bottom of the dish or cup. Cover the dish if you expect

rain and allow your bugs to populate the dish—the antifreeze preserves all the bugs and doesn't allow a higher level bug to eat all the lower level bugs present.

Burlese Funnel

This test focuses on sampling the smaller soil organism population. Pour ethyl alcohol or antifreeze into the bottom of a cup, so it just covers the entire bottom 1-2mm deep. Using a funnel or the cut top of a two-liter bottle inverted, place a small screen in the bottom of the funnel, and then fill it with soil. Suspend an incandescent lightbulb over the soil 10cm (4"). Within in 4 days time in a sheltered area or indoors, the heat from the lightbulb will drive out all the smaller soil life down into the cup. Use a magnifying glass or a microscope to view and count the organisms.

Use a Microscope

Break out the microscope, pipettes, test tubes, and glass slides and slide covers - you can sample your soil, dilute it in water, and view it under a microscope to see how much relative life you have. You might see a great diversity: this is good! You might see one species dominating the soil food web, or you might see an overall lack of life: both these scenarios are not good, but they can be turned around by adding in beneficial life and the foods that feed them.

Test your Water

How clean is your water? Does your filter remove all the contaminants in your water? You'd be surprised what the common carbon or ceramic filter doesn't remove from water. Knowing what you are dealing with will inform your procedure for working with your water. In our area of the Sierra Nevada foothills, there was a neighbor who's wife was ill for years until they spent thousands of dollars on a specialized filtration system that removed a specific iron bacteria that was affecting her health. In some areas, a biochar or even moringa seed filtration system could be enough to clean your water but not in all cases. Rainwater carries a payload of toxins nowadays that must be addressed in situ. Test your ground water for heavy metals, nitrates, lead, mercury, Giardia, and contaminants of all kinds - likely the same procedure should be done with the rain with the understanding that the rain's contents will be in almost all cases more variable than your groundwater. Using rainwater judiciously and using biology, biochar, and aeration to purify it - most contaminants can be sequestered into soil, even in a regenerative aquaponics system.

Some tests we can do at home on our own and get quick and helpful insights. Our well water was pH 5 in Coarsegold, CA in 2014 which is surprisingly acidic and not ideal for drinking, and our filtration systems didn't change the pH either. Test your water to know what you are dealing with. There are so many cheap pH test kits available. You can test your pH with a soil pH kit without any soil. Pool water test kits test pH too. You can also acquire pH specific home test kits, use a simple pH strip used for spit or urine testing, or send water into laboratories.

Research the Social & Legal

Are the neighbors onboard? Is the community supportive of your regenerative idea? Is your spouse supportive of this venture? Are you 100% in? Do you have all the permits you need? Is it insured? Is it legal? What are the laws in your region in regards to water harvesting, dams, raising animals, running a farm, or even having a garden?

Context vs Desire

We have to be careful to not let our desires cloud the context's possibilities. We can't impose a solution; we have to let the context suggest it through observation, listing, and study. By gathering lists of the possibilities without engaging our specific desires, we can get an objective selection of options to work with. In this way we can safely, confidently, and quickly generate solutions because we've begun by limiting the colors on the pallet we are painting with - all our solutions will be painted with same color theme. After you've created your lists, go back and review your holistic goals and then study the actions you can take to see what will fit and in what configurations from your lists. The possibilities are only limited by your imagination, so dream big!

Action: The Reality

Reviewing our maps and lists and using the frameworks, we can create a spectrum of strong ecological arrangements to choose from. A specific area could be an orchard, a garden, or an agroforestry system that embraces both annuals and perennials - how you prepare that area presents a series of choices again that will influence all the other elements in your system. This section focuses on actions, both in management and installation, but it will influence your design and as you adapt your choices to the changing landscape and new information - for instance, you decide to rip a field only to discover as you begin that there's an old septic leach field in place that must be traced and addressed before you prepare the field for planting. In real life, plans will change, but our goals may not, and we may shift the design to accommodate them. I hope you use this book to make decisions, to review decisions, keep a running set of lists, and find quick solutions to those unforeseeable complications that are guaranteed to come into all systems. So don't stress - just keep in touch with your holistic goals and your spectrums of options from your lists and maps.

You can Turn your Dreams on Paper into a Regenerative Reality!

Water

Water is life. Life requires Water.

Slow It. Spread It. Sink It. Slow the water, so it lessens erosion and allows the water to sink in. Spread it out so the entire area gets hydrated and sink it to hold it in the landscape. It is the classic permaculture water mantra, but perhaps we need to add in a few more: Store it, Test it, and Clean it. We all need water, and many sites and areas get enough rain for their needs - they just need to start catching and storing the rain. Using the calculations we made in our research, we know how much water we can expect and how big we need our storage to be. In addition, all water today everywhere faces potential contamination, so it should be assumed that untested waters are unsafe for use or consumption until proven otherwise. Luckily, there are things we can do to test and clean the water. Ideally, all the water leaving our sites should be clean and healthy with beneficial life.

No matter how dry or how wet your area is, understanding your site's water cycle patterns and planning properly will be critical to your design and site management. This workbook is designed to give you tools to make better decisions - you shouldn't feel obligated to do "everything" - sometimes ponds are inappropriate for example. Through bringing in a geotextile pond liner to guarantee it can become possible to have a pond in that area might also be inappropriate. It depends on your circumstances, needs, and interpretation of the ethics in your particular situation. You may need to put in a pond to setup a graywater biological filtration system to guarantee water leaves your property as clean as possible and that's why you are creating the pond - it all depends.

Remember: You may need more than that 55 gallon rain barrel…

Designer's Water Checklist

- Slow, Spread, Sink, Store, Test, and Clean All Water.
- Find where water enters into the site and assess its quality and quantity. Add it to your maps.
- Determine the directions of water-flow on the land - graywater, blackwater, roofwater, road runoff, swale overflow, etc. Map out all the water paths on the site.
- Calculate the graywater and blackwater weekly and monthly output rate.
- Develop a plan to clean and store or sink all water coming onto the site - if it's open water moving through your property, slow, aerate, induce meander, clean, and spread it as best you can.
- List the site's water needs to identify areas of usage and projected usage rates.
- Use gravity to save energy and stack functions - store water as high up in the land as possible to avoid pumping water as much as possible.
- Develop a list of plants that don't require irrigation to shade and populate the landscape.
- Design ponds, swales, diversion drains, roads, and rainwater harvesting systems with the worst case scenarios of flooding and precipitation in mind.
- If needed plant trees to soak up excess water, stabilize the earthworks, and to desalinate the water and soil.

Mapping Water's Paths

Using a topographic map and the locations of where water enters the site, we can map the trajectory of water and its path. It's the same principle behind the catchment outlining: water travels the fastest path down always. Tracing the point of entry 90° to the next contour line and then onward in the same manner down the slope on the map will show the probable path for the water but not necessarily the spread. Hardscape in the landscape can alter water's path as well as produce unexpected springs. Rocks, bedrock profiles, manmade earthworks, or a beaver dam can all change the way the water behaves in a landscape. Adding this information to your maps will help you see where you can use which elements and begin to shuffle through the possibilities.

Slow, Spread, Sink, & Clean Water with Earthworks

Using just a shovel, we can reshape our landscape to capture enormous amount of water. We can magnify that same act with earth moving machines and minimize the activity to a fraction of the time. Instead of months of digging, it's just a day or two, renting the machine or hiring a professional. To better understand earthworks and hydrology, we need look no further than the Loess Plateau restoration project that installed terraces and perennials to stop erosion and infiltrate and hold moisture. The ability for level earth to absorb water is powerful - especially water that increases the pressure on the ground, increasing absorption. The ability for level earth to pacify moving water to end erosion and allow runoff to drop their silt and nutrient loads is also equally beneficial and amazing. There are many solutions to slowing and sinking water in the earthworks toolkit though they all have their own caveats and contexts, so use them carefully to minimize error and having to redo earthworks which is always harder later on.

Cleaning water is also equally variable and particular: a specific toxin might require a specific fungi to remove it from the runoff coming onto your site, and you may even have to remove their fruits, the mushrooms, and compost them separately from all else because those toxins are being embodied in that fruit body (as is the case with some radioactive substances). As you review these techniques it is always important to keep in mind that we want to do the least amount of disturbance for the maximum amount of holistically positive effect over the longest time frame. You might find keyline ripping is the gentlest for your situation; you might find that you need to channel water into a centralized harvesting area to get the water you need. You might have a swale. You might have orchards design using a keyline methodology that you setup initially during this earthworks phase.

Do you need a Swale or a Keyline Plow?

This is often a debate in online forums, but it simplifies something that requires complexity. A swale is a tree planting system that harvests water exceptionally well - it is not an erosion solution though the CCC used to advertise it as such which led to P.A. Yeomans critiques and Keyline water harvesting concepts. The trees are there to hold the berm together, but if the water comes too fast and hard early on, it all can erode before those roots are holding it in place. Planting fast growing perennial grasses like clover can help with this, but always do a test site for the earthworks you are wanting to build and observe the soil in large water events: make a small swale and flood it. Time how fast it takes to absorb at a few inches deep, and then keep flooding it: does it overflow or does the absorption keep pace with the hose?

Keyline Ripping | a Swale

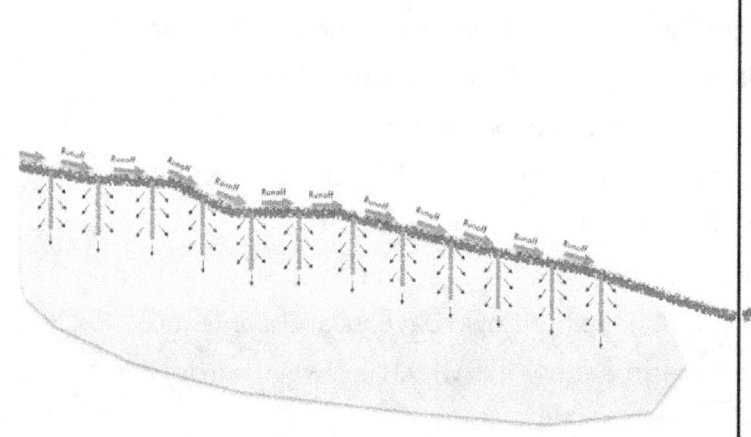
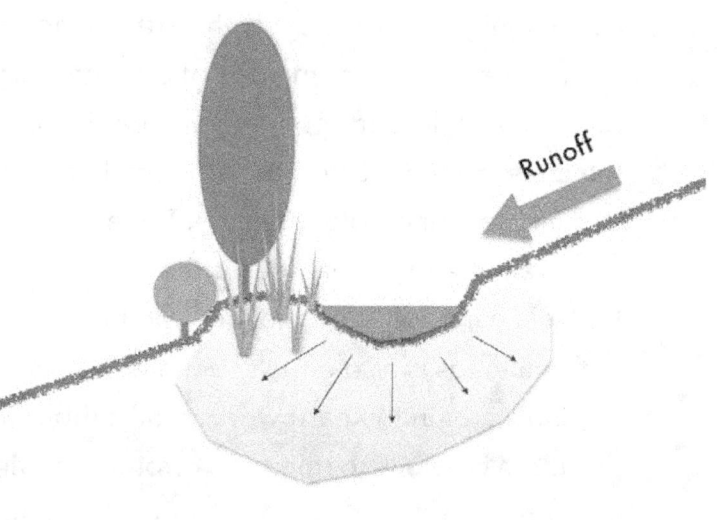

ThePermacultureStudent.com

Where's the water going? Walk down below the small swale and look for a new "spring" or a flooded gopher hole now turned into faucet. Is it all being absorbed or is it draining? You may already have had some insight from working with your soil samples, but the subterranean creatures can sometimes provide some surprises:

During our heaviest rains in California, I was outside watching my swales perform in the last El Nino and heard an audible pop and then slurping sound: a ground squirrel hole's plug had finally been overcome by the water pressure and drained. The entire swale catchment area which was our garden path (100ft x 3 ft) was drained to a meager puddle in seconds. A week later all the swales but one were dry. In that one area, the puddle remained for weeks: implying a potential pond site.

Swales are highly effective when used properly and equally visual - such that people see them working, but they are not always the best option for a site and, in some cases, are overused by designers and can lead to subpar results and needless expense. Ripping soils on contour in contrast allows water to infiltrate almost upon contact instead of forming runoff flowing between swales, but subsoil ripping requires machinery and an area that the machinery can navigate within. Ripping works best in a grazing, pastoral situation, but it's versatile too: it can be used between orchard rows and on slopes. Swales work superbly with alley cropping, silvopasture, orchard food forests, and reforestation projects with soils that can absorb the water at a rate that supports the site's ecological goals and avoids erosion.

How to Build a Swale

To make a swale, soil is removed from the hill on contour and placed below that contour line forming the berm. As we dig down, the berm builds up. The path or road is perpendicular (at a 90° angle) to the flow of water—it's a full stop and completely flat. An enormous amount of water can be captured and soaked in with swales. Based on your research and planning, the swale should be designed to handle the largest rain or flood events in your area—but bear in mind that some areas already get enough moisture. Consecutive swales down a mountain side or hill can recharge dry springs and change an ecosystem fundamentally without irrigation. This occurs naturally often in a forest where trees fall at or nearly at perpendicular—they intercept and slow the natural pathway of water downhill, so in that area, it soaks in more deeply. We all can do this big or small—micro or macro. It will work to save the California Sierra Nevadas and other desertifying forests as well as urban areas in arid climates. It is a universal law that water is pacified when it is level and undisturbed, and it is also true that it soaks into unsealed earth easily. It is in essence a groundwater recharging catalyst.

Swales can be made with only a shovel, among already developed trees and rocks. They can be made where large machines cannot go and can be adjusted to size the situation. They can restart springs, though in humid pastoral settings or places with fast draining soils, too many springs can become an issue for animals and erosion. Ripping is usually done on production farms and always with machines while swales are cut in all settings and can be done by hand on homesteads. Ripping is most often done with a keyline plow (similar to a chisel plow) as part of a keyline water harvesting farm planning design which is an extensive and logical perspective on landscape and a system to help land managers keep the water cycle healthy. Not only that but the keyline design can use swales if called for - it's a holistic toolkit of options as opposed to one technique. *Look for Keyline plows in your area.*

Continue Learning
- *The Keyline Plan* by PA Yeomans (1954). http://soilandhealth.org/wp-content/uploads/01aglibrary/010125yeomans/010125toc.html
- *The Challenge of Landscape* by PA Yeomans (1958). http://soilandhealth.org/wp-content/uploads/01aglibrary/010126yeomansll/010126toc.html
- *The Regrarians eHandbook* by Darren Doherty (2017). http://www.regrarians.org/product/regrarians-ehandbook-1-climate/

How can off contour sometimes be good?

When strict order is created as in systems with all things on contour, we sometimes end up creating wind tunneling, water harvesting overload, and even things like hugelkulturs on contour as swale berms rolling downhill since wood floats in those large rain events! We have to think about how we are designing the system for those larger patterns and trends. Offsetting our swale or row endings slows winds and increases their sheltering effects. Similarly off contour allows water to be slowed without building up water or force. Low level sills and spillways with on-contour systems can also work in this way.

Types of Water Harvesting Earthworks

Use these earthworks to slow and soak in water. Be as creative as you like but be observant: what works for the soil? What works for your plants and animals? What works for the wildlife? What works for you to install?
- Berms
- Benching
- Terracing
- Swales
- Net and Pan
- Diversion Drains
- Ripping
- Keyline Farm Planning

Identify your Keyline(s) & Keypoint(s)

"Keyline planning is based on the natural topography of the land and its rainfall. It uses the form and shape of the land to determine a farm's total layout. The topography of the land, when viewed in the light of Keyline concepts, clearly delineates the logical position of on-farm dams, irrigation areas, roads, fences and farm buildings. It also determines the location of tree belts to provide shade and give wind protection. Keyline concepts also include processes for rapid soil enrichment. The shape of a landscape is produced by the weathering of geological formations over millennia. The processes are always the same. And so the topography of agricultural land has a basic fundamental consistency. It is the inevitable nature of land shape that river valleys collect water from smaller creek valleys. They in turn are fed their water from still smaller valleys, until finally the water derives from the very first, or primary valleys of the catchment area. In any country, anywhere, when rain shapes the land over long periods of time, it inevitably creates and determines the topography of that land. Ultimately, at the extreme upstream of any river system there always [exist] thousands of primary valleys. The only variation to consistent topographical shapes occurs where geological features, such as hard rock outcrops modify normal surface weathering" –Allan Yeomans, <u>Priority One</u>, 2005.

You've made a topographic map, but have you found your keypoints? Your keyline(s)? These areas are the best places to harvest and store water in your area: they are the highest and first areas of possible catchment. Scrutinize your map and start tracing the different landforms and labeling them. Find those primary ridges and mark your keyline(s) and keypoint(s) on your maps. You are going to be either harvesting water at the keypoint, along the keyline as well as at the keypoint, or diverting the catchment from the keyline to the keypoint.

Applying Keyline Patterning in Practice

While some use swales on contour exclusively on their site with great results, many landscapes generate a lot of swale stubs, inconvenient narrowings or widenings, and dead end paths. Keyline patterning only uses the top or bottom contour of an area to determine the guide line for the rest of the rows, berms, roads, or fences. In valley systems, start at the top and then move down parallel to the original guideline (see diagram). In steep cultivation areas, start from the bottom contour and then make rows parallel to that contour guideline uphill at an equidistant spacing. This allows for standardization of access—the road or path is the same width the entire way and whatever equipment is being used can make turns easily at the ends of the rows or roads regardless of whether it is a wheelbarrow or a large tractor. Equidistant rows and the classic grid pattern is a time-tested system that can use contour as an initial guide but ultimately cannot follow the contours for every line or row. In a commercial setting, standardized rows give farmers the data necessary to more easily manage their farms and predict their yields, sales, water retention, carbon sequestration, and more.

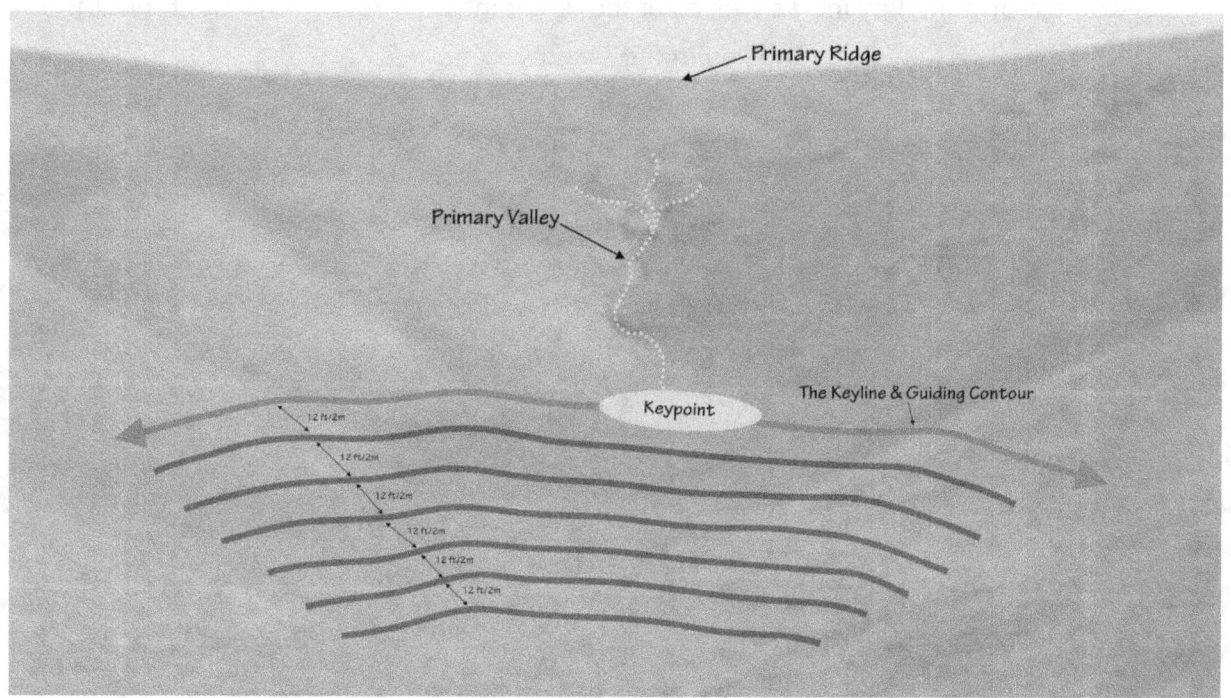

This example is not set to exact scale - it's designed to convey the concept.

Building a Pond

There are laws that govern pond design, installation, and usage in almost every town, city, state, and country. Permits are often required. Designers and home owners are responsible for adhering to those laws and guidelines. Pond building, if done incorrectly, can fail and cause harm - even fatal harm. Work with experts, follow the laws, get your permits, and always plan for climate change to increase the frequency and strength of large precipitation events.

> *"A good site generally is one where a dam can be built across a narrow section of a valley, the side slopes are steep, and the slope of the valley floor permits a large area to be flooded. Such sites also minimize the area of shallow water. Avoid large areas of shallow water because of excessive evaporation and the growth of noxious aquatic plants" –Pond: Planning, Design, Construction. NRCS, 2013.*

Find a Suitable Site

As Sepp Holzer asserts, any area of deposition can likely become a dam or water retention area. Looking at a topographic map, we can spot areas like thumb prints or round oval openings in the contours, with pinch points. These whorls with open centers represent flat areas with easy dam wall sites—the closer the pinch point, the more inexpensive the dam. The economic efficiency of a dam depends on the ratio of its back-wall length to its dam-wall length, since dam wall building is the most costly item. Always start by looking at the keypoints in the landscape.

Decide on a the Pond Type & Make a Plan

Will it be a turkey dam with a wall going all the way around? What will it look like (and therefore require)? Will it need a spillway - how big? Will it need a trickle pipe? How much freeboard will it need? Will you use pond liner or bentonite clay? Will you use animals, people-power, or machines? What will the pond's purpose be? Will it be for drinking, swimming, or fish production?

> *"Ponds that have a surface area of a quarter acre [1000m^2] to several acres can be managed for good fish production. Ponds of less than 2 acres [8000m^2] are popular because they are less difficult to manage than larger ones. A minimum depth of 8 feet over an area of approximately 1,000 square feet [93m^2] is needed for best management"*
> *–Ponds: Planning, Design, Construction. NRCS, 1997.*

Dig out the Site

It can be by shovel or machine. Time can be saved with machines but that option may not be possible for your site. Machines can also be run off of biodiesel made on site like Winfield Farm's lard-powered biodiesel tractor.

Build the Dam Core (Aquifuge) and Dam Wall

In a zoned dam wall there is a dense core inside the dam wall consisting of hard-packed earth that is often called the *core*, the *keyway*, or *aquifuge* (water barrier). Homogenous dam walls do not have a core; they are made completely out of impervious materials. Some dams only have an impervious lining along the pond foundation and inside wall but no keyway. Others have a miniature keyway inside the wall called a diaphragm. Sometimes there is a natural impermeable layer in the ground that can be connected to – but not always.

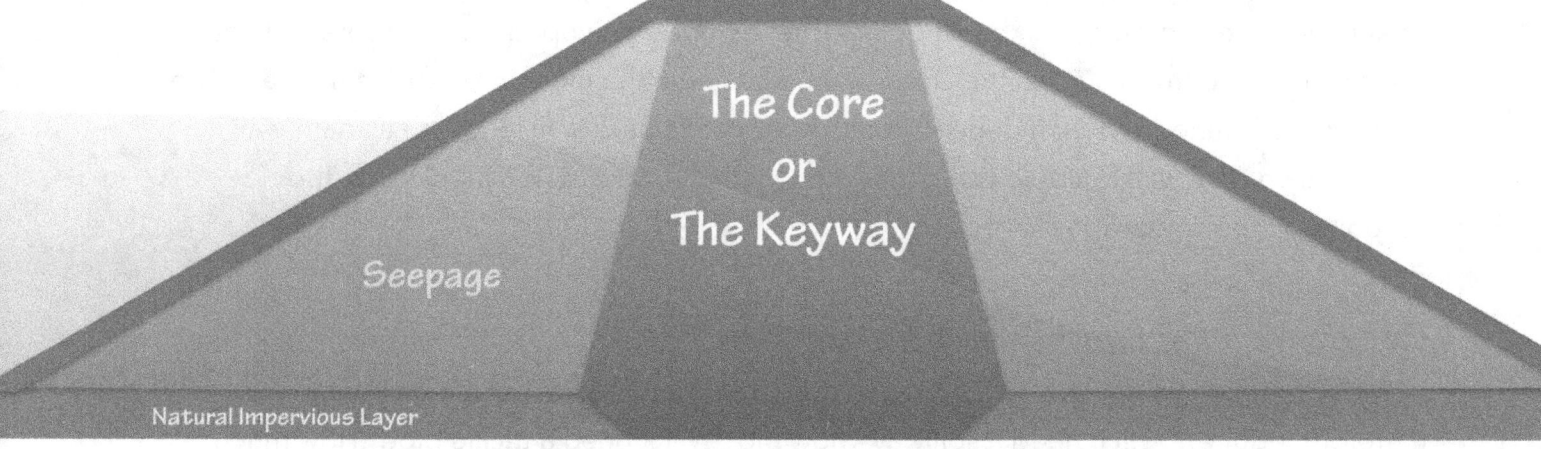

Based on Figure 29 from K.D. Nelson's *Design and Construction of Small Earth Dams*, 1991.

Keyways and other impervious constructions are compacted and impermeable. Clay and silt are needed in high enough concentrations to guarantee impermeability—30-40% clay approximately: gravelly clay, clay loam, silty clay, etc. It has to withstand the dam's full pressure – even in a flood event. Dams requiring a keyway are created with heavy machinery like a backhoe or excavator that drives over the keyway repeatedly until the soil particles are tightly packed together such that water cannot penetrate. Water seepage will naturally occur in the areas that are more permeable and even in the impervious core though at a much slower rate. It is key to maintain a dry top to the dam, or else this seepage could begin to erode the dam wall.

Seal the Pond

Sealing a pond foundation is simple if you have the right materials available: clear the area, fill in any holes with clay or other impervious material to seal them, disk or rototill the pre-moistened foundation area 16-18" deep (41-46cm), and then compress the soil by rolling over it with heavy machinery until it is compacted. You can always choose to seal just the dam wall to the impermeable layer in the subsoil as Sepp Holzer prefers. In this way, these water retention dams soak up water and allow it to infiltrate into the landscape until the landscape is saturated and only then does the pond fill completely as an indicator of the landscape being full of water.

Trickle Pipes (or Spillway Pipes)

A trickle pipe, or spillway pipe, is a pipe that acts as a release for small overflows that occur usually in the spring and fall. It helps maintain a set water level and keep the larger spillway sill dry. They redirect the water through pipes down past the dam wall and release it below where it naturally would drain to if there was no wall in place. Auxiliary spillways are for larger overflow events. The trickle pipe does not move nor can it be used to lower water levels as a valve release lower in the water profile would. Trickle pipes are permanent components of dam walls installed when the wall is built. They are built with anti-seep collars or rubber cut offs.

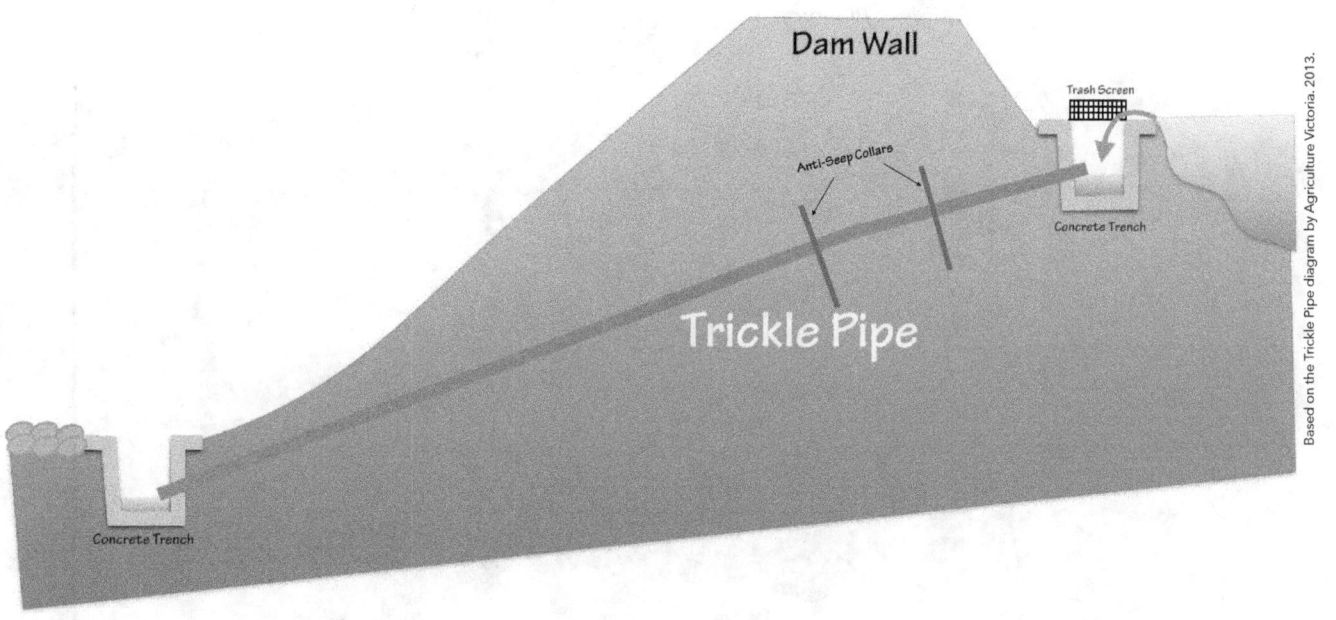

Building a Spillway

When water catchment is at its peak or during a flood, the overflow needs to safely run off from the dam over an auxiliary spillway that spreads the water out evenly in a sheet to prevent erosion and, ideally, catches it in another catchment system below to further slow, soak, spread, and store it. A grassy, absorbent area is ideal for below a spillway. Spillways can also be channels that direct the water away from the area in case of emergency overflow (as in large hydroelectric dams).

Spillway sills can be compressed earth or even concrete or plastic hardscape to prevent erosion. The NRCS recommends small dam spillways to be designed for the large 25-year-frequency rain events, and large dam spillways to be built for 50-year storms. With climate change increasing, the large cyclical storm events are going to be occurring closer together and, perhaps, with greater strength than our historical precedents. To determine the size and scope of a spillway depends on precipitation, runoff, the watershed, and the fetch of the pond (or the distance from the dam wall to the farthest edge of the pond).

"No matter how well a dam has been built, it will probably be destroyed during the first severe storm if the capacity of the spillway is inadequate. The function of an auxiliary spillway is to pass excess storm runoff around the dam so that water in the pond does not rise high enough to damage the dam by overtopping. The spillways must also convey the water safely to the outlet channel below without damaging the downstream slope of the dam. The proper functioning of a pond depends on a correctly designed and installed spillway system" –Pond: Planning, Design, Construction. NRCS, 2013.

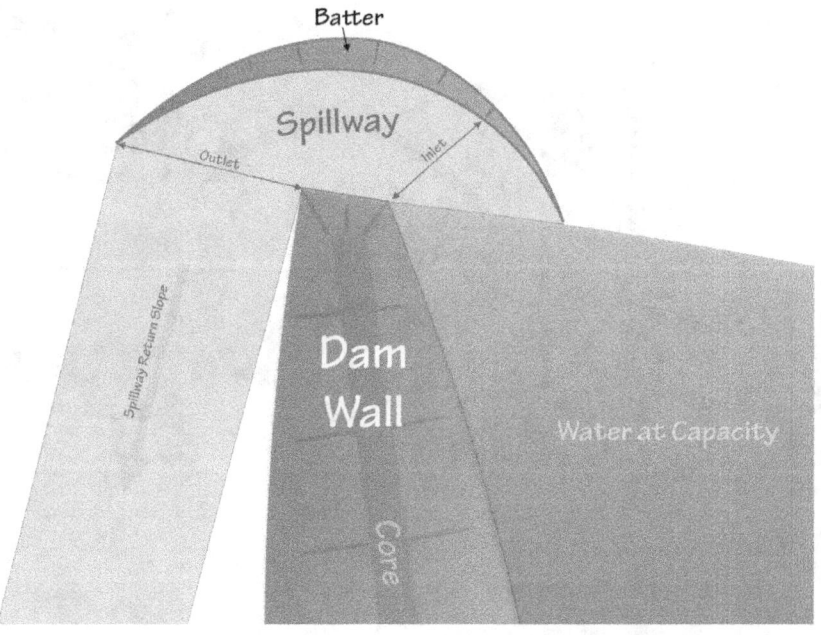

Based on Figure 36 Spillway Plan from K.D. Nelson's *Design and Construction of Small Earth Dams*, 1991.

45

Backcut, Side Slopes, and Freeboard

The back of the dam or swale where the earth has been cut is the backcut. The backcut of a pond or swale should match the slope of the land below the dam wall. This helps slow the process of silt filling the pond over time and keeps the slope more stable.

Side slopes can vary in their design, depending on the concentrations of clay and silt in the soil—some can be steep while others must be gentle to avoid erosion. The freeboard is the distance between the height of the dam wall and the height of the water when it is flowing into the auxiliary spillway. Maintaining a dry freeboard is critical.

"If your pond is less than 660 feet [201m] long, provide a freeboard of no less than 1 foot. The minimum freeboard is 1.5 feet [.5m] for ponds between 660 [201m] and 1,320 feet [402m] long, and is 2 feet [.6m] for ponds up to a half mile [.8km] long. For longer ponds an engineer should determine the freeboard"
—Pond: Planning, Design, Construction. NRCS, 2013.

Harvesting Roof Rainwater

An urban rainwater demonstration tank system at the Avis home in Calgary, Canada. This system purposefully has mistakes to teach students: the IBC tank is too small, and water tanks should be covered to prevent algae and bacterial growth.

To handle the amount of water you will harvest, careful calculations are needed in terms of the rain coming down, the square footage or meterage of the roof catchment, the amount of storage space, and the frequency and amount of rain; even with attention to detail, calculating exactly the catchment and infiltration of an area is always impossible. We can only approximate as closely as possible by taking into account as many factors as possible. We can budget our usage based on our storage and water catchment capacities.

Using a first flush diverter (pictured), we can divert contaminated roof water that is collected when rain initially hits a dirty roof. Limestone, marble, or shell in a mesh bag can be suspended in the storage tank to mineralize or "harden" the water by making it more alkaline. Rainwater is naturally "soft", as is lake water, and is lacking in minerals. Giardia and other organisms that present health concerns grow in soft water as well. Keeping organic matter, insects, etc. out of your tank and tank in-flow is important: use gutters that block out material and add grates and screens wherever needed.

Promising test results from Blue Sky Biochar suggest biochar can also be used to neutralize pathogens and algae in rainwater tanks - even in a clear plastic tank!

Cisterns are wells that are designed to catch and hold rain and runoff for irrigation and home consumption. It can be as simple as a hand-dug well lined with brick or stone that is 6-7m deep and 3-4m wide with a smaller opening near the surface. These buried stone or earthen tanks are an ancient, reliable technology.

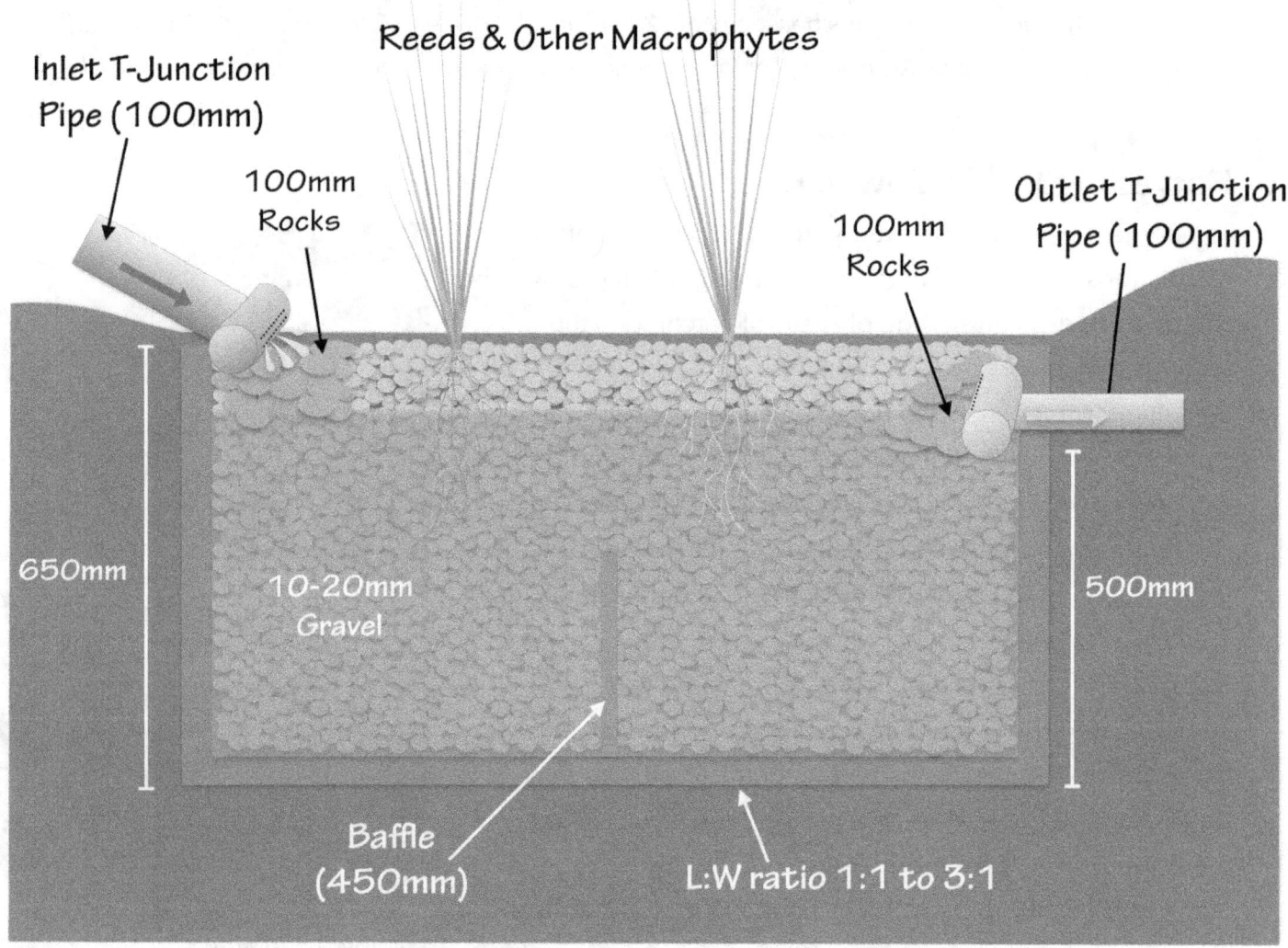

A Reed bed Gray and Black Water Treatment Bed.
Based on Lismore City Council's "Figure 2: Basic Reed bed Design (Lateral View)"
from *The Use of Reed Beds for the Treatment of Sewage and Wastewater from Domestic Households.*

Clean & Sink Your Graywater & Blackwater

Graywater Treatment Reedbeds

There are many different ways to use reeds and other macrophytes to clean gray and black water. The containment area can be sealed in a number of ways and the shape and pattern can be very creative, but the idea is very simple: contain plants and gravel allowing water to slowly filter through the system in a minimum of five to seven days in which anaerobic and aerobic processes occur. These kinds of plants pull some toxins out of the water and to a certain degree release them into the air while microbes digest pathogens and much of the heavy nutrient load in the gravel bed. Sometimes the surface has a layer of sand for the macrophytes. Lismore City Council has an excellent and thorough guide to setting up a home system. It can be found online here: http://www.canberragarden.com/water/Reedbed.pdf It is a great standardized method to start from that is proven, scientifically backed, and approved. Check with your local laws for what is preferred or approved for your area. The reed bed is only one stage of treatment.

For drinking, bathing, cooking, and garden water purposes, this partially cleaned water should pass through another biological filtration stage that is purely aerobic with a diversity of plants and animals and plenty of aeration. Testing is the only way to know how efficient these systems are. In heavy rain storms when things are overflowing perhaps or diluting or in times of winter when things are frozen, things change and processes slow down or stop. We have to have systems that can handle overflow safely and maintain movement and warmth in winter, and we have to test regularly, just like any home pool or pond owner would.

Compost Toilets

There are many different kinds of compost toilets currently available and possible to construct at home. The basic concept is that human manure (humanure) is composted by mixing it with a carbon-rich, high-surface area material such as wood chips, straw, hay, seeds, biochar, or sawdust. These toilets can compost the humanure directly below the toilet: drop, tumble, and aerate, or they can be removed to an external composting area which is often preferable.

In the simplest arrangement, one can add one's deposit of humanure to a plastic five gallon bucket and add carbon-rich, high-surface area material like sawdust or broken up animal bedding pellets. Adding biochar is a superb additional amendment to your mix, imitating the classic terra preta practice. Once three quarters of the way full, the bucket is taken to an outdoor composting area for up to three months. It is also possible to purchase a system with a high degree of sophistication with automated, electric toilets and even self-turning containment areas. These shuttle humanure through a specific composting process, conserving and returning its valuable nutrients and carbon back to the soil.

Composting of humanure can either be thermophilic (hot) and quick or cold (mouldering) and over a long period of time. Thermophilic composting creates a sterile product quickly while mouldering compost might allow parasitic eggs and pathogens to persist and would require thorough examination before that kind of compost would be determined perfectly safe. It is important for anyone looking to start working with composting toilets that they respect both the hazardous nature of fresh humanure as well as the management required. Carbon to nitrogen ratios must be maintained, and the mixture must be well-mixed, and often stirred, to guarantee even composting and a safe end-product.

An example from Hawthorn Farm in Washington, USA.

Mycoremediation

Fungal hyphae exude digestive enzymes that have the ability to decompose complex compounds often more efficiently than any other life form. As nature's greatest chemists and recyclers, fungi are critical to cleaning up the most complex pollutants in the environment. King Stropharia fungi form such a tight mycelial web that they can temporarily filter out microbial contaminants from flowing water systems - these systems need to be regularly harvested, composted, and replaced with new mycoremediation filters. These can be straw erosion wattles inoculated with oyster or king stropharia mushrooms placed in the flow of the water. Use wattles that are 50-75% myceliated, and try to keep the flow low and slow to let the water pass through the wattles as slowly as possible. Stagger the wattles on contour up and down the slowest and lowest flow areas. The flow may drag them away, so they may need to be staked and only partially submerged - 50-30% should be above the waterline. This way the fungi keeps working and can react to the stress with actively growing hyphal tips rather than a mature mycelial mass that is now considering fruiting instead of continued consumption. We want the fungi to continue to work on the substances around it as well - we don't want to drown it. This concept can also be used between stages of water treatment to help remove pathogens and excess nutrients.

Rewilding Water

Induce Meander

The more meander there is to a channel of water, the more flood control it naturally has. The back and forth also develops shallow and deeper areas which increases biodiversity, temperature range, filtration capacity, and more. Straight channels tend to incise into the subsoils, disconnecting the flood waters from the flood plain. To slow, soak, and spread the water for long-term storage, rivers and streams must be able to meander. Using baffles, erosion can be encouraged with weirs or rock dams between the baffles to imitate the natural deposition areas. Over time the channel will shift and begin to meander. Extending the rock dams as the water slowly shifts will speed up restoration. Refer to the image on the next page.

Continue Learning
- *Let Water Do The Work* by Bill Zeedyk and Van Clothier (2009). Paperback.
- Craig Sponholtz of Watershed Artisans. *http://www.watershedartisans.com*

Urbanized Stream ReWilding

Often streams, rivers, and creeks are channelized or straightened and lined with concrete. This prevents the water from infiltrating into the ground and prevents vegetation from growing around the channel. It also speeds up the flow rate and prevents settling of sediments. This unnatural design prevents sinuous curves that slow water and lacks a flood plain. Creating a 4-level floodplain system around the channel is critical: 1 - base or low-flow channel, 2 - normal high-flow channel, 3 - floodplain, and 4 - flood-prone areas. The floodplain can be planted with riparian species and a wetland can even be dug out—water will seep through the ground into that area naturally or be filled by rain or flood events. The flood-prone area can be planted with trees, shrubs, and other selected perennials adapted to an area frequented by flooding. Excavation opens up more area lower in the land profile to accommodate more water, making flooding events more manageable and safe. It also

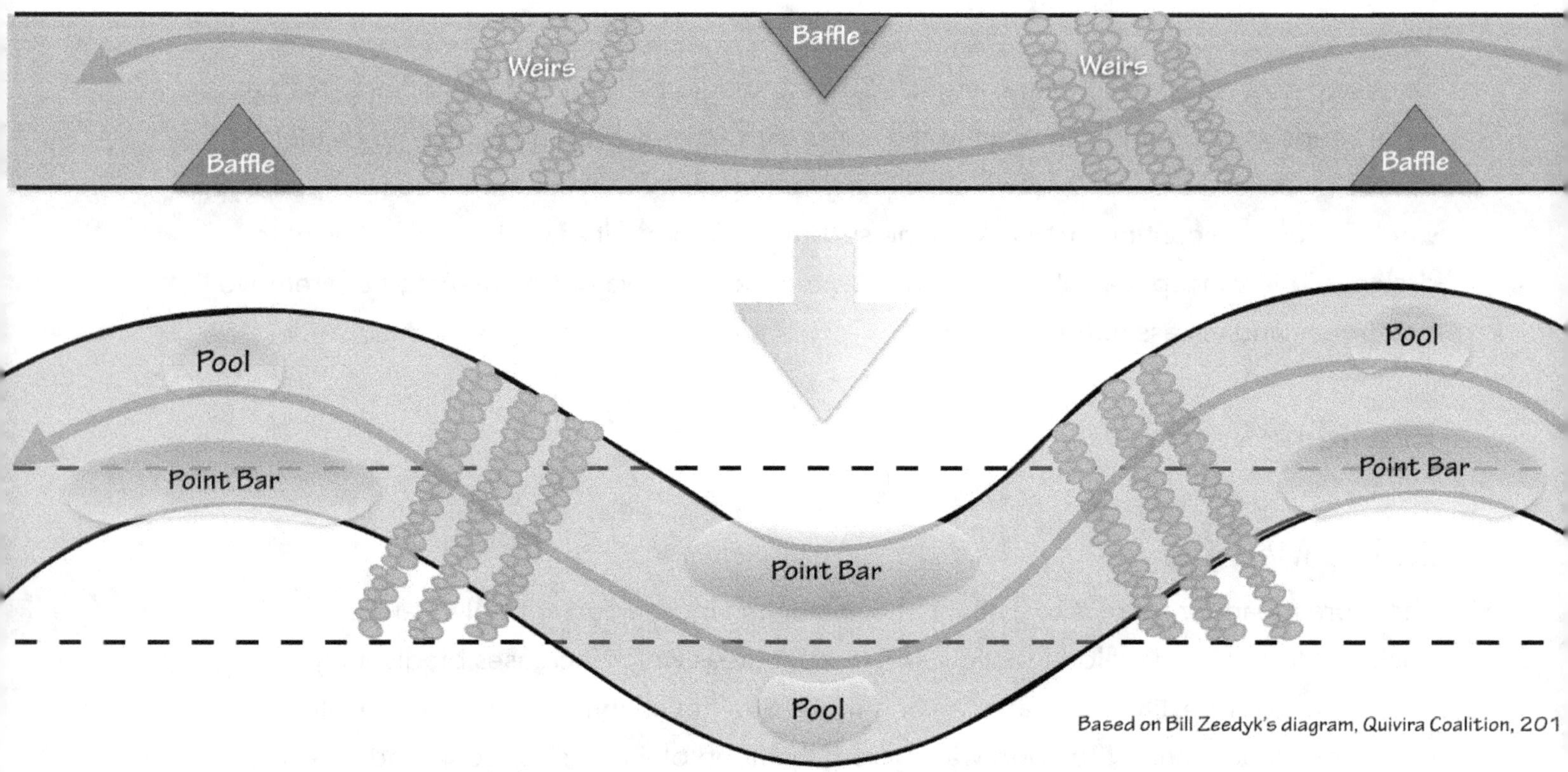

Based an actual project conducted by Bill Zeedyk in the American Southwest, this model of using one rock dams and baffles to induce meandering <u>and erosion</u> purposefully will restore the natural shape of the channel. As the channel shifts, new rocks need to be added to the dams. Read more about Bill's work in the book: <u>Let Water Do The Work</u> (2009).

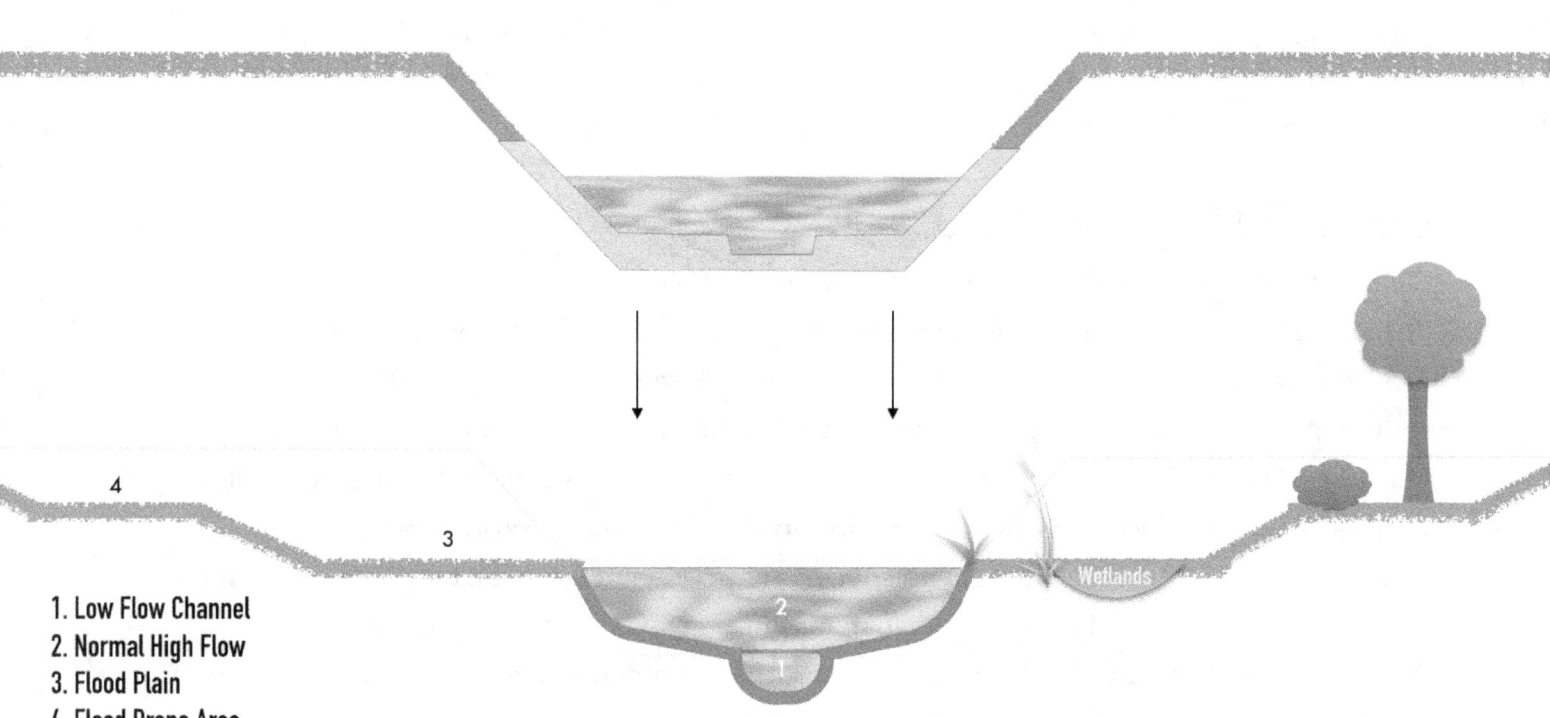

1. Low Flow Channel
2. Normal High Flow
3. Flood Plain
4. Flood Prone Area

increases wildlife and deep infiltration of water. The sinuous meander of a natural stream is needed to control flood waters, slow and infiltrate water, and to support the development of biological systems which clean, slow the water more, and grow more life. *Refer to the image on the previous page.*

Aeration

In all these efforts, aeration is key: it promotes life and cleans the water. Falling water, circulating water, disturbed water, and water with bubbles being releasing into it - there are innumerable ways to add oxygen to water.

The Key Will Be Conserving Water
If we use less, the water we do receive and store can last longer.

Continue Learning
- *Create an Oasis with Greywater: Integrated Design for Water Conservation* by Art Ludwig (2015). Paperback.
- *Let the Water Do the Work: Induced Meandering, an Evolving Method for Restoring Incised Channels* by Bill Zeedyk and Van Clothier (2009). Paperback.
- *Rainwater Harvesting for Drylands and Beyond* by Brad Lancaster (2013). Paperback.

Soil

How's your Soil?

Using your map and jar soil sample results, categorize all the soils on the site. Where is the soil rich, loamy, and dark? Where is the soil heavy in clay? Where are the sandy spots? Where is it compact? Where is it wet constantly? Where is it always dry? Where is it eroding? Where is it heavily vegetated? Add these areas and their soil types to your maps. These areas can be seen as individual microclimates requiring different management techniques and design choices for each area. That clay deposit could represent a pond spot or where you can dig out cob building material - it depends on your situation. You may simply increase the organic matter in the soil, so it holds moisture longer in the summer's heat.

Where is Soil Needed?

How deep do your soils go? If your topsoils are only a few inches deep, your carrots will stunt, and your roots will have a tough time penetrating the hardpan or bedrock beneath. Most gardens need soil or in the very least to develop their own soils to match the fertility of their gardening ambitions - corn and tomatoes both require a lot from the soil and the gardener! Figure out how much soil you need and set out to make it possible. Map out the places that need soil, calculate their area in square meters or feet, convert it into yards, and order or prepare to make that amount of soil - you can do this even if you just have a shovel and a friend with a truck!

Calculate How Much TopSoil is Needed

If the area is a square or rectangle:
Length x Width x Height of the Soil = Volume of the Soil
10 ft x 5 ft x 0.5 ft (6 inches) of soil = 25 ft³
10 m x 5 m x 0.1 m of soil = 5 m³

m³ x 1.0936133 = yd³
ft³ x 0.037037 = yd³
5 m³ x 1.0936133 = 5.47 yd³
25 ft³ x 0.037037 = 0.92 yd³

Make a Soil Remediation Plan

Depending on your climate, your site's soils will have specific ranges of attributes, weaknesses, and strengths. Depending on your goals for a particular site, the ideal soil types will range as well. Are you in the garden, in the wilderness, in the fields, in the cities, in the desert, in the tropics, on an island, in the mountains, or by the sea? Does your soil need organic matter and soil life? What kind of soil life? What kinds and ratios of Fungi? Bacteria? Nematodes? Protozoa? Microarthropods? Nitrogen fixing bacteria or phosphate uptake enhancing mycorrhizal fungi? Make a plan and tailor your soil building to addressing the issues you found in your earlier soil research and towards your goals for that soil and site.

If you are faced with lifeless dirt, you can make soil out of it using disturbance for infiltration and aeration, adding organic matter, and adding life via compost tea, Korean natural farming, EM, bokashi, Organics Alive's products, or any of the numerous other methods currently available - you can even add in worms and organic matter. Biochar is an excellent addition as it helps create structure for soil, longterm carbon sources for soil life, and habitat for soil life.

Where will you get the soil life you need for your site? What kinds and concentrations of life are you focusing on? From where will you source a diversity of organic matter? How will you carefully disturb the soil to prepare for infiltration? How will you deliver your soil life to the soil? How will you cover the soil or keep the soil covered after you deliver the soil life? How much mulch will you need? How much organic matter total?

The Remediation Plan

- Soil Life
- Organic Matter
- Aeration
- Infiltration
- Coverage

Build Soils

Thermophilic (Hot) Compost

For a compost to be effective, the ingredients must be as precise as possible. The initial pile is made of: a third brown organic matter (high carbon, dead, dried plant material that has already gone to seed), a third green organic matter (these are plant materials that haven't gone to seed, so they still contain enzymes, nitrogen, protein, and sugars—they can be dried or fresh), and a third manure or another nitrogen-heavy component. This even split is the ideal composition for a pile that is at minimum one cubic meter in size. The larger the pile is, the easier it will be for the microbes to go to work but the harder it will be to turn. Large operations use heavy machinery to turn their piles. (In the summer heat, smaller piles are possible).

Compost piles need more carbon when you use hotter manure sources. A pile that is a third chicken manure will have a higher nitrogen content than one that is a third cow manure simply because of the nature of the waste itself. Wood chips likewise contain more carbon than straw; they are higher in density. Hotter piles burn quicker and provide less compost as their end product, so if you notice yourself turning it more often, mix in some saw dust or well-shredded, dried plant material for more carbon to balance out the excess nitrogen.

When we arrange the materials it is best to start with a carbon layer on bottom to provide aeration pathways while it heats up initially. In layers, add brown, green, and manure layers, and then water it all until it leaks. Wrap it in a wire fence to encourage aeration and contain the pile efficiently. Cover it with a tarp. Wait 3 days and then turn it every other day from

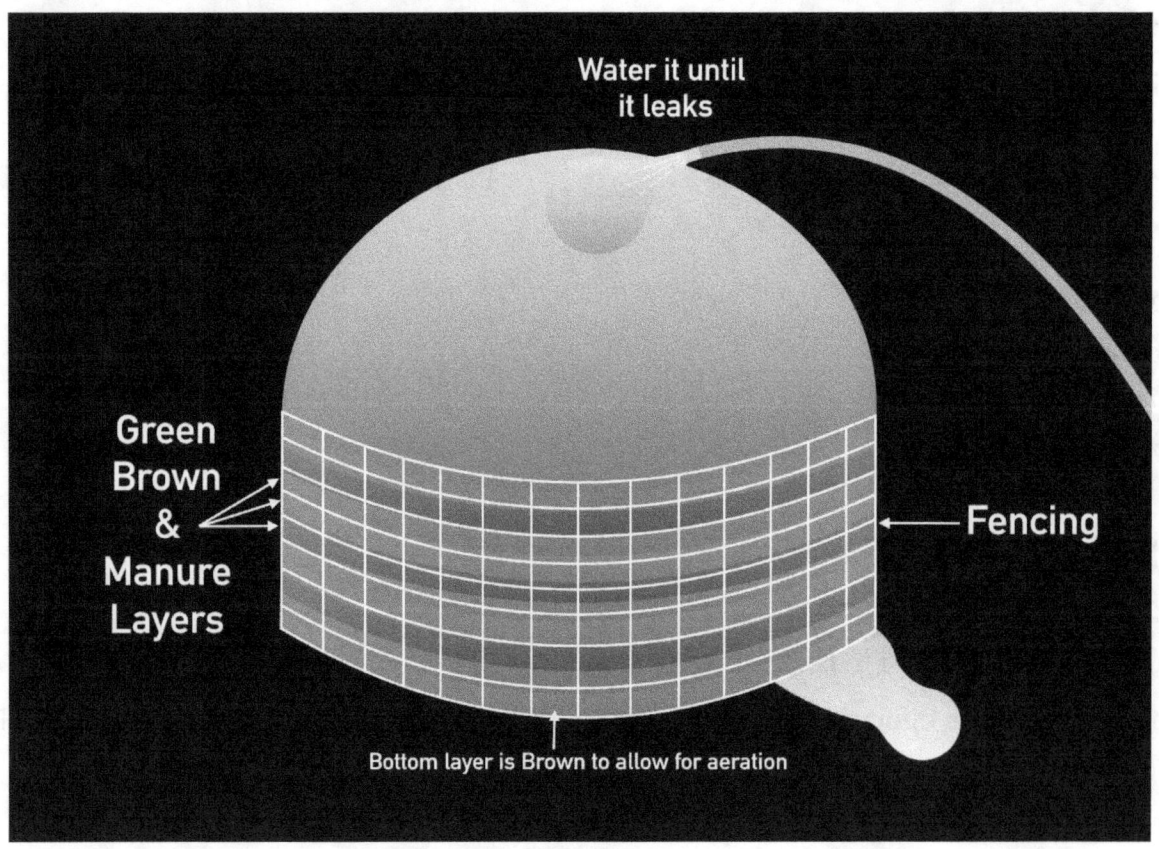

thereafter, as long as it maintains a 131°F-140°F (55°C-60°C) temperature range. If it is too cool, either don't turn it as often, so it builds heat, or add more manure and possibly greens to speed up the reactions and resultant heat.

For perennial systems, a woody compost is ideal because it will require fungi to breakdown the wood lignin, and the resultant compost will be more fungal-dominant. You can also feed a fungal compost chitin and fish emulsion - both attract fungi in large numbers. You can add indigenous fungi sampled from a thriving local ecosystem at this time as well (it doesn't have to be a large sampling for it to be very effective). If instead we add extra fresh cut grasses or weeds and a few tablespoons of organic blackstrap unsulphured molasses, we can easily create a bacterial-dominant compost which is ideal for more bacterial-dominant gardening soils.

Don't forget—it's hot! It should stay between 131°F-140°F (55°C-60°C) for 15 days, turning at least 5 times. The heat kills the pathogens, parasitic eggs, and the weed seeds. The pile also needs time to cool off unless you are going to burn the plants or weeds in place by adding hot compost to the garden beds—some choose to do this. Dr. Elaine Ingham prefers to let hers cool and then use it on the garden or to make compost tea or compost extract.

Vermicompost

Using earthworms and compostable kitchen waste, we can create a bacterial-dominant compost of worm castings. Liquid extracts from the castings and the castings themselves can be used to bacterially inoculate soils or to start a bacterial-dominant compost tea. It's important to recognize that worms from different areas in the soil profile support each other. For instance, the deep burrowing worms come up to the topsoil to feed on the the worm castings of the commonly used red wigglers who then feed on the mineral rich castings from the deep burrowers. Include as many worms and members of the food soil web as possible in balance. Also, be aware that their diets do matter: Organics Alive uses a specific diet to get castings with bacteria that feeds on chitin and cellulose, commonly the focus on fungi! There's a lot more to be learned in the world of worms.

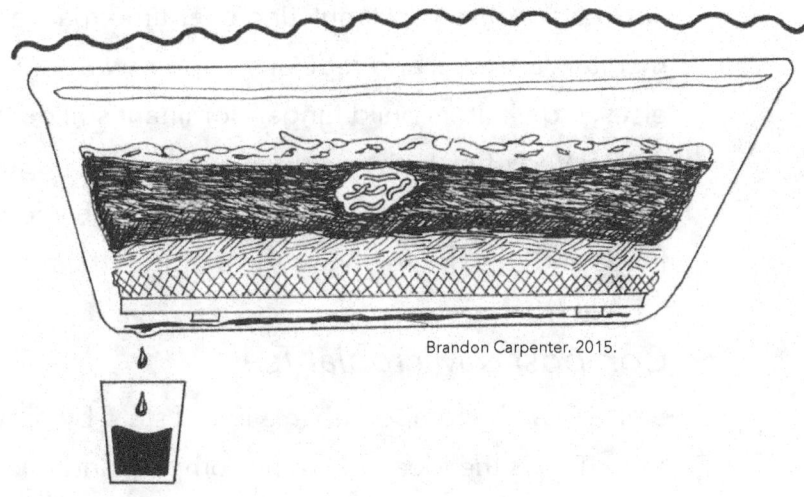
Brandon Carpenter. 2015.

Using an old tub or a waterproof container that allows liquid and air to pass through freely, we can add kitchen scraps to a base layer of manure (ideally seedless) populated with compost-loving worms and over time (approximately three months) the container's contents will be transformed by the worms into a finely processed earthworm compost.

Continue Learning
- Organics Alive's Website: https://organicsalivegarden.com
- *Worms at Work* by Crystal Stevens (2017). Paperback.

Mouldering Compost

Mouldering composts often are found by worms but are not necessarily part of the initial setup. It is more like a yard and kitchen waste heap that breaks down aerobically and anaerobically in contrast to all the other compost heaps which rely upon disturbance to keep things aerobic. Mouldering composts vary in their success due to their context and composition.

Earthworks

Earthworks like hugelkulturs, terraces, and swales build soils. Swales and terraces pacify water in rain events which allows the water to drop whatever it was carrying. This leads to a rich flood plain of soil accumulating over time that can be left in place on a terrace or harvested to maintain the level and regularity of the swale and to be used in a garden area somewhere else. Hugelkulturs build fungal-dominant soil quickly by imitating deadfall in a forest. Associated often with Austria's Sepp Holzer, hugelkulturs are mound-cultures in translation: you mound dirt on top of a wood pile which speeds up decomposition of the wood and feeds and to a degree heats the plants in the mound.

Compost & Microbial Teas

Soil life can be ramped up in a liquid state by providing the foods they prefer in a soluble form. This is the idea behind all compost and microbial teas. You can select for which element in the food web you'd like to promote by adding their favorite foods to the brew.

Compost teas are aerated with air pumps, usually the kind for aquariums, that have the smallest surface area because they need to be cleaned between each batch and sterilized - this is why the porous stones often used go anaerobic so quickly. The aeration keeps things aerobic, but when biofilm from the last batch remains, anaerobes can still ruin a batch. Compost tea can be fungal- or bacterial-dominant (depending on the compost sample), and it can be used directly on the soil or as a foliar spray. Compost teas are usually diluted to a water-to-tea ratio of between 2:1 to 4:1. A little compost can go a long way in the form of compost tea.

Brewing can take one to five days depending on the volume of batch, aeration rate, and temperature - the last being the most important factor after aeration. In the heat of the summer, brewing compost tea can happen in under 48 hrs easily. Use the brew within six to eight hrs of brewing completion. It takes time observing and smelling regularly to know when a tea is ready, but anyone can identify the bad-smelling anaerobes that indicate a brew that is no longer beneficial for plants and soil. The margin for error is quite large, and soil life is vigorous to begin with, so dramatic effects can often occur with even amateurish attempts at compost tea.

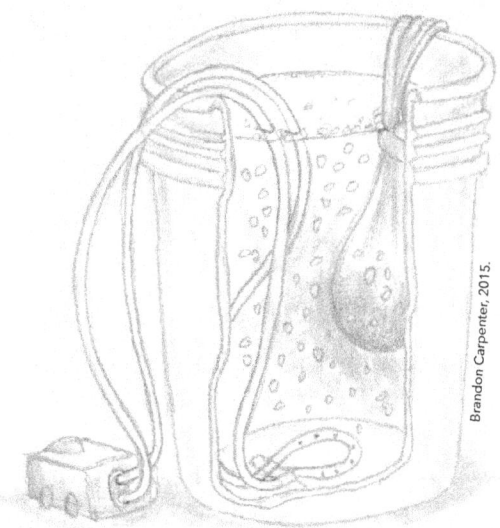

A 5-gallon (19L) bucket can be used to aerate compost to make compost tea.

There are many other beneficial foliar sprays we can create at home that are natural and non-toxic. Some act to nourish, some to repopulate, and others act to protect, as in the example of a physical barrier like diluted clay on fruit trees; however, living microbial brews are the most versatile and beneficial overall.

Bacterial Dominant Compost Tea

Simple sugars and fresh organic matter that is "green" or still growing vegetatively bring in the bacteria in a compost! This is why folks turning recently cleared pine woodlots into gardens are using molasses and hot composts made with grass clippings in their compost tea brews to boost the bacterial growth and tip their pH and soil life away from the heavy fungal and acidic side.

Fungal Dominant Compost Tea

Complex carbon compounds are what feeds and draws in the fungi into an aerated compost brew. This is why folks are adding fish emulsion, chitin, and kelp. By training the microbes with these specific highly complex and mineral rich foods when they are released into your soils, they will seek out those foods in the environment and pull them from the non-living elements of the soil - clay, sand, silt, and organic matter. It's important to note that there are bacteria that can digest cellulose and chitin - just because the fungi are found in greater numbers in a fungal dominant situation doesn't mean bacteria are absent or incapable of feeding or contributing. The same in reverse is true: fungi are necessary for bacteria to take hold in an area on land. Adding freshly harvested mycelium from a healthy local ecosystem is often a best practice as it can provide the best microbes possible: the indigenous microorganisms (IMOs). Practices like Korean Natural Farming and Bokashi partner with IMOs in their composts, ferments, and brews.

Compost Extract = Humic Acid

Often sold in stores at high prices, humic acids can easily be generated at home with native soil biology. After the compost has cooled, water can be gently run over some compost and through a sieve, the brown water, the compost extract, that trickles out of the sieve is rich in humic acids which are fungal foods.

Continue Learning
- *Life in the Soils Class* with Dr. Elaine Ingham: https://environmentcelebration.com/education/classes/
- *Teaming with Nutrients* by Jeff Lowenfels (2013). Hardcover.
- *The Field Guide I and II for Actively Aerated Compost Tea* by Elaine Ingham, Phd. (2001-2004). Paperback.

With Animals

Grazing animals are vital to growing soil in a pasture setting. Using animals in a succession to clear an area and build the soil is incredibly powerful. Master holistic manager, Joel Salatin recommends in a *Salatin Semester* to clear an area with animals to start with goats which mostly browse on trees and shrubs and then to follow with sheep that mostly browse on shrubs and graze on grazes, and finally followed by classic Salatin animal rotation: cows grazing on the grass followed by chickens to consume the insects and sanitize and spread the manure patties followed by turkeys that will continue the insect removal. The area is then rested until the classic rotation can return: cows to chickens to turkeys then rest and back again. This builds the soil and improves biodiversity season after season.

Another method recently popularized by Geoff Lawton and Justin Rhodes involves using chickens in a mobile electric fence to prepare garden areas in stages. They are amazing at clearing land and adding high nitrogen fertilizer directly to the soil, so it works exceptionally well. This can also be used in a composting situation - they can turn the pile for you and enjoy the heat from the piles especially in winter! As you have the chickens clearing an area you add the organic matter and manure - they add their manure, consume some of it, and undo the pile. Just keep rebuilding the pile until they are no longer interested and from there to finish it you have to turn it yourself or use it as a partially composted mulch that can be used to hot compost on top of an area - you can throw some seed or feed onto the pile to get them re-interested pretty easily too.

With Plants

Cover crops that get chopped and dropped or tilled into the topsoil along with plants that sequester large amounts of carbon into the soils while they grow both serve to build soil. Combining the two can create soil extremely quickly: growing a C4 grass like corn or sorghum with a nitrogen-fixing biomass accumulator like cowpeas. Cowpeas actually fix the most nitrogen and create the most biomass among all tested plants as a companion crop with corn. Use annual legumes inoculated with their associated nitrogen fixing bacteria and other annual cover crops like daikon radish and buckwheat to generate topsoils rich in nutrients and minerals, specifically boosting carbon, nitrogen, and phosphorous levels. None of this is done by the plants alone: soil life unlocks the nutrients in exchange for the root exudates (mostly sugars from photosynthesis). That being said, once you do have the proper soil life, the plants can perform at a much higher level and thus facilitate even more soil life activity. Half of the carbon dioxide a corn takes in during photosynthesis turns into its structure (97% of its structure) and the other half goes into the soil as carbon chains (sugars) and is traded into the soil food web economy! The more growth; the more soil building. If the biomass is chopped and dropped into a field inoculated with the proper life already, a majority of that biomass will not be oxidized but will be consumed - especially if finely chopped and dropped as with a flail mower or harrow and then sprayed with compost tea with chitin and cellulose digesting fungi and bacteria in it. That will become soil quickly with a greatly reduced loss of nutrients and carbon into the atmosphere - if biochar were added, the loss would be even less.

With Biochar

Biochar is biologically infused charcoal. Charcoal is made at high temperatures in a low-oxygen environment (pyrolysis). Biochar is made when the charcoal is soaked in compost tea or combined with compost. When charcoal is created all the life and moisture is removed; what remains is like a porous carbonaceous electron-sucking vacuum. It provides habitat for soil life, but charcoal alone as a soil amendment will rob the humus of water and nutrients. It should be noted that biochar has a unique electrical capacity abilities such that it can store information like a silicone chip can - scientists are eagerly researching and testing biochar for new applications currently. We are also just learning that different specific heats for making biochar create different types of biochar - and the plant mediums used make a difference as well. The Redwood Forest Foundation, for example, makes superb biochar at a specific heat in a specialized kiln of 600°F/315.5°C, but that doesn't mean that superb biochar can't be made at other heats, each for a specific purpose. Cannabis biochar has even shown promise as a semiconductor in recent research.

Using a moisture meter, we can test our wood to see how dry it is. 15-25% moisture is ideal to burn. The more moisture, the more smoke. Some larger burns use an alcohol accelerant to get the fire to heat quickly and thoroughly. The burn releases volatile organic compounds and leaves behind pure carbon honeycomb structure.

Biochar was inspired by Terra Preta, a dark, rich, man-made soil from areas of the Amazon that was created using charcoal, fish bones, pottery, humanure, and bones. Biochar is gaining attention as a carbon sequestration method as it takes biomass that would be burned and instead turns it into a durable carbon compound that improves soils. In some areas, terra preta is the best solution to depleted topsoils.

It should be noted that making biochar is a biomass-intensive process as it requires organic matter for both the compost and the charcoal. For those in the tropics or the temperate climates where biomass is plentiful and constantly generating, it can be a powerful tool for building soil. If the site only has its standing living carbon to be turned into biochar, it has to be imported - luckily, it's superbly lightweight and becomes a nearly permanent soil amendment. It can help in desertifying regions; they shouldn't use up the last of their trees to make it though. Many sites in contrast has an abundance of biomass that can be turned into biochar.

Biochar can be made quite simply by stacking your dried wood or organic matter so air can pass through the pile, small sticks at the bottom, bigger sticks in the middle, a bird's nest of sticks on top, and then lighting it from the top. Top lighting, or Conservation Burning, is a cleaner burning method than lighting from the bottom especially if you are a farmer burning agricultural waste already - top lighting produces much less smoke (estimated 98% less particulates); it is a clean burning method according to Sonoma Biochar and Blue Sky Biochar, and while it does create biochar, it is one of the crudest methods. Light from the downwind side, so the fire is both sheltered and fed by the wind. The conservation method burn converts unburned biomass into approximately 15% charred biomass. There are other methods where heat is applied around the wood in a kiln and the wood never catches flame but still turns into charcoal. Arresting the burning process is critical. Spray the pile down with water before the charcoal starts to burn into ash which is the 2nd stage of burning. Spraying it down with microbial infused waters also immediately imprints the char with life - Cuauhtemoc Villa of the Sonoma Biochar Initiative uses EM infused water to cool his biochar piles. The char should be very brittle and glassy looking - use a shovel to break up the char to create more surface area (though try to avoid pulverizing it since biochar dust is nowhere near as effective).

Continue Learning
- Wilson Biochar Associates http://wilsonbiochar.com
- Sonoma Biochar Initiative http://sonomabiocharinitiative.org
- Redwood Forest Foundation Biochar Project http://www.rffi.org/Biochar.html

With EM®

Effective Microbes® (EM®) are a consortia of selected microbes discovered by Professor Teruo Higa in Japan, and they are a trademarked brand owned by EMRO. These microbes are lactic acid bacteria (LAB), yeast, purple nonsulfur bacteria (PNSB), and other naturally occurring microbes that enhance the behavior of indigenous microorganisms in both soil and water. It is not a strictly aerobic group of microbes but rather a mix of facilitative microbes that encourage growth and health in aerobic food soil and water webs (they can also produce foods for each other within the consortia symbiotically). Yeast breaks down the organic matter using fermentation to keep nutrients bioavailable while lactic acid bacteria (an active ingredient in pickling) keeps pathogenic microbes at bay and the pH at a low, acidic, level. Purple non-sulphur bacteria (PNSB) is a remarkable bacteria: it can feed four ways. It can feed off of heat, toxic materials, light, and carbohydrates (sugars). PNSB is a thermophilic bacteria that can thrive in cattle manure lagoons, the edges of ponds, the digestive tracts of worms, and toxic waste dumps, but it can also consume CO_2 and release it as oxygen, amino acids, and folic acids. Like AMF, it is ancient and defies convention, leading many to theorize it to be one of the earliest microbes one earth. EM®'s amazing team of microbes do their work and then bow out of the food web after they finish their work: they stimulate the IMOs and then get consumed by them. EM® is used to purify water, improve soil, enrich aquaculture systems, invigorate animals, and help plants grow.

Make your own Biofertilizer Mix at Home
a Cuauhtemoc Villa recipe with LAB recipe from Chris Trump

Ingredients:
Yeast - from home-brewed kombucha or kefir

PNSB - from worm castings

LAB - from rice wash-water that has sat covered for 3 - 5 days (until it smells slightly sweet), and then combined 1 parts fermented rice wash water to 10 parts milk, and then covered for a 48 hrs until there's a clear separation of the milk curds from the whey which is a lactobacillus-rich liquid. Remove the cheese curds and then strain off the whey serum. Store the LAB in the fridge and make cheese out of the curds.

Molasses - organic blackstrap un-sulphured molasses

Water - ideally water from a thriving ecosystem: avoid chlorinated water from the tap.

Combine equal parts of the kombucha, LAB, and worm castings and then add molasses equivalent to the mixture amount. From there, dilute the mixture 1:20, mixture to water. Culture the mixture in an airtight container - it should be an anaerobic condition. pH should drop within 7-10 days to below pH 4 (ideally pH 3.5).

To Extend:
1 part Biofertilizer Mix or EM®

1 part Molasses

20 parts Water

1 tsp Super Cera Powder (a bioceramic powder) or Sea Salt

"Lactic acid bacteria, yeast, and phototrophic bacteria contained in EM have the ability to ferment organic substances and prevent putrefaction. Therefore, for example, when making compost with EM, putrefying bacteria will be suppressed and, due to the fermentation action of EM, it is possible to manufacture compost with less turning than usual. Also, compost fermented by EM is rich in amino acids and polysaccharides compared with compost produced by the usual methods. EM prevents the production of ammonia during protein decomposition, metabolizing proteins in such a way that amino acids are produced instead. These amino acids can be directly absorbed by plants. Also, under normal circumstances, cellulose will be decomposed and broken down to form carbon dioxide. However, due to the fermentation action of EM, low-molecular polysaccharides will be produced and these will be absorbed by microorganisms and plants. Generally, proteins are synthesized from nitrogen. However, if the plants can directly absorb amino acids from their roots, they can repurpose the energy that would have gone into producing amino acids and proteins, thereby producing fruit with more sugar."
- How EM Works, EMROJapan.com (2016).

With Bokashi

Bokashi means fermented organic matter, but more specifically it is organic matter inoculated with EM®. Bones, dairy, and anything organic can be digested by the bokashi EM® fermentation. It is commonly used on kitchen counters in Japan to digest organic matter of all kinds. Two

---

How to Make Biochar Bokashi

There are many methods, but this is the method taught by Cuauhtemoc Villa in *The Advanced Permaculture Student Online* and synonymous with the TeraGanix recipe on their site. Combine 1:1 biochar to organic matter (this can be compost). You can add ingredients like wheat or rice bran, insect frass, brewer's spent grains (beer mash), compost, seabird guano, cow manure, worm castings, agricultural waste, nut husks and hulls, and more to add in unique biology.

- *50 lbs (22.7 kg) bag of wheat or rice bran*
- *Equal parts biochar to bran*
- *4 gal (15 L) of water*
- *2 - 6 oz (59 - 177 ml) EM*
- *2 - 6 oz (59 - 177 ml) Molasses*

Combine the ingredients and mix them until just moist all the way through - 25% moisture, so you can squish out just a bit of liquid when you squeeze the soil. In an anaerobic condition like in a sealed barrel, ferment the mixture 21 days. You can then apply this to the soil or use it in a bucket system to digest your kitchen waste - including meat and dairy.

weeks after it has fermented in the bucket, it can go into a hole in the ground and covered lightly for two more weeks, and after that, it is nearly completely decomposed.

Continue Learning
- TeraGanix's EM-1® Bokashi Recipes from small scale to large scale https://www.teraganix.com/EM-Bokashi-Recipe-s/262.htm

With Korean Natural Farming

This is an entire farming fertility, waste, and pest management strategy that relies upon indigenous microorganisms and biomass, usually agricultural waste. Chris Trump is a Korean Natural Farmer in Hawaii that uses KNF methods on his family's farm for fertility, soil health, and to fight

---

How to Make KNF IMO Preps

IMO-1 - using a woven basket or a box with holes in it (that are covered with screen), we can inoculate undercooked rice with IMO (primarily mycorrhizal fungi but an entire spectrum of microbes will be present) by filling the box 2/3rds full, and placing it in a healthy soil area where mycelium is present and visible. Cover the box by stapling on breathable paper or use the basket lid. Check back in 4-5 days to look for white fluffy mold. That's IMO-1.

IMO-2 - combine and mix the harvested rice and mold with equal parts brown sugar in a large glass jar. Seal the jar with two layers of paper towels and let it ferment for a week. Now you have IMO-2!

IMO-3 - similar to bokashi, two ounces (60 ml) of IMO-2 are mixed into 60 lbs (27 kg) of biomass like flour, bran, or even macadamia nut kernels and shells. Compost the mixture for 7 days at below 110°F (43°C), and you get IMO-3. IMO-3 can be used to make a compost tea for foliar application and soil soaking.

IMO-4 - combine two parts IMO-3 with one part field soil and one part native ecosystem soil with 5 gallons (19 L) of water. Compost for a week, and you will have IMO-4.

IMO-5 - combine IMO-4 with a nitrogen-rich biomass like manure or the leftover biomass from producing black soldier fly larvae with 4-5 gallons of water depending on the moisture levels of biomass. Not too much moisture - it should just hold and then breakup easily in the hand. It will get up to 130-140°F (55-60°C) and then cool off quickly, and be ready to use in the garden in approximately a week. This prevents the nitrogen from gassing off, trapping it in the fungi, and prepares the fertility to be more bioavailable to the plants and the soil food web. This is IMO-5!

These are just the basic preps - inputs can be added along the way that aren't described here. There's a lot more specifics to KNF and even more abbreviations! Chris Trump's Youtube channel covers his practice and all the preps in-depth. Tune in to his channel or attend his courses for more information.

ubiquitous problems other macadamia nut farmers face in his area - he has an entire series of freely available KNF videos showing step by step how to create all the KNF preps at home using resources almost anyone can access or replicate. The basic concept is IMOs are captured in thriving wild ecosystems to be scaled up using a variety of methods akin to mushroom cultivation but without the sterilization or pasteurization usually required, but there's even more to it: there's ferments and other products used, and it's not just about soil. KNF pig operations have odorless pig pens, and KNF agriculture is always no-till.

> "We go up into the forest and we look for an indigenous biology bloom or mycelium that we can see with our naked eye. We take a collection - actually we take several collections, samplings of that indigenous biology. We bring it down, and we bring it to our farm in the place where we grow food. Here when we apply it to the soil, it changes things… By introducing indigenous biology, we boost the entire ecosystem that is happening under the soil. One of my mentors or people I listen to Elaine Ingham talks of it as the soil food web."
> - *Chris Trump: Korean Natural Farming in a nut shell* by Chris Trump, Youtube.com (2016).

Continue Learning
- Chris Trump's Youtube Channel: https://www.youtube.com/channel/UCus0ZO165qzh6KPIULSzs4w

Scale It Up

Once you play with these concepts for a bit, you begin to realize that there's yard waste, agricultural residues, commercial waste, and even municipal waste everywhere that could be transformed into something beneficial. There are also real-life examples of people doing this. San Francisco is trying to get to zero garbage and composting all organic matter is a key component of their program. Vermont Compost Company uses chickens in large flocks to help tend their giant hot compost heaps which they turn with tractors. Large scale bokashi operations are in the early stages of planning and development on the west coast of the United States - there is ample opportunity to dive in. The key is to have a way to turn large amounts of organic matter (or aerate it from below - whichever is less energy intensive for your context). Compost on an industrial scale is commonly made in windrows, long raised earth berm rows, and turned with a machine called windrow turner. Using worms, chickens, or EM makes it easier, but you will still have to turn it somehow. If you the answer to aeration issue, nothing will stop you! Compost and soil builders are needed everywhere, so look for a problem in your bioregion, and turn it into a solution!

Fungi

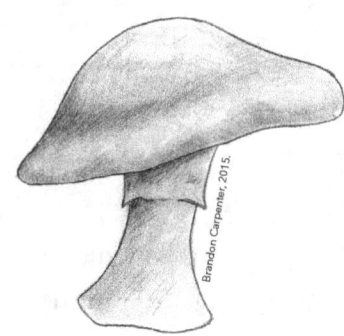

Fungal Site Analysis
What evidence do you have of fungi on the site? Is it in the soil? Are mycelium threads visible in the soil beneath trees in the shade? Are there mushrooms? Lichens? Where are they situated? Are your soils fungal dominant on the site? What's your soil pH? Is your site deficient in beneficial fungal relationships? Add the insights to your maps.

Create a Fungal Remediation & Application Plan
Where are the needs fungi can address in the system? In the garden, in the compost, in the kitchen, in the pasture, in the animal feed, in the medicine cabinet, in the graywater systems, and anywhere else you can find any lack: there's a fungal solution. Fungi are the alchemists and subtle architects of massive change and complex ecologies. Using only fungal pathways, we can address a myriad of challenges - some of which only fungi can address. Once you identify areas where you can partner with fungi, consider the options for remediation, choose a course of action, and then gather the resources needed. You may create a fungal dominant compost, create a fungal dominant compost tea, inoculate an area with king stropharia or an IMO prep, or start growing mushrooms indoors for medicinal and culinary purposes. Fungi will follow you wherever you go and provide numerous benefits.

Did you know that homegrown mushrooms are the amazing? There are many routes to take to grow your own: you can order fully myceliated blocks that sprout mushrooms soon after they are purchased, you can inoculate wood, you can grow it in your garden among the vegetables, or you can grow the mycelium yourself and use it in any of the ways mentioned here and more. Mushroom cultivation is a rather new practice despite humans coexisting with mushrooms their entire existence, so we don't know what's fully possible yet - fungi keeps surprising us!

How to Cultivate Fungi Indoors

Grown on sterilized or pasteurized substrates, the greatest diversity of fungi can be grown in an indoor environment.

Indoor Cultivation Practices

- *Agar* - a traditional cultivation and fungal strain preservation method. It is viewed as more difficult or tedious than liquid culture, but it is also time-honored and the only way to keep a library of preferred genetics at their most robust state. It requires a sterile space to work.
- *Liquid Culture* - this is a recently invented way to scale up mycelium quickly at home by imitating and miniaturizing commonly used commercial liquid cultivation systems that utilize giant vats. Home liquid cultivation uses mason jars with modified airport lids that allows the fungi to breath but keeps it sterile while it allows for mycelium to be added or sampled via the self-healing injection port. LC is much less costly and cumbersome in comparison to the agar system but doesn't have the same ability to store a library of genetics. Using a combination of agar and liquid culture systems is ideal for ease and options. LC allows you to raise fungal mycelium that may never fruit in an indoor setting, but it then can be used outdoors or in medicinal preps.
- *Wood-based mushrooms* - so many mushrooms grow on wood that it makes sense that sawdust would be such an excellent medium. Nutrified sawdust allows for an enhanced and tailored diet to make it even more versatile. Sawdust can be scaled and fit to any form.
- *Manure-based mushrooms* - these decomposer species of fungi break down manures and other composts. These were the first commercially raised mushrooms in Europe: most commonly known as the button mushrooms found everywhere in grocery stores. Many other kinds of mushrooms - some delicious, some psychotropic, and some medicinal - are also grown on manures.
- *On Waste Materials* - Coffee grinds, cardboard, paper-waste, tissues, municipal waste, agricultural waste, and more can all be inoculated with fungi like oyster mushrooms and turned into mushrooms and eventually soil. The edibility of the mushrooms depends on the substrate used and the growing conditions - always use caution!

Mycology Lab Setup & Equipment

Flow Hood - applying the same principles used in expensive laboratories, flow hoods can be made at home for a fraction of the cost of a clean room laboratory with materials found in some home garages, easily ordered online, or bought at the right stores. The principle is the same in all of them: sterilize the area and then pass clean air over the space in a uniform rate at a large volume to create a sterile field. A simple system is to rig a strong fan like a "squirrel cage" blower up to a HEPA (High Efficiency Particulate Air) filter to generate a sterile field directly in front of the filter. Having the filter facing outward horizontally towards the area where the person will be standing is vital. To lessen the mixing of outside non-sterile and inside sterile air, extend and enclose the work area from the HEPA filter outward on all sides but leave open the one side you'll be working (see illustration). This is an ideal space for working with agar at home and even with other stages and modalities of cultivation because it is so clean.

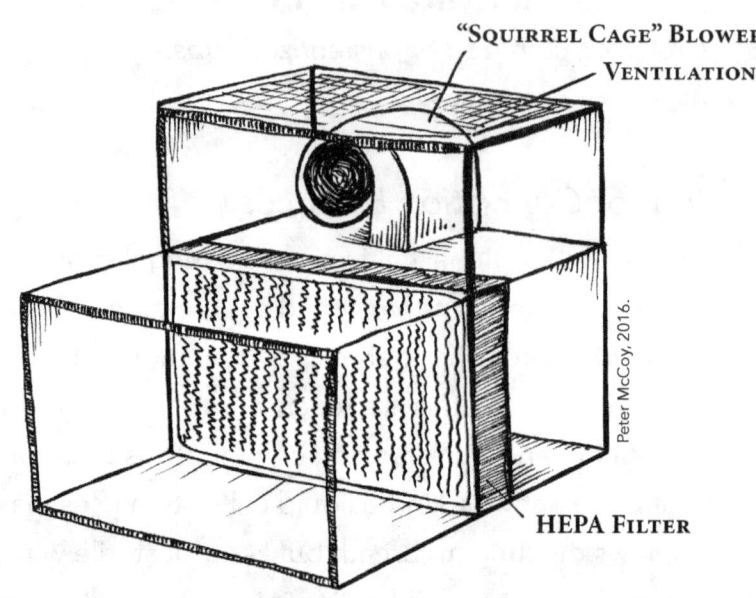

Glovebox - these are enclosed boxes with glass or plastic tops that allow viewing and holes with long gloves attached to them that allow working with materials within the box. By sterilizing the space from within while it is sealed, a sterile environment is established. In this way agar can be worked with even in a small space. Glovebox's are usually much more portable compared to flow hoods.

Pressure Cooker - to sterilize and pasteurize, you need a kitchen, and if you are doing more than pasteurizing, you will need a pressure cook or autoclave. You can make homemade pressure cookers and pasteurizers, but most home growers utilize recognized, reviewed, and tested pressure cookers to work with because a pressure cooker exploding is like a bomb going off, so always go with the best equipment possible and test everything for safety's sake! I echo Peter McCoy when I urge everyone to visit their local county extension office or your area's equivalent, and get your pressure cooker and pressure gauge properly tested before using them.

Supplies - these range the gamut: using a detailed guide is essential. I recommend using <u>Radical Mycology</u> by Peter McCoy; it is encyclopedic and easy to use at the same time. It's important to remember that your cultivation methods will determine your supplies for substrates, inoculants, supplements, containers, and more, so do your research before you purchase supplies.

Indoor Growing Activities

Liquid Inoculation Jars with Airport Lids

Using just mason jars with modified canning lids, we can cultivate liquid cultures of mycelium at home or almost anywhere. The liquid broth is primarily comprised of sugar water, but other ingredients such as yeast, peptone, or gypsum are also often added (for exact recipes and guidelines consult <u>Radical Mycology</u>). Sugar types can range from honey to malt to dextrose to even corn syrup. 500 ml of water is used in a standard quart canning jar. With an airport lid and a sterilized jar with sterile liquid culture inside, we essentially have a portable clean room (or sterile field) inside the jar. This means that liquid inoculation jars can be worked with in almost any circumstance with minimal concern for contamination—though you still have to sterilize your syringe and port site.

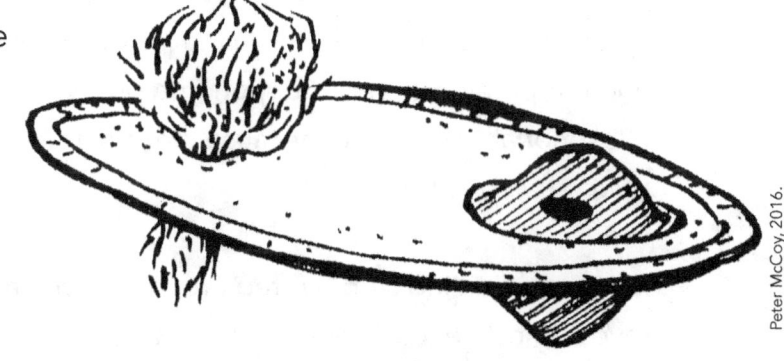

Mycelium grows best in liquid because it can grow in all directions rapidly. This method is also more time-efficient with less preparation required from the cultivator, and it is more efficient at inoculating substrates over other home cultivation methods because it can be sprayed on and soaked in. Inoculated agar or grains can be used to start liquid cultures or even just clean samples of mushroom tissue can be used since the entire body of a mushroom is made of mycelium!

Scaling Up in Different Mediums

From this liquid stage, things can go anywhere: back to agar slants for preservation of the genetics, further exponential scaling up in the liquid stage, or forward into organic matter substrates like wood, manure, agricultural waste, insects, and more. You can spray it on anything and have it inoculate fast because of its liquid nature.

Sterilized Substrate Jar Growing

Sterilizing the jars and the growing medium at the same time in a pressure cooker is easy and efficient. Mixing the substrate beforehand is much like mixing a batch of chocolate chip cookies (but for making the liquid culture substrate, it is more like preparing the honey liquid for mead). Add 0.5 inches (1.25 cm) of water to the bottom of the pressure canner (never let a canner run dry!) Once the substrate is in the jars, airport lids are added, and then they are put on a rack inside the pressure cooker. The pressure cooker is brought up to heat until a steam steadily comes from the release and then the weight is put on or switch is flipped, and the pressure begins to build. Once the desired pressure is reached (usually 15psi or 1055 gram-force per cm^2) the temperature is adjusted to maintain that pressure for the prescribed cook time, and then it is allowed to cool and depressurize at its own rate over night. This procedure works with all sorts of substrates din all sorts of containers. The jars are then inoculated via the injection port with a sterilized syringe containing liquid culture mycelium. The substrate in the jars is then consumed by the fungi completely before it forms any mushrooms. The myceliated substrate can be used to inoculate another substrate (to scale up further), to sprout mushrooms while still in the jar, or to consume as medicine or food. The growth rates and temperatures ranges depending on the mushroom being grown, but this technique is exceptionally successful because the substrate can be specific to the fungi and contamination is so rare if one is careful.

For more detailed step by step processes with all the variant possibilities for all your mycological needs refer to *Radical Mycology* by Peter McCoy. The caveats and particulars involved in each step, each fungi, and each method count, so dive in deep with a full reference and understanding with Peter's book or through his online and physical school, the first mycology school ever: Mycologos.

Continue Learning
- Mycologos, the School of Mycology https://www.mycologos.world
- *Radical Mycology* by Peter McCoy (2016). Paperback.

Pasteurized Straw Growing

Pasteurization is easier than sterilization because it doesn't require a pressure cooker - you can cook the straw for 60 minutes on the stovetop in an old pillow case at 140 – 160°F (60 – 71°C), drain it, and use it to grow many desirable and delicious mushrooms. These might be in beds, in sacks with holes in them, in buckets with holes drilled in their sides, or in long plastic tubes hanging from the ceiling with holes that allow flushes of mushrooms to poke out along their length. Because straw is so easy to work with, it allows for creativity in how it is used. Experiment and have fun with pasteurized straw! Start out with Oyster mushrooms; they all thrive on pasteurized straw.

Commonly Cultivated Mushrooms
with their Preferred Substrate & their Temperature Ranges

	Indoor Substrate	Outdoor Substrate	Temperature Ranges
Reishi (Ganoderma lucidum)	Pasteurized Sawdust, Nutrified Sawdust, & Agricultural Waste	Alder, Elm, Hemlock, Maple, Oak, Pine, Plum, Spruce, Sweetgum, & Willow	Incubation: 70-80F° (21-27C°) Pinning: 65-75F° (18-24C°) Fruiting: 70-80F° (21-27C°)
Lion's Mane (Hericium erinaceus)	Nutrified Sawdust	Alder, Beech, Chestnut, Elm, Maple, Oak, & Walnut	Incubation: 70-75F° (21-24C°) Pinning: 50-60F° (10-15C°) Fruiting: 65-75F° (21-24C°)
Shiitake (Lentinula edodes)	Nutrified Sawdust, Straw, & Agricultural Waste	Alder, Ash, Beech, Birch, Chestnut, Douglas Fir, Eucalyptus, Hickory, Hornbeam, Maple, Oak, Plum, & Sweetgum	Incubation: 70-80F° (21-27C°) Pinning: 50-60F° (10-15C°) Fruiting: 50-70F° (10-21C°)
Pearl Oyster (Pleurotus ostreatus)	Nutrified Sawdust, Pasteurized Sawdust, & Straw	Alder, Aspen, Beech, Birch, Chestnut, Cottonwood, Elm, Maple, Oak, Poplar, Sweetgum, Tanoak, & Willow	Incubation: 70-75F° (21-24C°) Pinning: 50-65F° (10-18C°) Fruiting: 60-70F° (15-21C°)
Turkey Tail (Trametes versicolor)	Pasteurized Sawdust & Nutrified Sawdust	Alder, Ash, Aspen, Beech, Birch, Chestnut, Douglas Fir, Elm, Eucalyptus, Fir, Hickory, Honey Locust, Maple, Oak, Plum, Poplar, Spruce, Sweetgum, & Tanoak	Incubation: 75-85F° (24-30C°) Pinning: 50-75F° (10-24C°) Fruiting: 65-75F° (18-24C°)
King Stropharia (Stropharia rugoso-annulata)	Pasteurized Sawdust, Nutrified Sawdust, Straw, & Agricultural Waste	Conifer or in a Garden Bed with wood chips	Incubation: 70-80F° (21-27C°) Pinning: 50-60F° (10-15C°) Fruiting: 60-70F° (15-21C°)
Maitake (Grifola frondosa)	Nutrified Sawdust	Alder, Beech, Chestnut, Cottonwood, Elm, Honey Locust, Larch, Maple, Oak, Poplar, & Willow	Incubation: 70-75F° (21-24C°) Pinning: 50-60F° (10-15C°) Fruiting: 70-80F° (21-27C°)

Sourced from *Radical Mycology*, 2016.

These commonly cultivated mushrooms are just a thin slice of the range of fungal possibilities on a given site, but even with these few, a broad range of wood types and substrates can be consumed turning potential burn piles into amazing mushrooms, worm food, and rich soils.

How to Cultivate Fungi Outdoors

- *Decomposer Mushrooms* - saprophytic mushrooms can easily be grown outside on manure piles or in garden-style beds. You can even grow King Stropharia in your garden paths with a mixture of manure and conifer-rich wood chips.
- *Wood-based Mushrooms* - feeding fungi wood is one of the most ancient practices, coming from Asia where growing mushrooms outdoors on wood has the longest tradition. Annual trimmings can become animal feed yet often the branches are left behind by the carefully browsing goats or sheep. These piles of wood accumulating on sites all over the world can

become mushrooms by matching the wood type to the fungi that consumes it. The wood can be processed into sawdust.

- *With Plants In Situ* - some fungi like arbuscular mycorrhizal fungi need a living plant partner and a reason to be present. These can be cultivated only with their symbiotic partner in situ. Just like as when rhizobia are in a field with

enough nitrogen present, they are inactive and not partnering with the legume roots to form nodules, so do fungi require a purpose often to present themselves in large numbers. This is why special ingredients are added to compost teas, fermentations, soil mixes, and substrate mixes: it queues the kind of life you are seeking by priming the brew with their preferred foods.

Outdoor Growing Activities:

King Stropharia Garden Path

Like Oyster mushrooms, King Stropharia mushrooms do not necessarily need sterilized substrate: they can outcompete competing bacteria and other fungi. King Stropharia, also called Wine Cap Stropharia, is a delicious mushroom that can grow on cardboard or wood chips in and amongst garden plants. It is incredible easy to establish and continuously feed and harvest from. A mushroom bed can quickly be made anywhere large or small, in any shape or design, by laying down alternating layers of inoculated substrate and wood chips, finishing with wood chips on top. Just keep it moist and it will continuously generate large, delectable mushrooms.

Oyster Paper Digestion

Using grains or sawdust inoculated with oyster mushroom mycelium (grain spawn or sawdust spawn, respectively), we can easily grow mushrooms on a roll of toilet paper or even cardboard and coffee grounds. Grain or sawdust spawn can be ordered online or made at home.

First, sterilize the growing medium by either pouring boiling water over the toilet paper and letting it cool or by soaking the cardboard in non-chlorinated water and then letting it drip out. Fresh coffee grounds are a great substrate as they are essentially pre-treated during the brewing process. Please note that Oyster mushrooms are one of the few types that can readily outcompete bacterial and fungal competitors on these non-sterile substrates! Observing this happen can be both fascinating and educational.

With clean hands, stuff the spawn into the center of the toilet paper roll, and then seal the roll up in a plastic bag that has many small holes poked into it. Alternately, cardboard, coffee grounds, and grain spawn can be layered in a clean yogurt container or bucket until it is full. The container is then placed in a cool, dark area with its lid loosely applied. For either project, the mycelium should grow over the material in two to five weeks.

What causes fruiting?
- Increase in Humidity
- Increase in Oxygen
- Decrease in Temperature
- Increase in Light

To initiate fruiting, place the bag or bucket in a cool area. Mushrooms will start to form from the opening in the container and they need to be lightly misted with water to keep from drying out. A bucket of mycelium can produce at least two to five flushes of mushrooms (each one to two weeks apart) before it is exhausted. The inoculated cardboard can be used two to three times more to inoculate more cardboard, but after three to four flushes of fruit, they tend to lose their vigor. Oysters can be found fruiting in the wild at daytime temperatures of 40-50°F/ 5-10°C but mostly prefer warmer temperatures.

Shiitake Logs

Using wooden dowels inoculated with Shiitake mushroom mycelium, we can grow mushrooms on a hardwood log. Inoculated mushroom logs can fruit for 5-10 years! Logs should be cut from a living tree while the tree is dormant or at the end of the growing season. They should be 4-8" (10-20 cm) in diameter. Using a drill bit the size of the dowels, holes that are 1" (2 cm) deep are made a palm's width away from each other. The

dowels are gently but firmly tapped in with a small hammer. Avoid damaging the bark. Hot beeswax is then applied over the pegs, sealing the hole to protect the fungus, keep out competitors, and retain moisture. In 12 to 18 months, try soaking the logs overnight in cold water to induce fruiting. You can also hit the logs with wooden mallets to stimulate growth! Shiitakes grow in a wide variety of climates outdoors. Sawdust spawn can also be used as well as other methods to grow medicinal and plentiful Shiitake mushrooms.

Medicinal Recipes

Disclaimer: As with all the medical references and physical activities in this book, ask a doctor before taking any new medications or strenuous physical activities, and recognize that none of this information is medical advice but informational only. I am not a medical professional. The medical benefits listed here are easily researchable, yet all medications and therapies as with all permacultural methods and techniques as said in the beginning of this book depend on the context: one person's medication is poison to another; one person's earthworks infiltrate while the other's creates erosion. All things in their context; all things in their season. Consult a doctor for medical advice and treatment.

Cold Water Soak - Mushroom or mycelium is rinsed then soaked in a room temperature water bath (1:10, mushrooms to water ratio) for 6-12 hours, shaking occasionally.

Tincture - Mushroom tinctures use liquids like strong alcohol or vegetable glycerin to separate organic compounds like terpenes, amino acids, and polypeptides not released in water from the mushrooms or mycelium. Submerge the mushrooms or mycelium (1:10, mushrooms to alcohol ratio) in strong alcohol for 6 weeks, shaking or stirring the mixture every day for a few minutes.

Decoction - Like a mushroom tea but with either fresh or the leftover mushrooms from the tincture making process, a decoction is made by simmering the mushrooms (1:10 mushrooms to water ratio) in hot water (158-176°F/70-80°C) until the liquid is 50% evaporated.

Triple Extracts - Combine all three of the above extractions in one bottle, and you have triple extract which contains all the elements derived by each stage.

Mushroom Tea - You can also use dried or fresh mushrooms to make a tea similar to the decoction but not necessarily as concentrated. You can add other elements to flavor it as well like ginger or holy basil.

Dried LC Mycelium

A very interesting thing that is possible with liquid culture mycelium is that it can be dried and used as an extremely potent medicine. All store-bought mycelium-based medicines rely upon carriers for the mycelium or active components like alcohol, glycerin, or dried substrate like rice - this lets the carrier drain away as it dries and leaves just the medicine behind. Dried on glass, the mycelium can be pulverized and encapsulated in pills for a fraction of the price of the store-bought medicines. The medicinal benefits of mycelium and mushrooms are well documented and increasingly expanding as more research occurs.

Lion's Mane "Milk"

Radical and currently making waves, a patent for making a new form of mushroom extract has recently been made with a focus on improving potency. It involves blending myceliated substrate and mushrooms in water with a bit of edible oil like olive oil then straining out the resultant milky liquid. Using a high-power blender is ideal. While it's true our digestion cannot break down raw mushrooms, the "juice" of the mushroom and mycelium are digestible and medicinal. A recent thoroughly cited article in *Fungi* magazine describes how the medicinal process works in detail: it's really remarkable (the article is linked below). In essence, the molecular weight of the beneficial molecules in the "milk" of lion's mane, reishi, and others allow it to pass through the blood brain barrier to treat previously impossible to reach problems - though it should be noted that the positive effects are largely reliant upon continued usage. It is all in the early stages of research, but the benefits that have already been demonstrated are very promising in treating those who suffer from Parkinson's disease, lupus, depression, anxiety, chronic fatigue, Fibromyalgia, and Fahr's disease, and on top of all that, it's a medicine that can be made at home cheaply and safely.

Continue Learning
- *Medicinal mycological preparations having improved potency,* patent https://www.google.com/patents/US20160206670
- *Neurodegeneration and Medicinal Mushrooms,* article https://www.academia.edu/35165675/Neurodegeneration_and_Medicinal_Mushrooms

Scaling Up

Using the methods listed here you can scale up your home diet and medicine cabinet as you cut costs in both areas, or you can turn it all into a business. Peter McCoy's books and courses are the best resources for scaling up from any starting point. He covers DIY to professional levels of cultivation indoors and outdoors online and in-person. Refer to *Radical Mycology* by Peter McCoy for best practices in indoor and outdoor cultivation of fungi of all kinds and dive deep with *Mycologos*, the first ever mycology school.

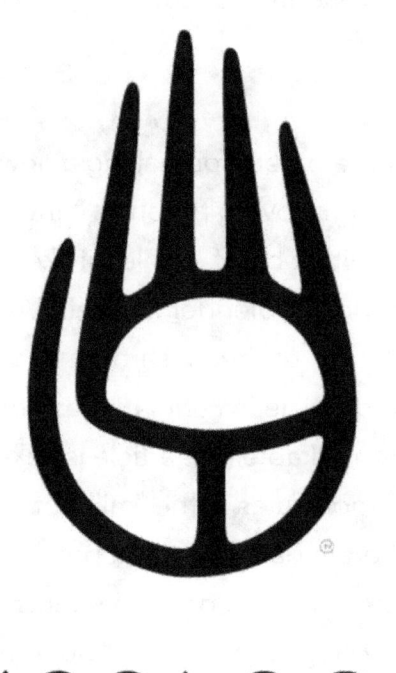

Earthworks

Mentioned earlier in more detail in the Water section, earthworks are used to harvest water, clean water, pacify water, channel water, spread water, raise crops out of water, stop erosion, provide level ground, provide earthen walls to structure, and provide a barrier to unwanted sight or sound.

Earthworks Activities

Essentially these are the colors you get to paint your landscape with to accomplish your goals, but not all the colors fit that final picture in your mind - you have to wisely choose what will illicit the reaction you'd like to see. The more experience you have with earthworks, the more confident you will become in choosing what to go where and in what arrangements.

Earth Berms

Raised earth with raised beds in gardens, below swale paths, and around areas to create privacy - these are versatile and simple structures that can be made with a shovel after an hour or with machinery in seconds.

Hugelkulturs

Classic soil building systems that turn burn piles into soil building events instead - wood is piled and soil is mounded over it. In sandy soils, the wood should be sunken into the earth. In soils with more clay, semi-sunken or even on top of the surface is viable. How deeply or not deeply embedded is also dependent on the context—if you are on a slope or get a lot of rainfall, you will want to bury the wood at least enough to give it a stable resting point in case of flooding. Wood floats, so hugelkulturs on undisturbed hardpan in flooding events have been known to float and then roll downhill, which is dangerous!

Swales

Classic permaculture design water catchment go-to, this is not always ideal and in fact ripping on keyline may be vastly gentler, more effective, and cheaper in some cases: do your research and analyze your site to know where these can go and whether these are right for you. The best places for swales are always the highest and lowest areas first and then the longest swale possible on the site. How to build one is mentioned earlier in the water harvesting section but we can continue here in further detail.

Swales are tree-planting systems at their core; the tree roots hold the berm in place. The more shade you have over the swale path and berm, the greater the water retention. It is therefore ideal to keep the width of the berm narrow enough to be under the canopy of the largest trees growing in the berm itself. They can also be ideal when designed into food forests, orchards, and perennial gardens with some annuals.

Swales can be used with grazing animals in the swale path. Just remember: any compaction in the soft berm area negatively effects the rhizosphere, or root area, of the plants living there —no grazing the berms. Grazing is ideal in large swale corridors with perennial grasses in the pathways (where the water is caught) with electric fencing lining the soft berms on either side, so that animals can graze the swale path and browse the edges of the berm without trampling the berm, but they must be moved through quickly to avoid compacting the soil and reducing water infiltration.

Swales can be smaller or closer together—especially on a hill where it is steep—dig them less deeply into the hill, and, conversely, the berm will be smaller. In order to fight erosion and capture as much of the water flowing over steeper slopes as possible, we need more aggressive trees, perennial ground covers, shrubs, or bushes to hold the soil together, stay in place year round, and spread vigorously (but not invasively), so they cover up the soil completely. We also need the plants to be synergistic—complementary in their inputs and outputs as in beneficial polycultures.

To aid in absorption, the entire area can be ripped below the soft berm, along the swale path, or even the area where the berm gets made prior to cutting the swale. Ripping consists of running a straight furrow 1-2 ft (~.5m) deep into the earth—it doesn't overturn the layers, just rips a tear. This allows for water and root infiltration. Keeping compaction to a minimum is ideal even on the path—the more absorption the better. In sandy soils, wider shallow swale paths are ideal while in clay soils deeper and narrower swale paths are needed.

Seeding swales with annual legumes and planting nitrogen-fixing perennial seedlings or bare root stock and valuable tree seedlings or bare root stock (timber, fruit, nut, fiber, fuel, etc.) is a superb way to start a food forest. We can choose trees that will grow to shade the berms within three to five years or grow from seed, which takes longer. Their leaf drop, seed drop, and accumulation of organic matter like fine silts, pollen, insects, etc. through their action as windbreak will then provide the organic matter needed to feed the soil life to feed the trees and shade the entire swale end to end. This has a cumulative effect. Much in the way lenses in a telescope enlarge a distant object or the way they focus light in a laser, water can be focused in the soil with swales stacked above and below each other on a slope. The integrity and strength of each water-lens in the swale-stack depends on its shade, how wide the swale path is, how well water can infiltrate into the soil, and how much water is entering the site at any given time. It should be noted: swales must be able to safely overflow—spillways are vital.

Feeding swales with diversion drains will magnify the amount of water entering the swale area which can reduce or eliminate irrigation costs. In this way, swales can be used to catch road or any hardscape runoff and absorb it effectively into the landscape while feeding a productive ecosystem that provides an abundance of value to the community. Pitting the swale path is also an option (and can help with clay soils)—these pits can be filled with manure or compost or inoculated wood chips to feed the plants, support soil life, and aid in soakage. Paths should be wide enough to move materials along them.

Diversion Drains

Earthen diversion drains and banks differ from swales primarily in that they channel water towards a pond or swale to absorb or hold it, but within a few seasons in the tropics or humid climates, an earthen diversion drain's compaction is relieved by soil life and plant roots leading to it becoming absorbent, like a swale. Swales can even be used inside of large diversion drains to absorb water in the diversion drain beds themselves. All water has to continue safely in an overflow event and as much water as possible should always be soaked into the ground for storage—our earthworks will always be a pattern and a marriage between these two concepts.

Compacted earth, un-compacted earth, or impermeable layers: it depends on your needs, the local environment, and available resources. The amount of water coming into your area must be understood in order for an appropriate design to be made. If more water than the system can hold is coming in and if you don't have spillways, you could have a broken swale, plant damage, and unexpected and potentially dangerous flood paths. Using the largest rain event on record as a baseline, we can figure out what to expect when 50 or 100 year cycle storms hit. If we are prepared for these events and include spillways and large soakage areas, we can expect our earthworks to perform well in these times.

Clever additions can be made to the drains that act as portable or stationary spill gates to release water strategically, but good design initially is better than using more energy to intervene later on. The less we do, the more energy we save and can use in other areas of interest. That said, if these spill gates are used on a farm, two people can water many acres of land with minimal effort. Pipes through the diversion drain berms can also provide quick water release. Wildfire controls can be used with sheet irrigation (water released on a level sill) with automated gates set to infrared sensors to flood out forest fires early on and before any human response can reach that area.

Interceptor drains are sealed diversion drains that only direct water. They are sealed by ramming the earth, compacting it to the point that not even salt can seep into the soil. They can act and look like diversions drains or a swale but they are sealed. These are especially important in drylands where salting occurs. Extremely salty water must be diverted and cannot soak and seep into the soil.

Terraces

These are large level areas separated by embankments. Build from the lowest terrace upward, reserving the topsoil from the first terrace for the last terrace. Once the first terrace is dug, the topsoil is pulled off the second site above it and used to finish the first terrace. This pattern repeats until the end when the first terrace's top soil is carried to the top and finally used. The level nature of the terrace pacifies rain and flood waters, makes flood irrigation easy and even, and prevents nutrient loss.

Terraces are not advisable on very steep slopes or in soils that cannot withstand the slope and water pressure. Trees are used on the embankments between terraces to not only provide leaf litter and nutrients but to hold the terrace embankments together and keep the terraces level and intact. Living fences or hedges are ideal for protecting the embankment slopes from grazing animals. Ponds and aquaculture in general can be utilized on the terraces for great effect, as Sepp Holzer's Krameterhof demonstrates elegantly. Staggering terrace spillways also prevents erosion over time. Terraces are the longest-lasting and oldest agricultural artifact still being used in the world today—while monuments of stone weather away, Asia's terraces endure—albeit with maintenance and good management.

Yeomans Plow or SubSoil Ripping

Like invisible earthworks, ripping uses a straight sub-soil ripper attachment on a plow avoids turning the soil; instead the ripper creates a 0.5 – 1 meter deep rip in the land. A "shoe" at the bottom of the shank breaks up compaction in the sub-soil, which promotes subtle water catchment in pasture and can also be used to control wandering root systems such as honey locust in orchard rows. Ideally done on contour or near contour for the strongest effect, this allows deep water infiltration, deep compost tea application, and/or tree planting all on contour or in a keyline pattern. The trees or plants with aggressive root systems will break up the soils and allow for more water infiltration as they begin on the process of building up the organic matter. Compost tea applicators and seeders can be attached to the ripping setup as well!

Keyline Water Harvesting Farm Systems

Applying Keyline water harvesting to your design and using the Regrarians Platform, an expanded form of PA Yeomans Keyline Scale of Permanence, we can make wise decisions as to where our earthworks, ponds, water harvesting, fences, and everything else should be placed.

Chinampas

Documented by the invading Spaniards, *chinampas* are plant-growing systems originally used by the people of the Triple Alliance, often referred to as Aztecs. They are used in wetlands or in areas with high water tables. The soil is dug out and piled up above the water line until there is a channel of water and a strip of land. You can continue this and transform an entire area into small channels and raised beds. The anaerobic soils from below the water are very rich but take some time to become aerobic. Once they do, they can grow rich gardens that can be harvested by paddle boat or canoe. It's an effective solution to a high water table.

An illustration of the Triple Alliance (or Aztec) Chinampas

Earth-Sheltered Greenhouses & Homes
These are structures that use earth to mitigate outside environmental conditions. They can be as simple as earth banked on the northern wall of a greenhouse in the northern hemisphere, or a southern wall in the southern hemisphere—this prevents heat loss and makes a thermal mass storage in the soil that continues to warm the structure through the cooler night. It also works to keep structures cool in the heat, even though they are under glass in the sun.

The *walipini* is a submerged garden (8-10ft/3m) facing the sun path with a ground-level, glass or plastic roof oriented perpendicular to winter solstice's sun at noon (the time of least solar energy). Topsoils are reserved during excavation and returned over a graveled and graded floor to prevent water logging and to give plants healthy soils (since the subsoils at 8 ft (2.4m) deep are far from ideal for plant growth). This makes for a warm winter garden even in sub-zero temperatures.

This design is based on a general thermal constant of the earth. All over the world starting at 4 ft (1.2m) deep in the dry soil it is 52-54°F (11-12°C) constantly. When we cap that heat and add the sun's energy to it, we easily create enough warmth to grow food through the winter.

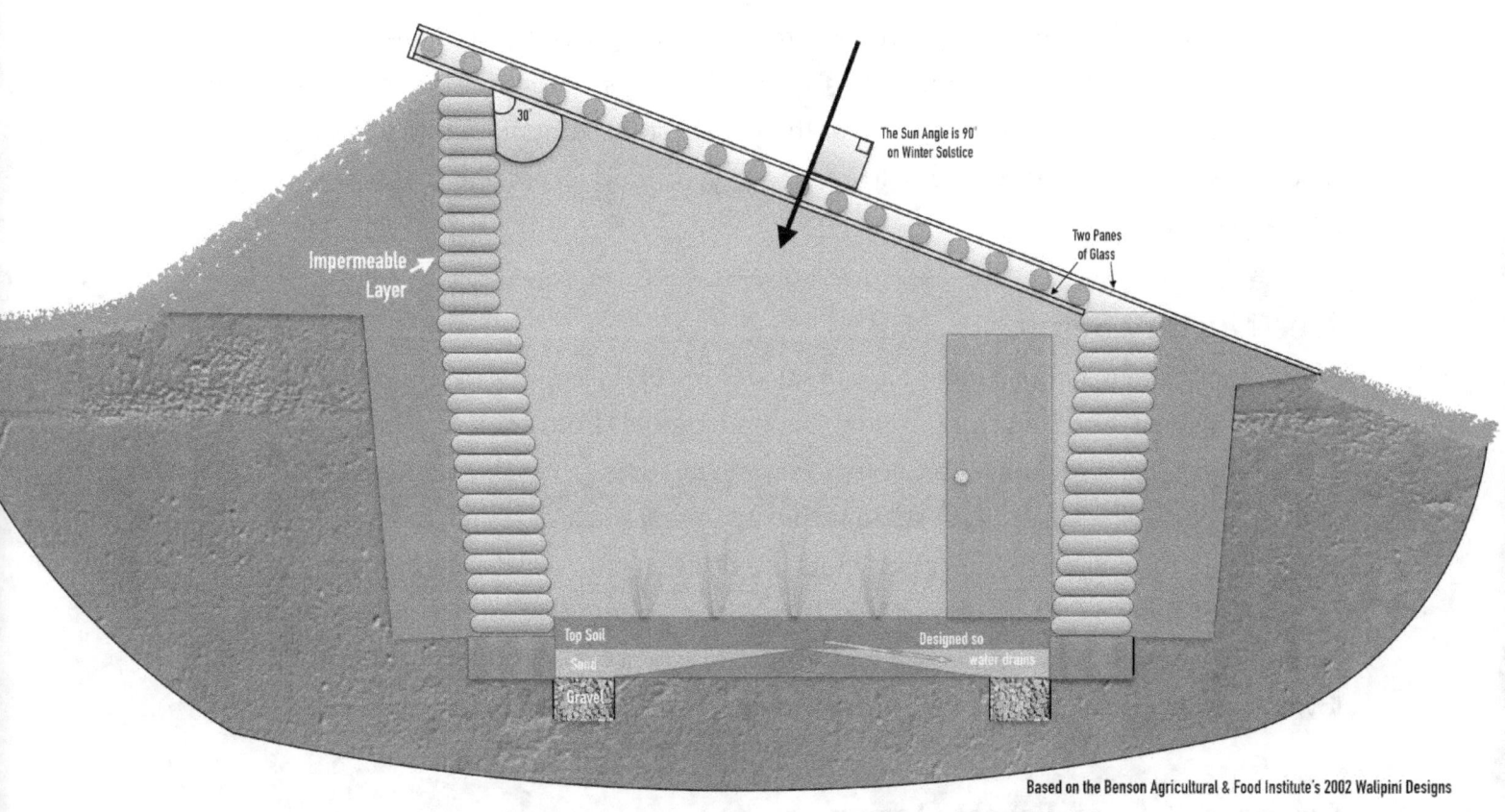

Based on the Benson Agricultural & Food Institute's 2002 Walipini Designs

Trees & Food Forests

Everyone wants a nearby food forest to forage in, but managing and designing it well makes the difference between a blessing and babysitting. The ideal system is one that requires no human interaction but those systems are always lower in food, fiber, and medicinal production for human purposes. We have to direct and guide by our initial designs and with our continued management unless it is truly a wilderness restoration project and then very little interaction might be expected after the initial establishment. Within this section are guidelines and best practices to help you make your food forest one that serves you and future generations.

Tree Nursery Setup

Rooting out cuttings from pruning is a great way to capitalize on a free resource, a natural return of surplus. Growing trees, perennials, and annuals from seed or cutting in a controlled environment, like a greenhouse, allows for homesteaders to quickly generate more plants than they can use on their homestead within just a few seasons. Small greenhouses equipped with misters connected to hoses on timers provides an easy way to start your own home plant nursery. You can take it up another level by having the humidity monitored and use a humidifier to maintain a desired humidity level. Mushrooms and other heat and sunlight loving organisms can share the space as well.

Orchard & Food Forest Design

Planting All the Layers of the Forest

By including all the layers of the forest in our designs, we occupy any niches a weed or unwanted element might try to occupy. You can plant all at once, but when planting, keep succession in mind. The space will start out dominated by support species like annual legumes, green manures, mulch plants, and some fast-growing, nitrogen-fixing trees with small bare-root trees and perennial seedlings hidden among the explosion of growth. Use flags and colored sticks to keep track of your valuable tree and perennial plantings—they'll need intervention routinely as they develop to prevent them from getting shaded out or

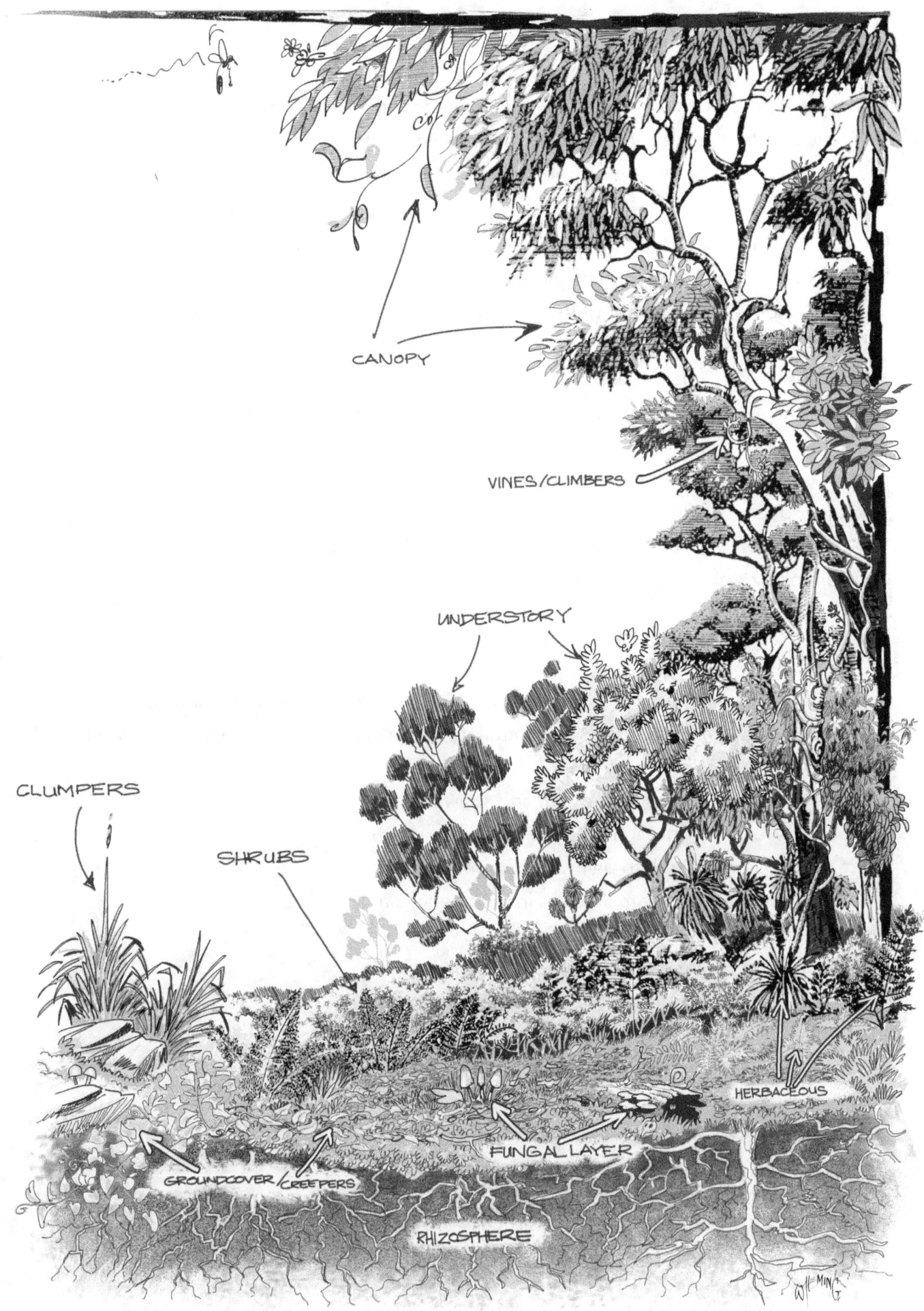

choked by vines. Once the valuable perennials and trees are established, the space will be largely occupied by valuable species with coppiced nitrogen-fixing trees and mulch plants found intermittently throughout the system.

- Canopy, the tallest layer (the large trees that for the "ceiling of the forest)
- Understory (small trees and bushes)
- Palms (some climates have both understory- and canopy-level palms, while some have none—such as in cold temperate)
- Shrubs (some climates have two layers)
- Herbaceous layers (in cold temperate climates there are two layers)
- Vines or climbing plants
- Ground cover plants or creepers
- Rhizosphere or root layer
- Fungal layer (both above and below ground and within plants and animals)
- Clumpers or plants that spread by division

Using Plant Guilds

A plant guild is a harmonious and beneficial polyculture or group of companion plants, focused usually around one or two central plants. An example could be an apple tree guild with onions or garlic for pest control, artichokes for mulch and phosphorous, nasturtium and strawberries for ground cover, and lastly, a small perennial nitrogen fixer like a Siberian pea shrub to pair with it. Plant guilds are creative assemblies that are limitless in their beneficial possibilities. There are lists of plant guilds as well as lists of companion planting pairs online you can use to start out, but few focus on the plant relationships or compile information on how plant guilds work. *The Natural Capital Plant Database* was created to serve this very purpose and features plants from across the globe researched by permaculturists for permaculturists. Free for anyone to use though advanced features require a small fee, the invaluable database shares research and data on plant guilds by region.

Likely the most popular and well known plant guild is The 3 Sisters: Corn, Squash, and Beans.

Continue Learning
- *The Natural Capital Plant Database,* the permaculture plant database http://www.permacultureplantdata.com
- *Dr. Duke's Phytochemical and Ethnobotanical Databases,* a USDA database https://phytochem.nal.usda.gov/phytochem/search
- *List of Companion Plants,* on Wikipedia https://en.wikipedia.org/wiki/List_of_companion_plants

On Contour, Off Contour, or on Swales

How will you plant your trees? What pattern? On contour? Off Contour? Even George Washington was interested in contour: he was convinced that contour plowing was key to saving America from losing its soils when he retired from the presidency - read more about that in <u>Dirt: The Erosion of Civilizations</u> by David R. Montgomery (2007). Contour planting holds the soil together and even without swales or any earthworks, planting on contour can harvest water like a swale or keyline rip. We can find answers to our questions in our earlier research: How much disturbance is required? How much water will be harvested? How cost-effective is each option? You might need to have water slow but not stop in your garden rows and so you might do a keyline pattern and have the rows slowly release the water to the sides from the naturally formed grade away from contour as the equidistant rows continue down the hill or up the hill away from the guiding contour line. Your area might be flat but very little on earth is flat (unless you live in a former rice farm plantation as some of my students do - those flood easily and require creating chinampas!)

The NAP Method

One of the methods employed by Stefan Sobkowiak of Miracle Farms. It is the most basic building block of his orchard system, the NAP polyculture: Nitrogen Fixer, Apple, Pear (or Plum). The idea is that every tree will have a nitrogen-fixer on one side. He prunes his orchard, grafts his fruit trees, and spreads a berry shrub layer with cuttings. He uses honeysuckle bushes to draw birds away from his cherry trees instead of using netting. An ornithologist by education, Stefan expects and welcomes sharing 5-10% of the farm's yield with the birds, animals, and insects is expected and monitored.

Continue Learning
- *The Permaculture Orchard: Beyond Organic,* video by Olivier Asselin featuring Stefan Sobkowiak's farm and teaching in Quebec, Canada (2014). http://www.permacultureorchard.com

Using Native Plants

Every area with settled indigenous peoples had ethnobotanical relationships with the native plants and ecosystems that we can imitate in our food forests. We can source the materials locally for a vibrant, hardy, and extremely beneficial food forest planting guild. With culinary, social, and medicinal focuses on native plants, animals, fungi, and more only increasing, we are going to see demand rise beyond the capacity of foragers to provide soon. Farmers will have to raise native plants to fill the demand. Mark Shepard's New Forest Farm seeks to mimic the oak savanna that used to dominate his area of Wisconsin. New Forest Farm has chestnut and oak canopies with cherry and apple trees in the understory, hazelnuts at the shrub layer with cane berries, currants below them, and grapes climbing throughout. It is a thriving oak savanna wonderland of food, timber, and fiber though it is a marriage of native and non-native. Sean Sherman is demonstrating what can be done commercially and in the kitchen with indigenous food systems education in NATIFS and The Sioux Chef as well as through his books and restaurants. The foraging alchemist Pascal Baudar writes books and teaches classes, encouraging us to eat the invasive plants in our areas to protect the native ecosystems which he also uses to make amazing foods and fermented concoctions.

Continue Learning
- NATIFS (North American Traditional Indigenous Food Systems), a nonprofit organization focused on North American indigenous food education and food access https://www.natifs.org
- _The Sioux Chef_ by Sean Sherman, a book filled with recipes using native plants (2017). Paperback.
- _The New Wildcrafted Cuisine: Exploring the Exotic Gastronomy of Local Terroir_ by Pascal Baudar, a book focused on recipes using wild plants for ferments, infusions, spices, and other wild food preparations (2016).
- _Restoration Agriculture_ by Mark Shepherd (2013). Paperback.

Net and Pan

This is a method for planting trees on steep slopes, especially in drier areas. Trees are spaced out evenly and planted in shallow pits (pans) then connected by even more shallow diversion drains. This allows all trees to be watered efficiently—all runoff is caught in the net, and all trees are included. Organic matter is carried and deposited along with the water, making it a compost tea of sorts which is shared by other trees when water levels exceed the individual pans. When all pans and diversion drains are full they release water in a sheet down the hill evenly.

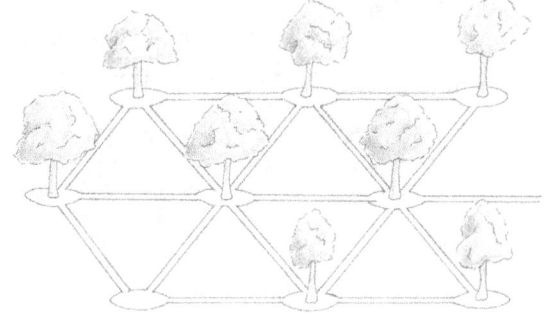
Brandon Carpenter 2015.

ORCHARD MANAGEMENT

Between the Rows

What will you do with the orchard row paths? How can you control the wandering roots of the legume support species? As you cut back your perennial nitrogen fixers, their roots will explode outward - in an orchard if the row paths are big enough, a tractor can pass through seasonally or more and to keep the area free of tree roots. Sheep, chickens, goats, pigs, and even cattle can be run through the area guided by portable electric fences while they graze on the grassy path, outreaching branches, and the fallen fruit which does much to interrupt the orchard pest life cycles. The row paths can also be cultivated with annuals like grains and garden vegetables.

To Prune or Not to Prune?

While there is much debate over pruning in general, pruning can help control growth, determine shape, and stimulate fruit growth. When pruned, many fruit trees like apples, stonefruit, and mulberries respond with an increase in fruit production—they panic and start producing overtime though the timing of pruning is critical and depends on the type of fruit. Most fruit trees prefer winter pruning but not all, so do your research!

When pruning, a classic method is to remove intersecting branches to prevent them from rubbing each other and damaging their bark. This also allows for airflow. Small branches are removed from within 6-8" (15-20cm) of the trunk, leaving only large branches and a relatively open area. Some growers use wires to hold the branches down after pruning for a couple of months. After this, they may grow downward, below horizontal or horizon line, which stimulates fruiting. The orchardists make sure to not leave the ties on the tree for longer than that, or else, the tree may start to grow around the wire. Other growers are tying branches to the

From Luther Burbank's experimental farm, espalier methods keep branches permanently laterally to promote a focus on fruiting.

branch itself or to the trunk in early spring for a few weeks or a month to stimulate bud growth. There are many different methods of pruning and training fruit trees, and many new combinations and methods are being trialed regularly.

For those that do not prune, they commonly control vegetative growth by pulling the branches down below the horizon line and holding them there for a month or two in late winter/early spring. This stimulates fruit growth instead of overall branch, trunk, and leaf growth. It channels the energy that would have gone into vertical (vegetative) growth into the fruit. Unpruned fruit tree arms weighed down with fruit tend to develop a drooping habit as well, as do trees with vines on them or late winter snow. Unpruned branches can touch the dripline of a tree intercepting critters that would have eaten the roots or bark of trees with pruned branches. Many argue that parasites from the soil can be transmitted this way, but the growers using this method focus on parasite and disease resistant varieties.

Orchardists who do not prune often cite vigor as the reason why. Vigor is caused by overwatering, over-fertilizing, and over-pruning. The sap that returns in spring is based on the quantity of branches, buds, and leaves that the tree had the season before. If the extra sap is a moderate amount, it can go into bud growth and form larger and more numerous fruits, but too much sap can turn into vigor: out of control vegetative growth which can lead to increased disease, weaker plants, and poor yields. This is why orchardists graft onto dwarf rootstock—it's non-vigorous! The branches that are grafted on are usually from vigorous varieties especially if they are heirloom. Trees want to turn water or nutrients into vigor and vegetative growth. In wet climates with heavy soils, no swales are needed for a line of trees on contour to act like a swale—a swale would create too much water and endless vigor!

Espalier

Fruit trees and vines can be trained up walls and along fences creating fruit walls on buildings or surrounding properties. They are especially useful in areas with limited space but many walls—like in urban areas. The espalier technique trains fruit tree branches horizontal to control vegetative growth and encourage fruiting instead. This makes for smaller trees but more fruit and less if any pruning. It is an elegant way to control vigor.

Grafting

Grafting is the art of taking a cutting from one tree and growing it onto the cut branch of another tree. This can create an all-season tree where each branch has a different ripening time period, so you can have early, mid, and late season fruit all on one tree. It is ideal for small areas, orchardists, or anyone looking to turn pruning cuttings into new trees. Every pruning from a fruit tree can be grafted onto a root stock or an already established tree's branch to diversify yields. You can have one citrus tree with lemons (*citrus limon*), limes (*citrus aurantifolia*), and mandarin oranges (*citrus reticulata*) on it or one tree with a dozen different types of apple.

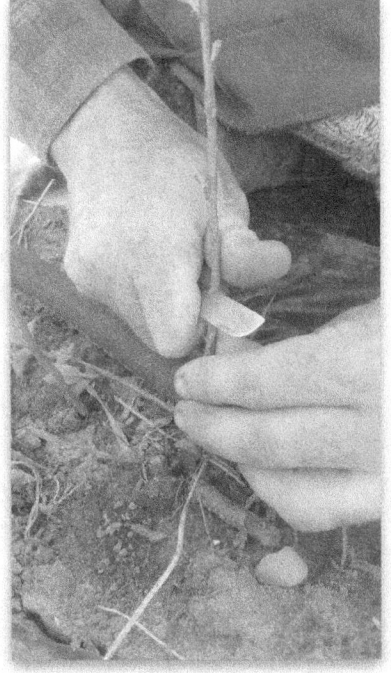

Rootstocks are chosen for their vigorousness, disease-resistance, and hardiness; they can also be linked to fruit-size and early fruiting. This is how it is possible to have dwarf and non-dwarf trees of the same variety: different rootstock. Pears (*pyrus*) graft onto quince (*cydonia oblonga*) rootstock to save time since quince trees don't take as long to mature as pears which can take 20 years! Plum (*prunus*) rootstocks can support grafts from all other *prunus* varieties: peaches, nectarines, apricots, and other plums.

Trees don't all readily graft onto each other—most are done within the same family. It is both an art and a science. Some use grafting tools that work like scissors while other use traditional grafting knives that are extremely sharp. There are several different styles of cut though the main idea is to have the bark from the cutting, or scion, and the rootstock touch. The pieces can range in size from a 6-8" (15-20cm) section of branch or larger, to a small 1-2" (2.5-5cm) section of branch (benchgrafting), to just a cut out bud from another plant (budgrafting).

When finished with a new graft, you can tie on or leave a final top branch for birds to land on. Otherwise, your fragile grafting can be ruined by any passing bird. At Miracle

Farms in Quebec, they use rubber bands to keep the grafts stable, and they seal off exposed wood with wood putty (as pictured).

PLANTING PRACTICES

From Seed

Arguably the best way to grow a tree on a site is to plant the tree from seed though it does take the longest amount of time. The seed's first roots will be in indigenous soils with the indigenous soil food web in place rather than in a greenhouse in an artificial environment. There's no chance of becoming root bound but they can entangle their roots if closely planted. Very little work is involved and the seedlings can be easily transplanted as bare root trees.

Do your Seeds require Special Preparation?

- **Stratification** - Winter seed dormancy can be broken by spending a short period of time in colder temperatures in a refrigerator, soaking in cold water overnight, or even outdoors.
- **Vernalization** - Some seeds require a longer cold period in the refrigerator or outdoors to simulate a full two to three month winter.
- **Scarification** - Some seeds need to be stressed to germinate through either heat or physical action like sandpaper scratching, fire, or nicking a corner with a knife.

Most of us will grow trees from seed in a greenhouse nursery setup often after stratifying, scarifying or vernalizing our seeds. A mister system on a timer can be used, but it can be just as easily hand watered as long as the temperatures don't spike and cook the young trees. After raising the seeds into young saplings, they can be transplanted to the food forest or into larger pots until they are large enough to hold their own in the food forest. Though plants do face some transplant shock potentially using this system, overall it is more efficient and productive than planting by seed in situ due to predation and uncontrollable natural environmental stressors: the seedlings get eaten, trampled, or outcompeted at a high rate.

Bare Root Trees

These are young trees that are transported in their dormant stage without soil as just a bare root tree. It's incredibly effective and efficient - the trees don't mind the treatment and they experience less transplant shock than from any other method. They can be shipped cheaply because they are small and light, and they can be planted quickly because they are small and their roots are accordingly smaller. Using a keyline plow, a rip can be made on contour while a few people in back of the tractor plant trees in the fresh cut and sow plant companion plant seeds - it can all happen in one pass. In this way, hundreds and thousands of trees can be planted in a day by only a few people.

GROWING PRACTICES

STUN Method

Mark Shepard has developed a system for getting the hardiest, most resilient, and vigorous plants for his area—with vigor being sourced from their genetics, not water or fertilizer. The STUN method stands for Strategic Total Utter Neglect. Mark plants his trees close together which makes it obvious which trees perform better than others and then aggressively culls out the weak plants. We can do this at any time in any system by using stress strategically to judge how strong or weak any given element is. Over time we can select for the best of the best over generations, leading to a resiliency and hardiness that far surpasses the original first generation of plantings, and we can fill out our entire systems with locally adapted, productive, and hardy plants.

Dry Farming

Dry farming, once quite common, has become something inconceivable to many gardeners and farmers in arid regions. This is simply the practice of using whatever rainwater you receive for watering your system – instead of pumping from aquifer-fed wells – especially not from those that are thousands of feet deep, as is common today. Irrigating with solely the rain you

Dry Farmed Huauzontle in Zone 8b in California in soils 120°F (48.8°C), US. Note the planting density and the shade generated by the native wildflowers and grasses.

receive in a year, or in some arid regions every year or few years, will determine plant choices and the length of the growing season. In desertifying areas, dry farming may be the only option for keeping farms profitable and ethical.

Dripline Irrigation

Used almost everywhere, dripline irrigation saves water, time, and energy, and over time it even saves money on hoses if the dripline is covered up from the sun which can quickly destroy hoses in hotter, drier climates. This can make management much easier by allowing the gardener or farmer to control how much water is released and at what times, and it allows them to spend more time on observation than on watering. This system also makes it easy to add nutrients and minerals via the dripline - just remember compost tea via a dripline will eventually clog it. Sending food soil web foods instead of life is ideal - this is exactly what Organics Alive has done. They are focused on problem solving and bridging the gap between permaculture systems and conventional agriculture and landscape management systems, so they are designing products that are compatible to the current agricultural modalities.

Continue Learning
- Organics Alive Homepage https://organicsalivegarden.com

Using a Refractometer *(also known as a BRIX Meter)*

Refractometers or BRIX meters are devices that refract light through plant leaf or stem sap, honey, or fruit juice to detect the concentrations of starches or sugars in that liquid - Gabe Brown even uses it on his eggs! Industrially they have many applications. They don't require batteries, just the sun's light. Its reading of sugar/starch levels indicates how efficiently a plant is producing exudates, interacting with the soil food web, and photosynthesizing. To avoid inconsistent data, do not take measurements in the early morning or on cloudy days—try to test at the same time of day when sunlight and temperature are similar as a form of control on the experiment.

BRIX readings are variable per plant per soil per location. Exudate, mineral, and overall nutrient offerings differ from place to place, so nutrient content is varied in both soils and plants, as is BRIX reading. It should be noted that refractometer readings correlate to overall plant health and nutritional density, but they lack the sophistication to give us the nutrient profiles and the concentrations of each individual nutrient. It is still a great tool for measuring overall plant health, fruit nutrition, and ripeness as it is used by viticulturists, beekeepers, and orchardists globally.

Professional Applications & Scaling Up

You can scale up into a tree nursery business quickly. *Permaculture Voices*, a now defunct podcast, featured many tree nursery businesses that began with a small backyard garden plot growing from seed or even a bulk order of seedlings that they tended and then sold once they were larger and more valuable. As with the fungi, you can hop in at any point in the growth cycle with trees: all stages of growth are sold online and often locally in season. The need for organic and regenerative organic tree nurseries is immense. Every year the perennials and trees sell out earlier from the organic and even non-organic outlets.

Continue Learning
- Permaculture Voices Archives https://www.permaculturevoices.com/blog-2/podcast-2/
- *Integrated Forest Gardening: The Complete Guide to Polycultures and Plant Guilds in Permaculture Systems* by Wayne Weiseman, Daniel Halsey, and Bryce Ruddock.
- *The Forest Garden Greenhouse: How to Design and Manage an Indoor Permaculture Oasis* by Jerome Osentowski (2015). Paperback.
- *Paradise Lot: Two Plant Geeks, One-Tenth of an Acre and the Making of an Edible Garden Oasis in the City* by Eric Toensmeier (2013). Paperback.

Gardening

Home gardens are more productive per square foot or meter than any industrial farm simply because of the diversity and hands-on nature of home gardening. We see what's going on with individual plants and usually early on. We know our gardens intimately. There is an immense amount of freedom we feel when we eat from our own gardens, and the ways in which we can manage them spans a huge range from market gardener to a natural farming styles. I hope you feel free to embrace any and all the styles depending on your situation, mixing and matching using what works for you and the landscape itself.

PLANTING

Throw Sow

This is both a planting technique, sometimes called broadcasting, and seed characteristic– seeds that grow vigorously when surface sown. They do not need to be hand planted (cover with soil). They will grow faster than birds will eat them (or have another form of protection). Throw sowing for plant adaption generates extremely vigorous offspring. Save seed each year from the best plants in the worst soils, and their vigor will increase with each generation. You can also train plants to self-seed by shaking out their seeds all over the soil once the seeds have set. Over time, it creates a seed bank in the soil that outcompetes any native or non-native weeds.

Seed Balls

Masanobu Fukuoka used seed balls, a mixture of seeds, clay, and compost or manure to prevent birds from eating the seeds after they were sown and to provide them with the fertility they would need to grow once sprouted. Seed balls also make planting easier. They can be used to plant out public space, abandoned lots, and other areas where birds or neglect are preventing recovery. They can be made and used by people of all ages and ranges of abilities because it does not require bending down to plant in the soil. Again though there is a range - in some instances Fukuoka's seed balls were mere clay coatings on rice seed which was enough to throw off the birds. Wild flowers do well with the full

Masanobu Fukuoka spreading seed balls on his farm.

concoction of clay and compost, but clay alone can be sufficient especially because of its water holding ability.

Continue Learning
- *One Straw Revolution* by Masanobu Fukuoka and edited by Larry Korn (1978).
- *Sowing Seeds in the Desert* by Masanobu Fukuoka and edited by Larry Korn (2012).

Direct Seeding

The most common form of planting in a garden or farm is direct seeding. This is where the seed is placed *directly* in the soil. Seed packets have measurements for seed depths and spacing, and these range in accuracy and necessity. Some seeds need to be directly sown solely to avoid being eaten by birds and can grow on the surface perfectly albeit vulnerably; others need a specific depth or their roots won't develop properly, and the plant will be weaker than it could have been.

Some plants are given the spacing we are directed to plant them at because of soil fertility, or, more accurately, soil infertility: they need to be able to work with a larger volume of soil in order to find adequate nutrients. Contrasting with this, there are examples of very close plantings in bio-intensive gardens with very high yields and large, beautiful plants. The soil structure and fertility are key components for determining the planting density and success of your seeds. The seeds with the highest probability for success are either thrown-sown or directly seeded. Most direct-seeded plants have large seeds that can be planted deep enough below the surface of the soil to not be visible. Seeds like squash, corn, beans, okra, melon, peas, and other large seeds can all be covered with soil. Many of the finer seeds, seeds that birds love, or more tender seedlings are grown in a nursery and transplanted more often—though certain fine-seeded plants like carrots don't like transplanting, so they need to be direct surface sown and watered gently.

Some seeds like corn can be soaked overnight in water before planting to speed germination while other plants need to be soaked in hot water or orange juice to germinate at all! Learning the needs of each plant and seed can seem daunting the first time you learn about it, but when you actually work with the seeds, it's hard to forget; they're just so amazing!

Pasture Cropping

As its name implies, this is sowing seed directly into pasture. Growing grains directly in the native, perennial pastures allows native habitats to be preserved, and the pasture can double as a crop field. When the grains are harvested, holistically managed herbivores like cattle can be used to harvest, process, fertilize, and trample the area—leading to more carbon sequestration, increased pasture biodiversity and soil depth, and higher quality products without any soil disturbance.

Continue Learning
- *Why pasture cropping is such a Big Deal* by Kirsten Bradley, on Milkwood.net (2010). https://www.milkwood.net/2010/12/07/why-pasture-cropping-is-such-a-big-deal/
- *What is Pasture Cropping* on PastureCropping.com (2018). http://www.pasturecropping.com/pasture-cropping

Rows, Beds, & Raised Beds

The most common garden growing design are rows which often leave very little room for root growth and can lead to compaction. Wider paths can help but then require maintenance regularly with a tool or a permanent path using stone, wood or mulch can be used. Double-reach rows are rows where one can reach to the middle from both sides which helps avoid compaction and give the plants plenty of room within a traditional row format. It should be noted that the more diverse, crowded, and deep your rows get, the harder it is to find and harvest foods though it is at the same time enormous fun as well to hunt in our garden jungles for food. Quite narrow in comparison are the biointensive 30" (72cm) beds that use Elliot Coleman's line of 30" (72cm) standardized tools. It should be noted that those systems often rely upon regular aeration to fight compaction. How you shape your garden depends on your space and preferences and can be, and often is, a combination of design techniques and management strategies.

Garden beds are growing areas that don't have to be any certain shape or size, and while these range in their expression, they often allow for more room for plant roots and greater expression overall. Raised beds can help those who cannot bend over - the typical raised bed is essentially a box of soil that is easy to access. They can be installed anywhere as long as they can drain easily. There are other raised beds like hugelkulturs that allow for easy harvesting from a large growing mound. Keyhole garden beds are circular beds that surround the gardener in an C or U shape. By only having enough room to stand and pivot, this gardening technique saves space and effort. Double reach beds are garden beds or rows that allow you to comfortably reach to the middle from either side (to avoid straining your back).

Management

How will you manage your system? Will you be walking through it daily? How much time will you dedicate to it? Who will help you? How will it change throughout the year?

Observation

The gardeners greatest asset as with every designer is their observation: if you are not observing and getting in close, you will miss the many undercurrents in your garden space. Pests that arrive to prey on your Peruvian golden berries are in turn consumed by their predators a few days later who discover them. Your golden berries just miss one flush of flowers - a week later another is up setting fruit. Was that enough water? Digging in the soil a few inches, feeling around in the mulch, and looking daily over a longterm - observational habits will come to you as you slow down and spend time observing and trying to understand your space.

To Weed or Not to Weed? Chop & Drop!

We've all done it, but weeding only calls in worse weeds over time as they are just trying to bring in the nutrients and soil life to address a soil issue in that area. The more we pull, the more weeds. If we chop them they will regrow, but there's mulch in that, and if we time it right, we can chop it before the seed heads form. There are only a finite number of times a weed can re-sprout from the root, and it also accumulates the exact thing that area was needing: organic matter that has accumulated or will attract life that can release the nutrients lacking in the topsoil. If your area has weeds it might be due to soil disturbance and uncovering weed seeds in lower layers, soil compaction, a lack of key nutrients, and/or it could be due to the soil pH which can all be remedied with either a fungal (acidic) or bacterial (alkaline) compost tea and aeration with a broadfork. Healthier soils have fewer and weaker weeds that yield wonderful mulch.

Using Animal Pressure

We can manage our gardens by routinely running animals through them in short spurts, or they can be used to clear an area at the end of a season or at the very start. Their manure also fertilizes the ground as they work. Some animals cannot be trusted to focus on just weeds or insects, but chickens tend to first focus on insects and some pigs like guinea hogs tend to focus on grass. Goats can be great for clearing areas and sometimes for managing weeds as well though they can just as quickly eat the kale and lettuce.

To Water or Not to Water?

Many folks can temporarily dry farm in their region at different times and still grow their favorite and familiar foods like in Sonoma county where they time their tomato growing season to taper off the watering, so the tomatoes rely upon the water table water only deep with their roots and in doing so create these richly flavored tomatoes - if they were watered regularly with their roots in that water table too, they'd taste watery and boring. In Iowa where dry farming is common, the rains come regularly throughout the season in a good year, and when it's not a good year, that's where the common meme of a farmer praying for rain comes from - that farmer in that situation is a dry farmer. If we want to grow without water in many regions we are going to have to change what we are growing and drastically change the way we are gardening.

Garden plants are for the most part 'needy plants' - they expect consistency, care, and protection. If we are going to go without watering our gardens or sections of our gardens, we have to prepare the soil, the area, and the seeds properly. Water harvesting earthworks along with drought-tolerant perennials and self seeding annuals in deep life rich soils will make watering increasingly unnecessary as things mature, but annual-only systems that are intensive require too much soil disturbance for them to hold moisture in the same way that a little to no disturbance system does. Lean towards a perennialized garden if you are in a region where water is restricted, and use dry farming wherever possible. Dry farming takes time, patience, experimentation, and adaptation.

For most gardeners, they are going to want to water their gardens regularly to get a consistent yield and strong plants. A best practice is to dig up the soil to a depth of several inches (8-10cm) to see if it is dry - or if your soil is healthy, just stick your finger in it. Is it dry or wet 3-5 inches (8 – 13cm) down? If it is dry a few mm below the surface, you have hydrophobic soils and the water is not infiltrating. You need to help force that water in - only time and pressure will make that happen unless you disturb it and add organic matter and life. If your soil is mud and holds water forever, stop watering and observe and use it only when needed. If your soil drains quickly and dries out, add compost teas so that drainage pathway is populated now with soil life that will now start to slow the water's passage and filter and retain the nutrients the water was carrying. Mulch on top of the soil will increase water retention. Water for less time and more often to lessen the stress on the newly established soil life and to reduce the distance the water will infiltrate and the rate at which it will occur. Use the mulch to slow and distribute the water as well.

Dripline vs Hoses

There are many ways to water a garden but the most common is with the garden hose, and often the most desirable method is by automated dripline. These two methods represent the full spectrum between automation and manual labor in the garden. Driplines are usually placed permanently in their location or at least for the duration of that growing season. They do deteriorate in the sun as do hoses, but you can bury them under mulch and have them last years longer - this also moderates water temperatures. Sometimes critters make holes in cheaper drip lines and depressurize that entire line. More expensive drip lines avoid this problem by being of tougher material.

Hoses in the direct sun in hot and dry areas can split within a season as well as deliver hot water to drip lines. Shading our hoses is critical to keeping water from burning plants and simmering topsoil life. The inverse is also an issue: cold well water on warm soils and plants can be shocking. Hoses also have to be carefully dragged everywhere we use them to avoid disturbing or killing our plants in the process of watering them, yet despite these drawbacks, hose watering is the most intimate, effective, and versatile. You can put it on mister on that one plant and soak on that other. You can pull the head off and flood that row or stuff it down a fresh ground squirrel hole. You can make sure everything gets the water it needs which can sometimes be an enormous amount if our soils are poor and hydrophobic.

Sprinklers on Timers

We can also buy more than one hose and use a hose splitting water timer to connect to multiple sprinklers and even drip lines in combination to water our entire growing space. Lawn sprinklers are very effective though they can be erosive on bare soils, too much water from above for some plants prone to mold, and difficult as plants grow bigger and minimize the sprinkler's range. You can place sprinklers on raised platforms, but test this in situ always and observe its sturdiness first before leaving it to run automated. There is also a loss of water when water is sent through the air in the form of vapor. This vapor is actually the most potent greenhouse gas, so minimizing vapor loss of water is important!

Flood Irrigation

An ancient form of irrigation - flooding either along side row crops or flooding entire fields, it is an easy and fast method for infiltrating water deeply into an area with very little labor involved though it requires large volumes of water on demand. The fertile crescent's farming communities were so efficient they drained the Tigris and Euphrates using flood irrigation to the point of capacity and beyond, causing a droughts, crop failures, and decline. We have to be careful with our water resources and avoid using them wastefully. That being said, most American households are already dumping huge volumes of water out daily they could be using - if all their gray water was put into a mycoremediation swale and their blackwater into a reed bed water remediation bed after some composting, there'd be an abundance of water in the landscape again and flood irrigation would naturally occur on laundry day!

Crop Rotation

There are many ways that crops can be rotated, and there have been many different crop rotation methods throughout history. Rotations range from changing heavy to light feeders, to switching botanical families, planting guilds, and stages of succession. There are many

BroadFork Farm's 10-year Crop Rotation

	Year 1	Year 2	Year 3	...	Year 10
Plot 1	Solanaceae Compost	Greens & Roots	Garlic Compost	...	Greens & Roots
Plot 2	Greens & Roots	Solanaceae Compost	Greens & Roots	...	Early Cucurbitaceae & Brassicaceae Compost
Plot 3	Early Cucurbitaceae & Brassicaceae Compost	Greens & Roots	Solanaceae Compost	...	Greens & Roots
Plot 4	Greens & Roots	Early Cucurbitaceae & Brassicaceae Compost	Greens & Roots	...	Liliaceae Compost
Plot 5	Liliaceae Compost	Greens & Roots	Early Cucurbitaceae & Brassicaceae Compost	...	Greens & Roots
Plot 6	Greens & Roots	Liliaceae Compost	Greens & Roots	...	Late Cucurbitaceae & Brassicaceae Compost
Plot 7	Late Cucurbitaceae & Brassicaceae Compost	Greens & Roots	Liliaceae Compost	...	Greens & Roots
Plot 8	Greens & Roots	Late Cucurbitaceae & Brassicaceae Compost	Greens & Roots	...	Garlic Compost
Plot 9	Garlic Compost	Greens & Roots	Late Cucurbitaceae & Brassicaceae Compost	...	Greens & Roots
Plot 10	Greens & Roots	Garlic Compost	Greens & Roots	...	Solanaceae Compost

Based on the work of Jean-Martin Fortier, *The Market Gardener*, 2014.

Botanical Family Key

Solanaceae Tomatoes, Potatoes, Eggplants
Liliaceae Onions and Leeks, but not Garlic
Cucurbitaceae Cucumbers, Squash, and Melons
Brassicaceae Broccoli, Cauliflower, Turnips, Radishes, Cabbage

rules of thumb that need to be considered. Often using slips of paper and rearranging them to see what works best for your system can be the most effective planning exercise.

Crop Rotation Principles
- **Alternate Heavy and Light Feeders**
- **Alternate Root Crops with Leaf Crops**
- **Brassicaceae, Solanaceae, Liliaceae, and Cucurbitaceae** - Rotating these botanical families gives each area a three year break between growing the same family there again.
- **Green Manure (usually Legumes)** - Grown during Fall/Spring, this field crop is tilled in and allowed to incorporate into the soil before spring planting.

For commercial annual production systems, crop rotation is invaluable at maintaining soil fertility and controlling pests and pathogens. Jean-Martin Fortier's farm is a working example of a market garden designed around a crop rotation (see chart).

The Harvest

Food Preservation
How will you preserve your harvest? Where will it be stored? How much do you need of what? Food preservation relies primarily by displacing or removing moisture or air to temporarily interrupt or slow down the decomposition process.

- *Drying* - one of the oldest and longest lasting forms of food preservation. It can often be the easiest too if done outdoors in the sun!
- *Salt Brining* - a preservative for meats, vegetables, and fish where they are submersed in the brine. Some pickles are salt brined.
- *Salt Curing* - a way to dry and preserve meat and fish using salt.
- *Candying* - a sweet way to preserve fruits and even some vegetables like rhubarb.
- *Canning* - though relatively new in its adoption due to its reliance upon modern technology, it is the most common form of large scale home preservation. Some pickles are canned in a brine.
- *Smoking* - this method uses smoke to dry and displace moisture in meats, vegetables, and even fruits. The smoke also seals and preserves the meat in a unique way that makes it less likely to go rancid.
- *Potting* - an older method that focuses on keeping air out of the container and was used often for meat.
- *Burying* - another ancient preservation method using burial that relies on preventing air from contacting the food and keeping the temperature a constant (52-54°F/11-12°C).

- *Fermenting* - this amazing ancient preservation method uses beneficial bacteria and fungi to transform plants, meats, and all kinds of foods into delicious stable preserves like yogurt, cured meat, wine, sauerkraut, and mead. Some pickles are fermented in a brine.
- *Freezing* - Another modern and common method, freezing is easy for all kinds of food. Freezing first on a sheet or screen allows for easy bagging without clumping once the outside layer is frozen.
- *In Oil* - similar to potting, plants can be submerged in oil and preserved - sometimes only the oil is used carrying the flavors of the preserved foods. These can be cooked in soups or dishes when the oil runs out as well.
- *In Alcohol* - alcohol is an excellent preservative. Tinctures are easy to make and a great way to preserve your herbal, medicinal plant, and medicinal fungi harvests.

Continue Learning
- The Art of Fermentation by Sandor Katz (2012). Paperback.
- The New Wildcrafted Cuisine: Exploring the Exotic Gastronomy of Local Terroir by Pascal Baudar, a book focused on recipes using wild plants for ferments, infusions, spices, and other wild food preparations (2016).
- The Resilient Gardener: Food Production and Self-Reliance in Uncertain Times by Carol Deppe (2010). Paperback.

Reverse Engineering Your Diet

A concept from Permaculture Gardening, the online course, in which we calculate how much we consume of an individual food per month and then reverse engineer our diet back to square footage or meterage of land and ounces of seed or number of plants needed to consume that food for an entire year. It reveals how much land our current diet actually requires. For most of us, we cannot even consider growing the amount of wheat, corn, and beef required for the common American diet, but we can grow a diversity of equivalents instead that can replace them, and we can grow more food per square meter at the same time.

Seed Saving

What seeds are you saving this season? Which plants are you saving from? The best seeds come from the best plants in the worst soils and growing conditions. They are your fighters: seed save from them. If you save seed from your losers and your winners and then mix them up, you'll be planting mediocrity within a few seasons! Eat your weaker plants, save your best plants for seed saving, and save from more than one plant for genetic diversity. If your seeds can be surface sown or throw sown, do it - the survivor seeds will have better expressions of

Reverse Engineering Your Diet

Step 1 - Calculate How Much You Consume of that Food per Month per Year
Step 2 - Calculate How Much Land Growing that Quantity of Food would Require
Step 3 - Calculate How Much Seed, Water, Compost, etc. will be Needed & the Total Cost
Step 4 - Calculate How Much Storage Space will be Needed and the Food Shelf Life
Step 5 - Calendar and Map Out Your Food Coverage: How Much Can You DIY?
Step 6 - What Other Foods that are Easier to Scale can Replace this Food?

1 lbs of seed potatoes typically grows 10 lbs of potatoes in 10 feet of garden row.

Step 1 - If you consume 10 lbs (4.5 kg) of potatoes a month, that is 120 lbs (54.4 kg) a year.
Step 2 - 120 lbs (54.4 kg) requires 120 feet (36.5m) of garden row
Step 3 - 12 lbs (5.4 kg) of seed potatoes can grow 120 lbs with good soils, regular water, and sunlight during the growing season.
Step 4 - It won't take up much space in storage.
Step 5 - It likely will not last year round but it may come close - the potato seeds will be fine. It would be easy for me to grow what I needed and not much harder to store.
Step 6 - There are similar roots and tubers that can replace or be added to the standard potato in our diet: sunchokes, beets, sweet potatoes, ground nuts, oca, turnip, radish, jicama, taro, and more.

9-10 square feet ($3m^2$) can yield 4 cups (946 ml) of flour in a season.
If your family consumes 2 loaves of bread a week, that's roughly 8 cups (1.8 mlL of flour a week.
A 1/2 acre (1/5th of a hectare) can grow 400 loaves of bread or 1600 cups (41 mL) of flour.

*

A mature standard apple tree can grow 500-1000 lbs of fruit in a season.
A mature standard peach or apricot tree can grow 150-300 lbs of fruit in a season.
A mature avocado tree can yield 60-200 lbs of fruit in a heavy bearing season.
A mature chestnut tree can yield 15-130 lbs in nuts in a season.

---

vigor and root development in subsequent generations. You'd be surprised by which seeds can be surface sown! Can you water the seed minimally? The less water, the more drought tolerant the next generation of plants. The information is encoded in those seeds. Can you test it? If you have a plant that is clearly sweeter or healthier, you can likely prove it with a BRIX meter with the fruit juices or plant sap. Select for the best plants for the best epigenetic expressions in the following seasons. Even if they are all genetically the same (like a selfing pea or bean), their epigenetics are selected for and reinforced by this process which is what controls the actual (phenotypic) expression of the plant. Save the most mature seeds - the larger the seeds the better. If the seeds are flat and deflated in comparison to other seeds of the same type, they are either duds or of very low fertility and vigor. Blemished and deformed seeds can still grow, but they are usually never the same quality, vigor, or resilience as a large, unblemished fully mature seed.

Do you have enough time in your growing season to finish the seeds properly? What seeds are your most expensive that you can grow? Can you save those seeds in large quantities? Can you save a large amount of seed all at once to make it less tedious? Do you have space to dry the seeds you plan on harvesting? Do you have a place to store them that is cool and dry? Do you have a spare refrigerator to use for seed saving, scion saving, and seed stratification and vernalization? Do you have a dehydrator that can go low enough for seeds 95°F (35°C)? Some areas are so wet, a gentle dehydrator is vital. How will you clean your seeds? Will you use screens? Bowls? Fans? Breath? How will you store them? In plastic bags, paper envelopes, glass jars, wooden boxes, or some other way? Are you storing them for longterm (freezing) or short term (cool and dry/refrigerator)?

How are you organizing your seeds? By family, alphabetically, by each type, by season, or planting time? How are you labeling your seeds? The name, the harvest date, number of generations locally saved, and where the seed is sourced from? The more thorough, the more valuable that seed can become in the future.

Don't have a great diversity of seeds? If we can focus and save a large quantity of one or two types of valuable seed, it becomes very easy to trade and sell those seeds to get the seeds we cannot grow ourselves. Seed swaps are marvelous ways to diversify our seed banks with locally grown seeds.

Continue Learning
- _The Seed Garden: The Art and Practice of Seed Saving_ by the Seed Savers Exchange (2015). Paperback
- _Seed to Seed_ by Suzanne Ashworth 2002. Paperback.

Caring for the Future
As we harvest we must always keep an eye to the future:
- Returning some seed to the soil

- Chopping and dropping crops to the ground
- Leaving some plants in place to self seed or to feed wildlife
- Bringing in organic matter, compost, compost teas, and then redressing the gardens with a new set of plants or a bed of mulch to protect the topsoils from the winter frosts
- Saving seed from the best plants

Make your garden a place where you never harvest too much - give back to the biodiversity in place above and below the surface, and it will give back to you; if not at first, then in time. What the biodiversity may require from you may be far above a fair share or surplus at first since the debt we owe to the soil and biodiversity at large is generations old and compounded as a result. Some sites are expensive to remediate in all different sorts of ways. Some sites are simple and only require removing impediments to regeneration. We must approach each site as an individual and care for its future with a unique plan. How will you improve your garden when it comes time to harvest this year?

PLANT BREEDING

While it can fill several books with its intricacies, plant breeding can also be a very simple and profitable hobby. Several famous heirlooms were made by mistake or by backyard gardeners hand pollinating their flowers. Many garden plants have obvious male and female parts (see pictures) that are easily hand-pollinated and then sealed off with tape or with a paper bag. When both a male and female flower are just about to bloom, (usually the night before) remove the petals of a male flower and cut it free. Open up the female flower, use the male flower like a paint brush on the female flower, and then seal the flower shut. This can be done with corn, tomatoes, squash, peppers, and melons easily, and with the aid of a paint brush and a microscope, smaller flowers.

While it is true that Mendel's inheritance chart works well with simplistic genetics like those found in peas, it does not work with other reproductive genetic arrangements. Potatoes, for instance, are much more complex in the way they reproduce genetically, and for that

Male Squash Flower

Female Squash Flower

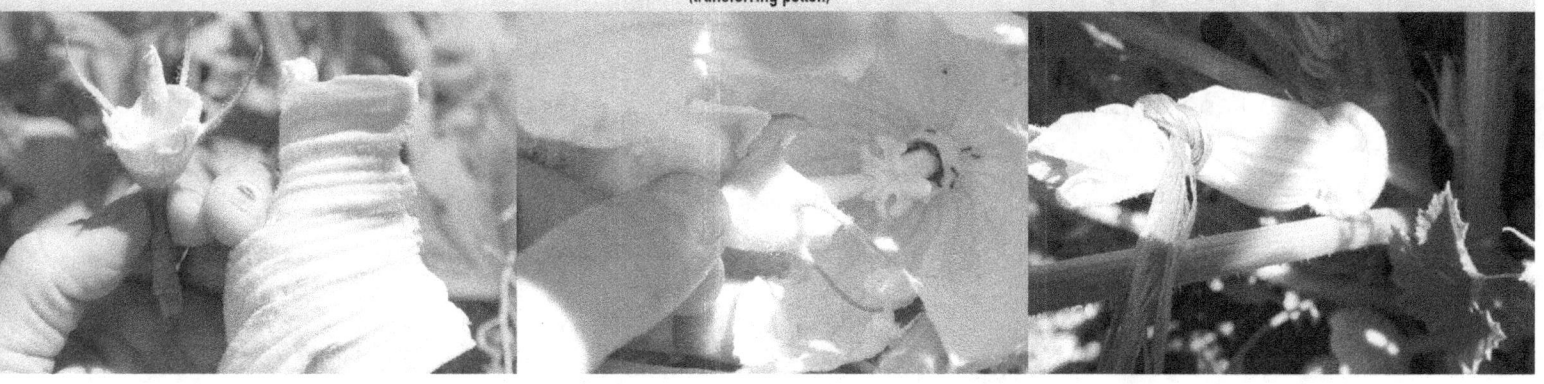

1. Remove the Petals from a Male Flower
2. Paint the female pistil with the male stamens (transferring pollen)
3. Seal up the flower & watch the fruit develop

reason they can reproduce either asexually (vegetatively) from their tubers or sexually via flowers, bees, and small tomato-like fruits. Most commercial varieties of potatoes rarely flower, but heirloom potatoes can mostly be relied on to flower, and you can start on your own potato varieties easily in this way.

Just remember the first generation of the cross between the two plants will be in the seed of the fruit from that flower the pollen was crossed for. When you plant that F1 or first generation seed, you get an expression of a cross, but that is not a stable expression: you will likely find a broad range of expressions within the seeds from that single crossed fruit. Only after 5-10 generations of choosing the traits you want to see expressed will a variety stabilize into an open-pollinated heirloom.

We can have a lot of fun breeding and creating landraces by allowing for open crosses and then selecting the best each year. This is how most plants have been bred for human use, but several are a bit more mysterious and complex. Use a guide to make plant breeding easy and fun.

Continue Learning
- _Breed your own Vegetable Varieties_ by Carol Deppe (1993). Paperback.

Professional Applications & Scaling Up

There are many pathways to scaling up your gardening operations into seed farming, seed companies, market gardening, a seasonal CSA offering, a dye garden, or the core of your diet. You might choose to use biointensive methods like close plantings and neatly organized scheduling. You might use hand tools only or small machines. There are several commercial examples that have clear guides to their methods in courses, books, and online videos.

Consider Curtis Stone's example: he is using every square inch and measuring the time, money, and energy put into each step of his operation. Seeds are closely planted to create a canopy that holds moisture in and shades and covers the soil. Every bed is exactly 30" (76cm) wide to fit his tools and to make for easier harvesting. He uses soil blocks, pressed earth instead of seed trays, to save money and produce no waste. While initially he does use a rototiller to turn over plots, from then on he only forks often and cultivates the top 1-1.5" (2.5-4cm) of soil. Curtis focuses on smaller-sized, high-value crops with a short growth cycle (60 days or less from seed to market) that can be sold to high-end restaurants, at grocery stores, and at weekly farmers' markets. This allows him to have a seasonal crop rotation where he grows three to four crops in the same bed in rotation in one season.

Consider Jean-Martin Fortier's example: they don't use a large tractor, but they do use a BCS walking tractor which many of their amazing machines attach to. They use a small amount of fuel in their tractor and delivery truck (which is biodiesel) as well as a small amount of propane in the greenhouse to jumpstart their season by warming the soil with hot water piped beneath the soil surface. Jean-Martin feels that they are more effective without a large tractor. He prefers using small walking-machines that adhere to the 30" (76cm) crop bed width and an ergonomic 18" (46cm) wide path. Using a stale seed bed method using either flame weeding or a black impermeable tarp for several weeks of smothering, they prepare the beds to have zero weed pressure on their crops and then plant their seeds 10 to 50x closer than the seed packaging recommends. The canopy this intensive planting creates holds moisture. When there is no bare soil, traveling weed seeds cannot find a place to germinate. The beds are all on a 10-year crop rotation plan alternating heavy and light feeders, using green manure, compost, and granulated chicken manure before heavy-feeder beds are planted.

They use wheelbarrows, shovels, hand tools, broadforks, wheel hoes, regular hoes, seeders, row covers, insect covers, biodegradable mulch, and more to minimize their reliance on fuel. However, they also use attachments on their walking tractor such as a harrow which horizontally mixes the top 1-2"(2.5-5cm) which is followed by a roller attachment, creating a uniform soil surface. This perfectly prepares the soil for planting without turning the soil over or pulverizing it as a rototiller would. A flail mower is also used as a tractor attachment; it shreds the green manure. They always use a rotary plow to reshape the beds and dig out the paths to cover the flailed green manure, so it can incorporate into the soil without tilling it in (which is commonly how green manure is used). Covering the row with a tarp will speed up the breakdown process, so that in only a few weeks, the area is ready for planting. The farm's main inputs are labor and compost.

Continue Learning
- *The Market Gardener* by Jean-Martin Fortier (2014). Paperback.
- *The Urban Farmer* by Curtis Stone (2016). Paperback.
- *The Market Gardener with Jean-Martin Fortier, Six Figure Farming* on Youtube (2016). https://www.youtube.com/playlist?list=PLCeA6DzL9P4uRadXW0_hj5Ct3EAqWH1zl
- *The Lean Farm: How to Minimize Waste, Increase Efficiency, and Maximize Value and Profits with Less Work* by Ben Hartman (2015). Paperback.

Regenerative Ranching

We've all heard overgrazing leads to desertification, but not everyone knew a lack of grazing can also lead to desertification until Allan Savory made it his life's mission to tell the world. With the right kind of grazing, ranchers today can lead the reversal of desertification in many areas all over the world (though in some cases withholding grazers is still necessary - at least initially). Using animals on the small scale to bring back fertility can be very powerful, but it often relies upon helping them mimic their natural environment.

Holistic Management with Cattle

Holistic management (HM) was created by Allan Savory to help farmers make better decisions through careful observation and reflection and imitating prehistoric grazing patterns. Joel Salatin, a widely known HM farmer, allows his cattle to mob graze a small patch of pasture, approximately 100 cattle on 1-2 acres (4000-8000m²), for 24 hrs, and then shifts the cattle onto a new patch of land. They will only return two to three times a season to that same patch. The daily cattle shift happens without coercion or force, only an invitation to greener pastures. Using portable electric fencing, cattle can be kept safe and easily shifted daily. Cows are not dumb, and they eagerly await the chance to chew on fresh pasture each morning, so all the managers have to do is peel back the electric fence and they will pour through in an excited bustle.

Portable fencing allows for creative adaptation to terrain, area, and timing. It is also cheaper than permanent fencing which doesn't accomplish the same goals at all. Joel says that if you don't move a fence for three years, you can make that permanent. You may have a series of small, permanently fenced paddocks that you shift cattle through, but then must rely upon observation and timing for when to shift the animals and at what densities. It is imperative to keep the right amount of pressure on the herd, so they graze indiscriminately, so the plants can be grazed thoroughly, and so they can fully rebound. It is also important to know the history of your grazing site: was it an area of intense or light grazing in the past? What herbivores thrived there? How can we imitate what was natural? How can we prepare for climate change with all this in mind? For some areas, an extended rest may be called for before grazing can resume as was the case with the Loess Plateau Restoration project.

Holistic management above all embraces the complexity of holism in an agricultural setting with careful planning and management principles and techniques. Understanding your animals, their digestion, their waste products, their inputs, their outputs, and anything else particular to your operation can improve your understanding and management of the business. Doing your best to work with complexity requires reflection, note-taking, developing metrics, collecting and analyzing data, and adapting in response to feedback.

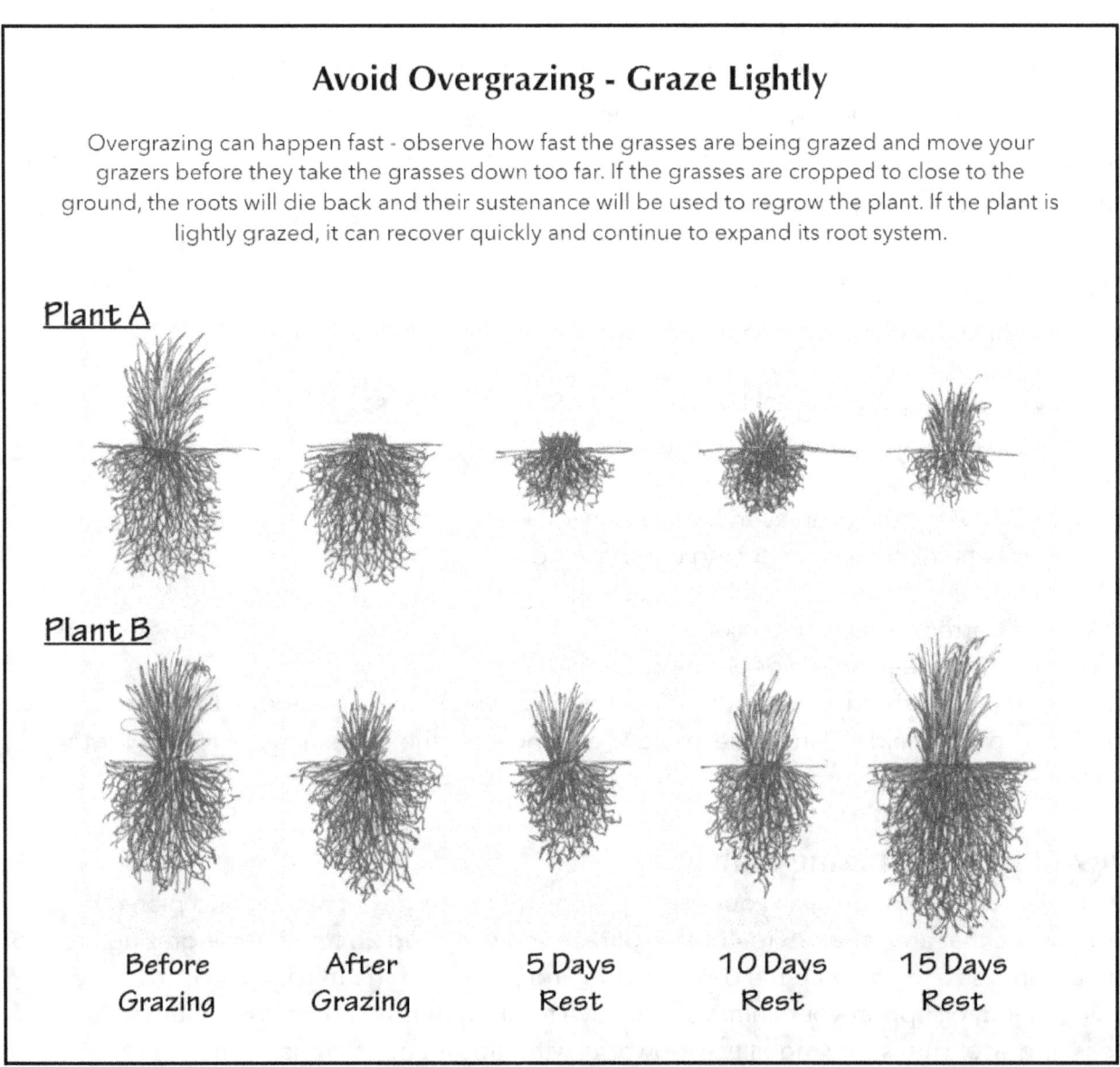

Based on Figure 38.3 of *Holistic Management* 2nd Ed. by Allan Savory (1999).

Succession of Grazers

Grazing with just one type of animal means just one type of manure, one type of disturbance, and one set of associated microbes and pests. That's often a recipe for weakness in a system -

having a succession of grazers can greatly diversify the services the animals can give, create more stability, and greatly enrich the landscape, the animals, and ourselves in the process.

- *Goats* - they can strip the branches off lower trees in minutes, making them great for fire prepping around homesteads and highways!
- *Sheep* - though sheep are grazers, they can browse as well and prepare the way for cattle.
- *Cows* - they become the restarting point when the system has rested enough once the area is initially cleared by goats and sheep.
- *Chickens* - they spread the manure patties, sanitizing the field in their search for fly larvae.
- *Turkeys* - they continue the job of pest control and graze on grass.
- *Rest* - a critical ingredient to success - the area must replenish itself in order to grow from the next mob grazing succession.

Grazing with Chicken Tractors

Mentioned earlier, using chicken tractors to prepare an area for the garden is similar to grazing chickens in a pasture setting. Chickens can easily turn remove more than necessary, so moving them quickly is ideal - their manure is very high in nitrogen - it's very *hot!* It can even burn green growing plants. With their scratching and pecking behavior and their manure pH, they can turn an area into a barren, alkaline, nitrogen-heavy moonscape in a week or two depending on the

A Salatin-Style Chicken Tractor

area and the flock size. Their manure is incredibly powerful and spreading it out evenly over a field will increase its vigor and increase the protein in the forage for the chickens or other foraging animals paired with them in succession.

Developing a Grazing Plan

If you plan on mob grazing all your grazing areas for only 1 day at at time and plan on returning to that area after 25 to 40 days of rest, you will need 25 to 40 other grazing areas of comparable size to continue the daily grazing and shifting of the herd. If you don't have enough land to support your animals, you have to bring them feed or bring them to new areas to graze. This is why mobility is powerful with grazing operations. If one area takes on a ton of water or becomes brittle, you may want to skip it in the rotation and visit another area earlier in your rotation. Always monitor your grasses to watch for when to shift your animals - Greg Judy will shift his herds multiple times a day. The rest cycles will determine the number of paddocks or grazing areas you stake out. The size and vigor of the grazing areas will determine the amount and types of grazing animals that the site can support.

Professional Applications & Scaling Up

Scaling up with animals usually means more land, and for most folks that can seem like an obstacle to growth, but it isn't true. Many people, including Joel Salatin and Greg Judy, utilize a mobile setup so they can utilize rented temporary pastures whenever needed. They can move their animals anywhere because they are mobile. It takes a crew of dedicated people to make it work, but it is possible, and it is being done masterfully.

Scaling up can also mean diversifying: adding more varieties of animals. By implementing a succession of grazers, a variety of products and benefits can be generated on the same piece of land. Consider the Polyface Farm System, possibly the best regenerative farm example in North America: approximately 100 cows graze 100 acres (40 hectares) about one acre (4000m^2 or 0.4 hectares) at a time using portable electric fencing. The paddocks are selected to have the same elevation approximately across each fenced off area since different elevations have grasses germinating and developing at different times and rates - an even maturation of grasses equals an even grazing pattern. They will return to the same area two to three times a season at most. They will only spend 24 hrs in any one space to avoid the second bite effect.

Following after the cows are the laying hens in an egg mobile, a simple, portable shelter that lacks an electric fence. They have feed, pasture, and the freedom to range, but they primarily focus on spreading the cow manure patties and eating the insect and parasite larvae inside. They spread them out and sanitize them by increasing surface area and exposing them to the air, sun, and wind—this means that the cows rarely have flies on them and never need any special treatments for parasites. The Salatins don't use vaccines or antibiotics; they cull sick animals quickly, monitor closely, and mimic nature which makes for strong genetics and functional immune systems that don't need vaccines or antibiotics.

Turkeys often follow the chickens, and then the pasture rests until the return of the cows, or they grow it out for hay. This system makes for delectable eggs, pasture-raised beef, and pasture-raised soup birds in a sanitized and carbon-sequestering pasture system. Joel's system sources lumber from his property that is sustainably cut and milled on-site. He does supplement his laying hens with local non-GMO grain which Joel admits is their weakest point.

In winter, the Salatins rely on a clever deep bedding method where the cattle feed on bailed hay from the pastures they visited lightly that previous season. They eat from troughs on pulleys that raise and lower to unload the hay from the top of the stacked hay bales as well as keep the feeding troughs off the rising ground. This all occurs inside a hay barn that is half stacked hay bales and the other half deep bedding. A layer of straw and wood chips with some grain mixed in gets laid down after each feeding to combine with the manure from the visiting cows. By mixing in grain with this new layer of bedding, it creates a compost heap littered with fermented grains which for a pig is a cross between a buffet and a treasure hunt. In their enthusiastic searching, they turn the matted layers into a fluffy mix making it easy for the farm interns to remove and relocate to where it can be fully composted. Most of the compost gets spread out onto the fields to support the foundation of the entire system, the pasture, but some goes into the Salatins' vegetable garden.

The deep bedding method of adding carbon throughout a season can be applied to many different animal systems. Their chickens overwinter living below rabbits inside a *Raken* (Rabbit+Chicken) house where they live in a deep bedding situation. The rabbit manure and chicken manure are mixed with a carbon source like wood chips or straw regularly to keep the ratios composting and sanitary; this leads to a rising floor. By using pigs to loosen the bedding initially and using a tractor to transport the bedding to a large compost area where it can be turned further with the tractor, Joel has created a system where labor and time are saved, and animals are utilized as much as possible in synchronization with their instincts.

Whatever you feel drawn to, study and research your ideas and reach out to those who are doing it in your area or climate analog. They will give you invaluable information if they have time - gone are the days of ranchers leaving cattle in a gigantic pasture for months and watching them from afar: these ranchers are on the ground know their animals. Study more from Salatin, Doherty, or Judy - visit them or intern if you can. See how it is done. Invest wisely and build a team. Build soils and raise healthy, happy animals.

Continue Learning
- *The Salatin Semester: A Complete Home Study Course in Polyface-Style Diversified Farming*, by Verge Permaculture and Acres U.S.A. https://salatinsemester.com
- *Holistic Management* by Alan Savory (1999). Paperback.
- *REX*, the online Regrarians course with Darren Doherty. http://rex.farm
- Greg Judy's Green Pastures farm site and books http://www.greenpasturesfarm.net/store.php

Regenerative Agriculture

What is Regenerative Agriculture?

Regenerative agriculture implies different practices in different scenarios, but for our purposes we can say that regenerative farming uses processes that continuously restore, maintain, and enrich the ecology of the area being farmed. In practical terms, "enriching ecology" means the farmed area contains more biodiversity, more water is available on-site (or wiser management of water is in evidence), and more soil is retained on-site. Meanwhile, farmers are making a profit with a marketable yield that is safe, nutritious, and improves and maintains the health of those who consume it. The recent release of the Regenerative Organic Certification expands that definition to include fair labor and humane animal focuses. While all the listed methodologies are similar in their goals and together embody regenerative agriculture, they are each distinct and represent different branches of study.

Regenerative Organic Certificate Goals from the Rodale Institute
- Increase soil organic matter over time, and sequester carbon in the soil
- Improve animal welfare
- Provide economic stability and fairness for farmers, ranchers, and workers
- Create resilient regional ecosystems and communities

Continue Learning
- Regenerative Organic Certification https://rodaleinstitute.org/regenerativeorganic/

Biological Farming

"Biological Agriculture or Biological Farming: Production of healthy plants and animals using management promoting a healthy soil microbiome, using natural processes to grow crops and animals that promote healthy animal and human microbiomes. Biologically-based production methods select for the desired crop and against weeds that might compete with the crop, promote natural processes of nutrient cycling so the soil is not mined of nutrients, leaching is prevented, soil structure is built, and plants/animals are protected from diseases and pests"
—Dr. Elaine Ingham, Phd. (2016).

Biological farming is a way of growing food and raising animals without amendments, as nature has done for at least a billion years. Biological farming respects the whole ecosystem while making a profit for the farmer and generating high yields of nutritionally-dense foods. At the same time, biological farming cares for the future by building soil and increasing biodiversity—which leads to economic stability for the farmer and ecological stability for the ecosystem their farm interacts with. A proponent of biological farming, Dr. Ingham uses microscopes and sophisticated, modern analysis and testing methodologies (some of those that she pioneered are now seen globally) to calibrate her compost to her exact garden needs down to the exact soil food web population densities and ratios in her compost, compost tea, or compost extract. Her methods are being adopted by commercial enterprises and small farmers alike the world over.

Steps:
- Analyze your Soil Food Web
- Create Custom Compost Tea
- Use Biology, Disturbance, and Observation to Continually Progress

Carbon Farming

Carbon sequestration is an important aspect of regenerative agriculture which increases the capacity of soils to sequester carbon in the soil. Carbon farming makes carbon sequestration and the tracking thereof the farmer's main focus, even as they strive for profitability and competitiveness. Regenerative agriculture processes most importantly feature returning as much organic matter or humus to soils as possible, where it can improve soil quality and foster plant and fungal growth, sparking a beneficial cycle of carbon sequestration from the overburdened atmosphere.

While carbon farming is often associated with land-based farming systems, our definition here also includes carbon farming in the oceans, seas, and other bodies of water through the growing of algae, fish, shrimp, plants, birds, and their deposit in sludgy, carbon-rich soils below. Pharmersea's seaweed farming is an example of an ocean-based carbon-sequestering farming operation in the fledgling stages - once kelp is mature on Dan Marquez's farm off the coast of Santa Barbara, California, it will be brought back onto land for fertilizer to return the lost carbon, nitrogen, and other essential nutrients back to the soil.

Steps:
- Analyze your Carbon Sequestration Capacity

- Use Compost, Compost Tea, Bacteria, Fungi, and Aeration to Add Organic Matter and Life to Facilitate Carbon Sequestration
- Grow Perennials Where Possible to Sequester Carbon
- Use Rest and NoTill to Sequester Carbon

Continue Learning
- *The Carbon Farming Solution* by Eric Toensmeier (2016). Paperback.

Natural Farming

Developed by Masanobu Fukuoka, natural farming is often called the Fukuoka method or "do-nothing farming". His no-till, no machines, no fertilizers, and no chemicals stance seemed idealistic at the time, but by mimicking nature, Fukuoka's methods accomplished surprising successes like growing rice without permanent paddies, naturalized annuals, an abundance of food, and productive fruit trees without pruning. He not only ran an economically successful and productive farm in a counter-cultural way but promoted his methodology worldwide.

While natural farming may seem the territory of the generational farmer or the rural guru, the methods of natural farming are understandable and replicable in any climate working with permacultural methods, scientific research, local knowledge, and minimalism as your guides. It is a philosophy in practice more than any set of protocols. Interestingly, it naturally sequesters carbon by design but has no specific protocol for carbon sequestering.

Steps:
- Analyze Your Current System and Reflect on What Work can be Avoided by letting Nature do the work
- Throw Sow Seeds and Chop and Drop to Grow your Food and Control your Weeds
- Use Clay Coating to Hide your Seeds from the Birds
- Grow in a More Dispersed and Rampant Annual and Perennial Mixed Polyculture

Perennial Farming

Perennial staple crop farming is what large groups of people used to rely upon for their staple foods before fossil fuels shifted our reliance onto a handful of annuals primarily—which predates the concept of carbon farming. Perennial crops such as chestnut, baobab, and coconut trees each provide a wide spectrum of foods, fibers, fuels, and medicines. Wisely, humans traditionally paired with long-lived, climax species.

Long-lived perennial crops need a polyculture around them for strong and resilient growth. Only a polyculture will support a strong perennial system as seen in nature. Mark Shepard's oak savanna system is a perfect example of imitating nature to create a perennial farming operation. Its resilience comes from imitating what naturally occurred in that bioregion before it was brought into dysfunction - similar to Veta La Palma's history.

Perennial farming can come in many iterations and under many names, from polycultural orchards to agroforestry to alley cropping to edge cropping. They all use trees, shrubs, or bushes to support and enrich the annual production and provide a second or third yield on top of the annual one—meanwhile saving soil, stopping erosion, preventing flooding, soaking in more water seasonally, and enriching the soil, the other plants, and themselves in the process.

Korean Natural Farming

KNF is a farming method that partners with indigenous microorganisms (IMOs) taken from local healthy forest ecosystems and sources on-site farming waste to create fertility, manage pests and diseases, and facilitate a closed loop, no-waste system that builds soil and sequesters nutrients. In Hawaii, Chris Trump's family macadamia nut farm, Island Harvest Inc., relies upon KNF to control the many and varied tropical diseases and pests they encounter in Hawaii naturally. Indigenous microorganisms are captured initially using undercooked rice in a basket placed in a dry area that is fertile like beneath a healthy large tree (IMO-1 Prep). Most of the organisms that grow on the rice are fungi though bacteria and other soil food web members would of course be present in a non-sterile environment. The long white hyphae that grow in these capture baskets are the hallmark of a good sampling. From there, the farmer can scale up the biology numerous ways into liquids and dry forms - all outside of a lab setting! KNF ends farming waste, ends nutrients gassing off of pig pens and chicken coops, ends conventional farmer's reliance on petrochemical inputs, and ends the cycle of degradation in farming - it is a probiotic farming method that is spreading like wildfire.

Aquaculture

Aquaculture has the highest possible yields per unit of surface area because gravity isn't pulling on the organisms in the water in the same way that it exerts this force on organisms out of water, and organisms are surrounded by nourishing water and nutrients similar to mycelium in a liquid culture. Ponds act as a nutrient trap, capturing silts and all organic matter that breaks down in the water, forming a rich sludge that can be removed and used in gardens. Using aquaculture to build soils and grow food is a powerful solution to depleted soils and hunger.

"A properly built and managed pond can yield from 100 to 300 pounds [45-136 Kg] of fish annually for each acre [4000m²] of water surface" –<u>Ponds: Planning, Design, Construction</u>. NRCS, 1997.

Site Analysis & Planning

What fish and aquatic plants do you want to grow? To eat? To feed your animals? To feed your soils? What can your site support? Some fish can be stocked one per gallon (3.7 liter) and some one per cubic cm or inch. How many fish can your system handle? What predator fish can you employ if the population grows too rapidly or can you harvest all the excess when needed? Do you have a separate area for predator fish? What plants can you grow to feed your fish and animals? What examples locally do you have of what you want to accomplish? Where are ideal sites in the landscape for holding water - are they also good areas for aquaculture? Can you use silt traps to clean the water on the way in? How will you keep it aerated? How will you feed your fish? Can bunny manure fall into the pond somehow? Can you line the pond with edible plants for the fish? How will you harvest your fish? What will you do in winter? Write down these answers and develop a year round plan for managing your aquaculture system.

Outdoor Aquaculture

Orientation and placement

If ponds are placed against the prevailing wind, allowing it to blow over them, they get passive aeration naturally. This also has a cooling and evaporative effect. Placement so that the sun shines on the pond for long periods of time each day turns the pond both into a reflector and magnifier of that energy in the area surrounding it as a thermal mass that will even keep frost off of the trees planted around it. It should be noted that oxygen levels drop as the temperature rises, so shade is often important to keep waters within tolerable temperatures during summer and spring, especially in hotter climates.

Size and Depth

Whether small or large, pond aquatic systems that are less wild (and thus less self-sustaining) need a lot of tending and inputs, and they tend to have more problems. The wilder, or the more self-managed through biological interaction, they can be, the better. Pond depths can range: some recommend they be 2m (6.5ft) or shallower, with deeper areas of 4-5m (13-16ft) to retain fish if the pond has to be drained or for cold temperate climates to help fish survive through the winter. Sepp Holzer, on the other hand, commonly creates ponds, or lakes, 10-15m (32-49ft) deep. While more commonly, most make ponds and water areas are much smaller due to the smaller living spaces most people work within. Deep areas allow for

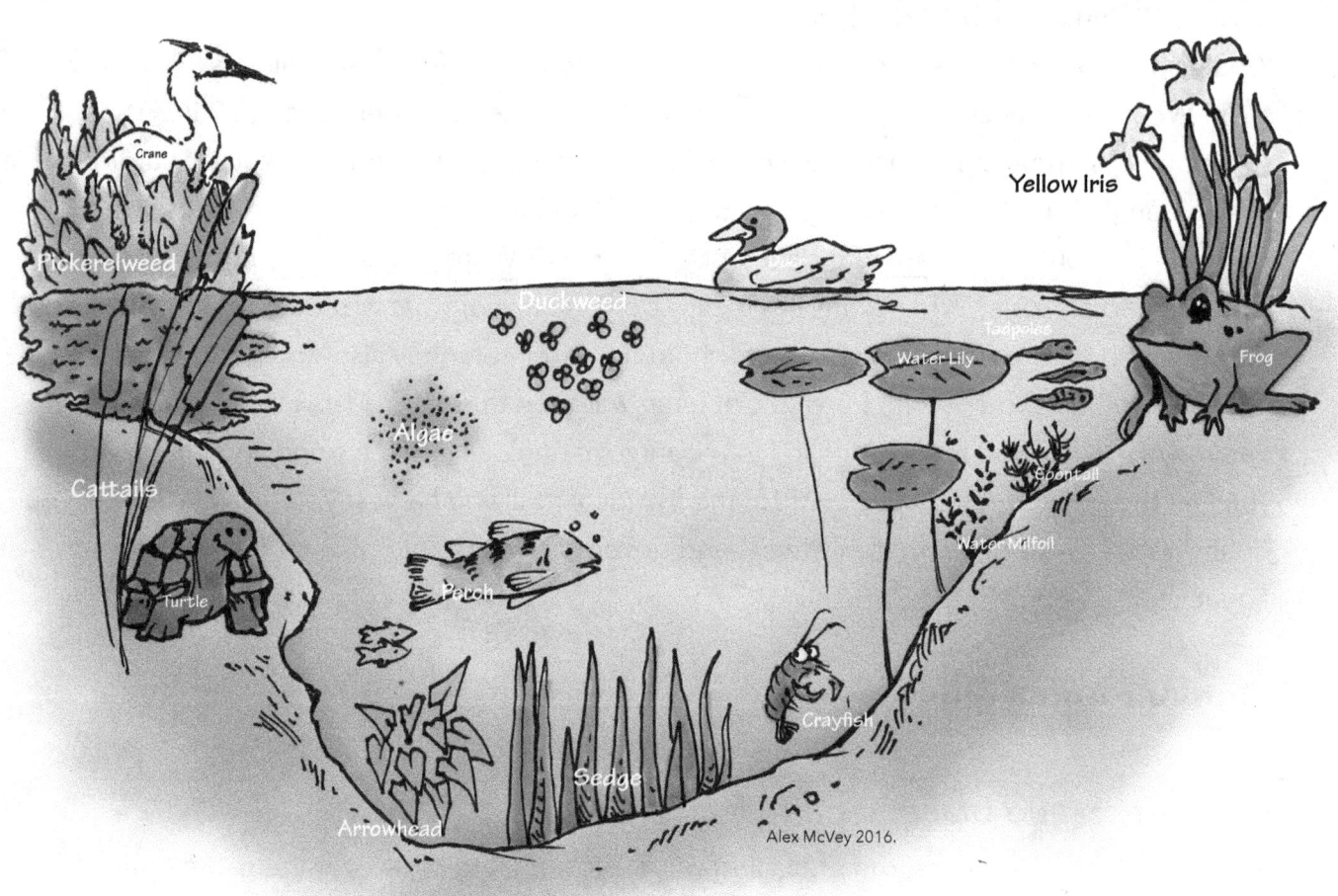

certain fish to spawn, protection in winter, and higher oxygen levels. Shallow areas allow for spawning of other fish, lower oxygen areas, and temperature and pH differentiation. Shallow and deep zones also support different species guilds. Overall differences in the depth allows for constant movement of the water as well, which keeps it fertile and oxygenated.

Plant Layers

- **Floating plants**
- **Edge plants**
- **Shallow-water plants**
- **Deep-water plants** - though no deeper than 8 ft/2.4m

Trophic Layers

- **Algae**
- **Zooplankton**
- **Plants** - Chinese water chestnut, kangkong, taro, cattails, water hyacinth, Indian water chestnut, lotus, arrowhead
- **Shellfish, crustaceans, mollusks, and echinoderms**
- **Fish** - Tilapia, Catfish, Bluegill, Bass, Carp, Trout, Perch
- **Small to large water mammals, reptiles, and amphibians**

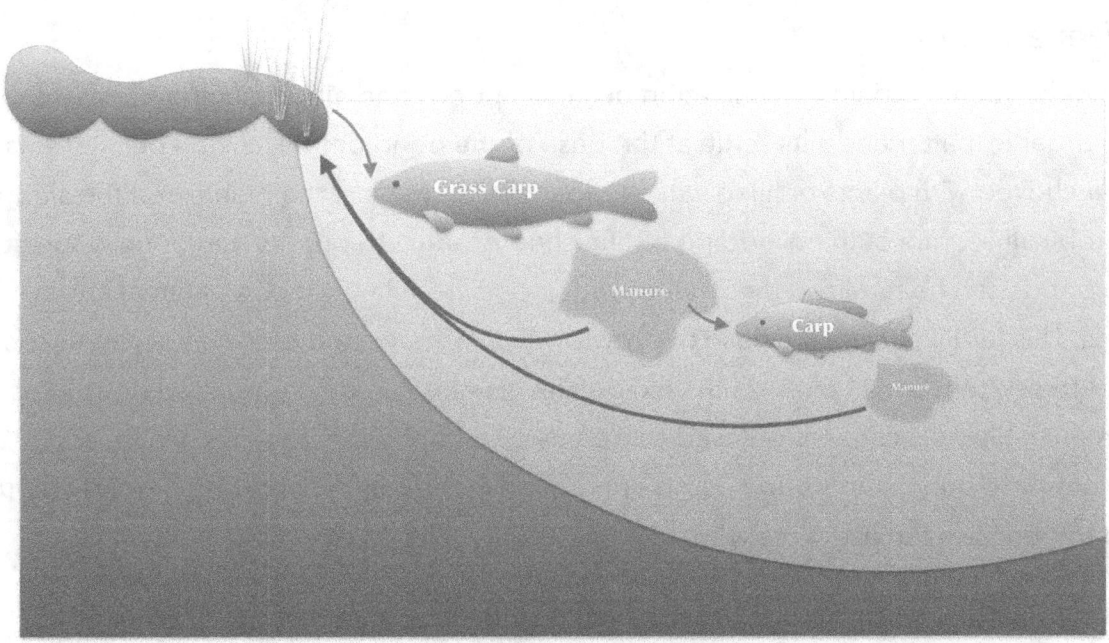

Grass Carp feed on vegetation along the edges of ponds while other carp feed on their manures, and plants feed on the manures of fish in general.

Food Chain

Algae feeds on sunlight and nitrates in the water. Zooplankton, a diverse population of microscopic animals, feeds on the algae. Crustaceans, macroarthropods like crayfish, crabs, and shrimp, feed on zooplankton. Fish feed on plants and crustaceans. Animals like birds and amphibians feed on plants, fish, and crustaceans.

pH

Ideally large systems should have a range of 6-8 pH. Fish, mollusks, freshwater crayfish, and shrimp prefer hard alkaline water while food organisms that feed into the aquaculture food chain need more acidic conditions, so areas of different pHs are desirable. This can be achieved with deep areas, shallow areas, still areas, and actively aerated areas. Finding the balance for your system between all those variables can take some tinkering and will in the end be unique to every situation.

The Pond's Edge

The more edge, the better—especially in pond design because it provides more areas for plants and sheltered habitats. A wavy meandering pond edge has nooks and crannies for frogs and other animals to hide from predators, to lay eggs in, to provide more organic matter input, to provide more food for fish, and to allow for different pHs to develop for more complete cycling of pond waste and nutrients.

Fertilizer and Soil

Rich and abundant nutrient accumulation occurs in ponds and all aquaculture systems over time as organic matter and silts settle at the base of the pond or tank. When our systems become choked with plants or filled with sludge, we can harvest the plants and the sludge and aerobically compost them, adding the finished product to our garden or food forest soils. In turn, ponds can be fertilized themselves with inputs from land, such as animal and bird manures. This fertilizer causes a flush of growth which is harvested before it occupies too much of the system and chokes off the oxygen levels—this can be composted or used as direct mulch. Mussels can also be used to clean and add phosphate to the water, and subsequently to enrich the sludge and plant growth in the pond. Fertilizing a pond and using a pond to generate fertilizer is easy!

Aeration

Water aeration can occur in a number of ways: oxygenated water input, water pumps, falling water, or orientation to the prevailing wind.

Remember:
More oxygen = more life
Warmer water = less oxygen.
More oxygen = more fish
More fish = less oxygen.

Always have a way to aerate your water. 1ppm oxygen is too low for almost all fish while 5ppm oxygen is a good minimum for overall pond health. On warm summer nights, heavily vegetated ponds may experience a dip in the oxygen level. Having an low-oxygen-detection system and automated aeration system may be desirable.

It is always best to aerate and filter water through gravel and plants as it enters a system. Gravels and other stone filters develop bacteria that digest nitrites in the water as it passes through.

Cage area

Having fish in a caged area allows food and natural elements to grow and flow through their area without letting those fish free to be eaten or eat other fish. It is a great way to control population growth, protect fish, and protect plants. This can also be useful to grow smaller fish or organisms to feed to larger fish, yourself, or other animals in another system.

Restricted area

Having a restricted area for filtering plants, smaller fish, and delicate habitats to remain protected from larger fish protects the entire ecology's health. This can be done with screens or even a simple rock wall that doesn't allow those larger fish to pass through.

Pipe releases

Warm surface water in summer as well as cold water from the bottom of the pond in winter can both negatively affect pond life—both can be siphoned off a pond with pipes and valves.

This can help keep temperatures tolerable for pond life during the extremes of the year. A pond can even be drained quickly with a valve just above the base of the pond.

Fish Feed

Fish can be fed using the plants in the ponds, plants on the edges, crustaceans in the pond, and insectary plants like mulberries hanging over the pond to drop insect-covered fruit to the waiting fish. Sweet potato and black soldier fly larvae together make great fish, duck, and chicken food as is done on Zaytuna Farm. Duckweed and other floating plants will feed fish as well. Fish can be fed other fish using screens, cages, or through multiple ponds with different stocking variations.

Different forms of waste attract different forms of fish food. Worms are attracted by kitchen scraps, ants by bones, and grasshoppers by the color yellow. Termites are drawn in by woody biomass, snails by moist areas of the garden, and even cockroaches by rough mulch. We can grow our own fish food and save money and energy.

Even a simple light over the pond at night can attract mosquitos for fish to feed on. Placing rocks beneath the light allows for smaller fish to exclusively harvest the mosquitos. This is a win-win for farmers and fish! Rabbits and other animals can be housed over fish ponds as well to provide passive feeding of the fish. Often this can only be done temporarily as too much manure can imbalance a pond.

Temperatures and Salinity

Every species has a range of temperature and salinity that it prefers and usually a slightly wider range that the species can tolerate. There are species that prefer freshwater, some that prefer saltwater, and some that prefer a brackish mix. These conditions exist in all climates. All designs must take these two factors into account for any diverse, self-managed system to emerge.

We can choose the most resilient fish while making the highest quality microclimate for our site—this increases our margin for success and reduces the margin for error, but in the end it is trial and error, with observation and reflection, that will ultimately guide any successful system. Start with researching the systems of your area, the fish that thrive there, their needs, and what you can mimic on your site.

Natural Swimming Pools

Natural swimming pools are pools or ponds that use biofilters to clean the water. There are numerous do-it-yourself models online as well as professional services for natural swimming pool installations. Hot tubs are being filled with plants and pebble beds to filter the water for the main pool area. Aeration is needed, but can be attained in several ways—especially if converting a standard, in-the-ground pool. Without

The plant filtration station for Frank Golbeck of Golden Coast Mead's natural swimming pool, designed and installed by Eddy Garcia of Living Earth Systems. Vetiver grass, onions, strawberries, herbs, and more feed on the fish manure in the water, cleaning it in the process.

altering the hardscape at all, a bio-filtration area can be directly next to the swimming area at a low cost, cleaning the water with plants before it is released back into the pool. The pool water can stack functions as a place to raise fish and store water for irrigation, human consumption, and fire fighting.

Frank Golbeck of Golden Coast Mead's natural swimming pool in Southern California. It is a converted standard pool with a liner, fish, plants, external bio-filtration system, and pumps.

Scaling Up

Consider the Ancient Hawaiian aquaculture - it was an incredible system that started water catchment inland and upslope using *chinampas* called *Lo-e* which were a system of ponds in succession that would feed each other all the way down to the shore where fish ponds, manmade lagoons, held fish for the Hawaiian chieftains. The *lo-e* would catch, slow water, and overflow into small bodies of water step by step down the slope, and fish, along with plants like taro, would be cultivated in them. Their shoreline aquaculture was most impressive —they used stones to create artificial lagoons that allowed small fish in but not larger predator fish. Many of these fishponds have freshwater springs in them which facilitates the growth of a specific set of species and plants that support a host of life in the fertile brackish waters. As the small fish grew in size in the safety of the lagoon, they were no longer able to leave the artificial lagoon and were then harvested when needed. They also used gates to regulate fish coming and going during the tides. Today, anyone who visits the restored fishponds of Molokai can see them for themselves. This design and concept can be locally replicated anywhere to create sheltered habitat - bring water into your landscape and ramp up the biodiversity and yields on your site. With your aquaculture systems, partner with nature and follow the Hawaiian example: start slowing water as high up in the landscape as possible, use the water as many times as possible, build soil, use life to clean the water and feed the next stage in the process, and use native plants and animals as your foundation!

Water & Ocean Restoration

Mentioned earlier in the planning section for water, now concrete actions must be taken to restore these sites. The ocean may seem impossibly large in scope but the majority of the ocean life resides along the coasts where we mostly live all over the world - we are in place to respond and regenerate these fragile and fertile ecosystems that support all life.

River & Stream Restoration
- Liberate Water
- Induce Meander
- Reintroduce Multi-level Channels and Flood Plains
- Reconnect to Wetlands
- Keep Runoff Clean
- Reintroduce Native Flora and Fauna

Riparian & Wetland Restoration
- Provide Place for Riparian Areas and Wetlands to Exist
- Restore Drained Wetlands
- Reintroduce Native Flora and Fauna
- Monitor and Support Reintroduced Biodiversity as Balance is Established

Ocean Restoration
- Clean and Filter Water as It Approaches and Enters the Oceans Using Shellfish
- Clean and Filter the Coastal Waters with Kelp and other Biology
- Farm Seaweed to Sequester Carbon, Nitrogen, and Other Excess Nutrients in the Water (drones can be used to know exactly when to harvest)
- Farm Shellfish in the Coastal Waters to Sequester Carbon, Nitrogen, and Other Nutrients as They Clean the Water
- Restore the Kelp Forests (recent warming killed over 90% of US west coast kelp)
- Build Artificial Reefs (reefs provide shelter and act like underwater windbreak as do kelp)
- Return the Harvested Kelp and Shellfish to the Soil to Return the Lost Nutrients and Sequester Carbon

How Will We Restore Our Coasts?

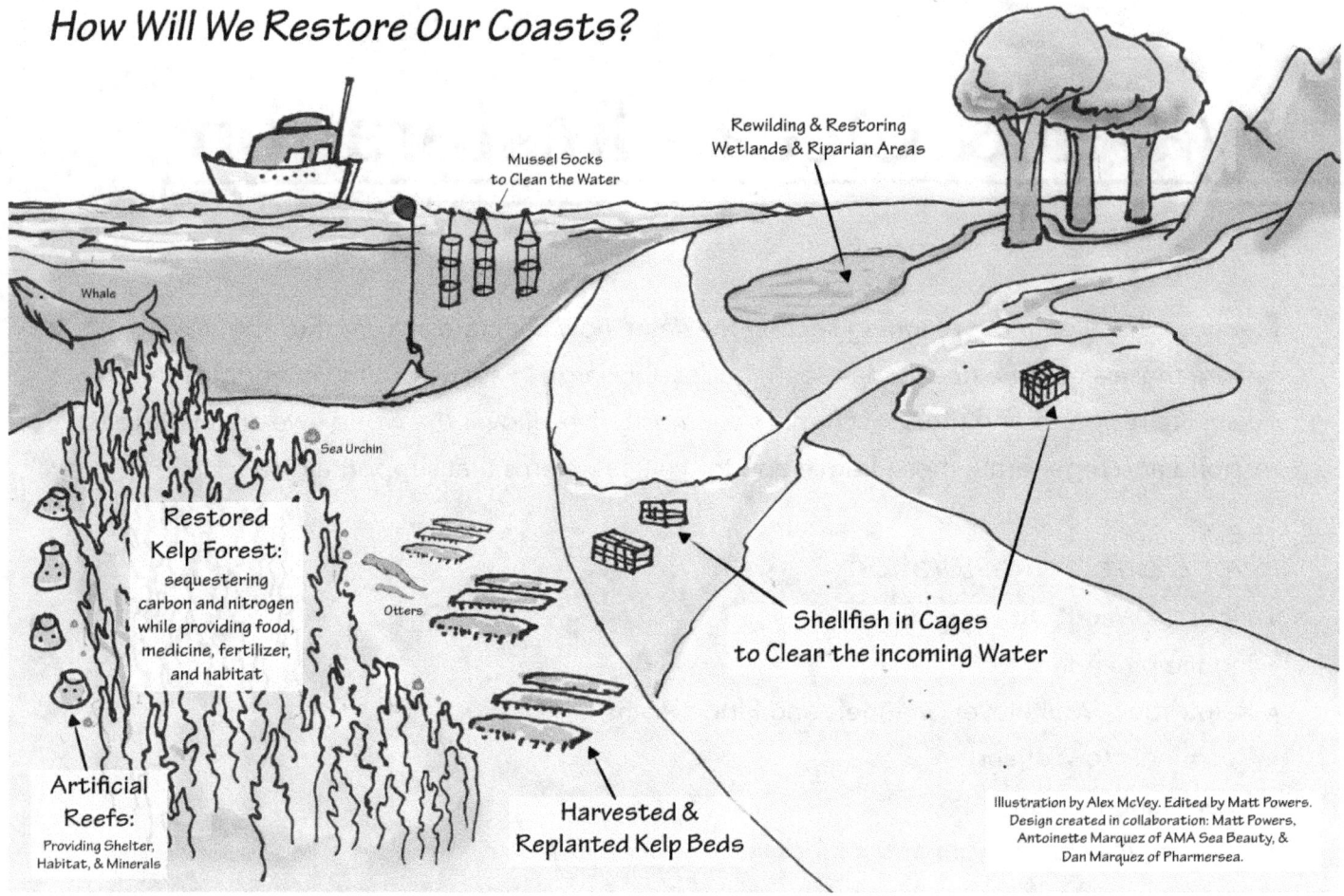

Professional Applications & Scaling Up

Become a Seaweed Farmer

This is not too far fetched - in California, an acre of coastal waters is only $50 a year to rent and only a few thousand dollars in fees and permits to get started - it is affordable! You can monitor your work with a drone - they can tell you when to harvest to the day by tracking the carbon sequestration rates. You can sell your products to food producers, beauty product producers, farmers for their soils, compost companies for their compost mix, ranchers to feed to their cattle to lower the rates of methane released by them, and even biofuel producers. A boat can be rented for installation, maintenance and harvest - everything can be monitored from a drone from on shore otherwise!

Restoring Wetlands for Hunting

Ducks Unlimited is a duck hunting organization that has restored over 14 million acres (5 million hectares) of North American wetland stretching from Canada to Mexico to provide the rest stops the birds need in their regular migrations. Ducks are considered by some to be the most studied animal in North America - they are photographed in Canada before the migration and counted. The count determines the hunting limits for the season - harvesting only at a rate that enhances the overall health of the species. Restoration and hunting together are providing habitat for all the other biodiversity related to these areas as well - it's a trophic benefit that is incalculable! The future of ethical meat could be focused on wild-caught and carefully monitored animals from a restored ecosystem.

Veta La Palma - Spain

Once drained for raising cattle, Veta La Palma returned the waters, restored the wetlands, and is now a fish farm that is 27,000 acres (11,000 hectares) of marshland and canals. It is a biologically-rich ecosystem that is nearly all edge. It is one of the largest private bird sanctuaries in Europe as well as one of the few fish farms that do not feed their fish. The shallow, sun-drenched canals frequently host algae blooms which leads to vibrant, healthy, and abundant shrimp and fish populations which in turn attracts incredible numbers of birds in great diversity. This is all happening as the farmers are harvesting fish to sell, yet they do not feel like they are in competition with the birds. The health and abundance of the birds themselves indicates the health of their ecosystem and the fish they are harvesting, and the best part is: there is always enough fish for all.

Their system is often referred to as Algae-Culture which is similar to Joel Salatin's Grass-Farming. By focusing on the photosynthetic point of contact as the support of their enterprise, they've organized systems that are both regenerative and sustainable for as long as the sun shines and the seasons turn.

Continue Learning
- *Let the Water Do the Work: Induced Meandering, an Evolving Method for Restoring Incised Channels* by Bill Zeedyk and Van Clothier (2009). Paperback.
- *The Regrarians eHandbook* by Darren Doherty (2017). http://www.regrarians.org/product/regrarians-ehandbook-1-climate/

Land Restoration

This is an occupation that will become more common in the future as land restoration becomes a central focus in all global cultures. We already have proven large-scale examples and scalable designs and technologies. We can repair large landscapes using biology, organic matter, disturbance, earthworks, timing, rest, and animal pressure - all wisely utilized in tandem. Because it is possible, extremely inexpensive, and often the only rationale step to be taken in many damaged areas, governments, nonprofits, and nongovernmental agencies are all recognizing land restoration as a viable option for turning desertified areas into thriving and stable ecosystems. It's a win-win; the biodiversity returns, the economy returns in these areas, the governments get tax revenues, and thus, even the international banks get paid their dues. This was the exact situation in China's Loess Plateau; it was a joint venture between the US government, the Chinese government, and the World Bank. It was such a success economically that it spread throughout China virally, changing Chinese law. There are several other examples featured in the Permaculture Action section of *The Permaculture Student 2* though none as large as China's restoration of half million square kilometers! With 3.5 billion hectares of desertified land, there is plenty of opportunity to go big with restoration.

In Saudi Arabia, Neal Spackman's example is one that can scale: his method for restoration can convert the entire coastal flood plains leading down from the mountains of Saudi Arabia towards the shore into a green dryland forest with no bare soil. All their water comes in one storm usually once a year but sometimes in drought it can take years for rain to come - this makes it key to use trees to restore this area because they can handle the long periods of drought. Using just the water they harvest in these rain events and no more, they mete out less than the equivalent that was captured from their wells through driplines to the trees until the next storm comes. Within 3 years, they've taken white and tan sand and rock and made it into a perennial food forest where no bare earth is found using swales, rock dams, gabions, and more to slow, spread, sink, and store the water. They've even discovered varieties that can be taken off the drip lines now! The deserts can be regreened - even those like Saudi Arabia that do not get the precipitation that other large restoration sites like the Loess Plateau receive.

It's possible - it's just up to us to organize the political or private will to support such a project. By engaging with our communities and community leaders, we can inspire and explain how large land restoration can positively effect all levels of a bioregion's people and biodiversity: economically, socially, environmentally, health-wise, emotionally, and more!

We can also learn with those who have done it: Geoff Lawton, Darren Doherty, John D. Liu, Neal Spackman, and more - all teach what they've learned in their experiences with large restoration projects, so others can emulate them and expand on their work. Partnering with those that have done it already can give you a massive head start, so study the examples we have, learn from those who have done it, and design and install in a large collaborative team of experts - the more minds the better, safer, and longer lasting! *Let's Restore Our World!!*

Steps to Land Restoration

1. Start with the Watersheds - Use Keyline Patterning: Find the Keypoints and Keylines
2. Slow, Spread, Sink, Store, Test, and Clean the Water - Use Earthworks, Keyline Patterning, and Indigenous Biology
3. Use Native Perennials in Native Polycultures in and around your Water Harvesting Areas and Inoculate them when Planting with Appropriate Soil Life
4. Reintroduce Native Wildlife, Allow Them Access, or Imitate Them with Holistic Management
5. Encourage Rapid Cycling of Life - Chop and Drop, HM Mob Grazing, Compost Tea, Fungal Inoculations, and Predator Introduction

Climate Specifics

Drylands

If it's hyper arid, you won't be able to start with perennial grasses. Drought tolerant trees and water harvesting earthworks are key to restoring arid areas. They are brittle but retain nutrients well. There's new technology in this area as well: Liquid Nano Clay (LNC) by DesertControl.com, which is made of just clay and water, is being used to even spread clay down into sandy desert soils. In the past, all attempts to incorporate clay into desert soil arrived at the same result: the mixture of clay and water would separate, and the clay would all remain on the surface and form a crust that would bake and harden in the sun. With the arrival of LNC, we have a new tool that none of the restoration projects have had thus far.

Though it requires clay to be transported to areas where it is not currently found, it can completely change the soil composition in hours rather than years by making it so soil life can rapidly inhabit the area, not get washed away, and start building soil. Using earthworks, biology, new tools like LNC, keyline design water harvesting, and trees, we can green the deserts.

Humid Tropical

Soils are shallow in the tropics - most of the carbon is standing forest. Once the forest is removed, the thin soils quickly erode and are washed away into the rivers and then out to the ocean where it can cause dead zones. The amazing thing is we can bring the soil back quickly too: using the area's own pioneer species in a quick chop and drop succession. While in the arid climates it might dry up and blow away, in the humid tropics, it will quickly be consumed by members of the soil food web and incorporated into the soil. Ernst Gotsch's example is superb: he used pioneer species that were also food crops and he chopped and dropped the branches and leaves from his perennials every few months until he had built up soil enough for more valuable food crops. The tropics move fast: they are constantly growing! If we are constantly working with them, chopping and dropping, we can quickly restore an area. You might need to use terraces, earthworks, trees, and other methods to stop erosion from the heavy rains, but it is possible! You can restore the humid tropics!

Humid Temperate

The humid temperate has by definition deep soils but people have been exploiting those soils for thousands of years. Using native plant polycultures led by over story trees, proper soil biology, appropriate earthworks, and the reintroduction of native wildlife, the humid temperate native ecosystems can be restored quickly and relatively easily in comparison to more brittle and arid areas.

The Challenges

People are the greatest challenge. We occupy the spaces we often need to be restoring: like shorefront properties in areas where wetlands were drained or ranchers who use national forests to range their cattle but don't support the reintroduction of wolves because they are afraid of losses to their livestock. We've been raised to fear the wild, even from a young age with books like Little Red Riding Hood and the Big Bad Wolf and many more. Our fears stand in our way from a self managing system that gives us perpetual clean water, air, food, and more. People stand in the way of conservation and restoration efforts because they are confused or ignorant- that can be fixed. People are the only ones that can make the changes necessary to restore these landscapes - that alone can be immensely empowering. We are the key and the most difficult component. If we are committed, anything is possible. The Social Permaculture section will provide some pathways to change in this area.

Professional Applications

Restoring Large Landscapes for Hunting

Before Tatanka, the American bison, was nearly driven into extinction, it enjoyed a massive range extending from northern Mexico to Canada to Northern Florida -it was called the Bison Loop. There were an estimated 65 million bison thundering across the continent when Columbus sailed towards the Americas. The indigenous American people were not able to dent that large a population with their hunting - it was resilient to hunting pressure. If we took the same policy that Ducks Unlimited took with ducks but with bison and other large animals like deer, we could hunt for wild meat from restored ecosystems or buy it locally. Deer are considered the most sustainable meat in the continental United States because they are so numerous and lack predators in so many areas where they thrive. What thrives in your ecosystems already?

Restoring Large Landscapes with the Regenerative Mead Cycle

With the introduction of sour mead and improved dry mead to the market through the sustained efforts of Frank Golbeck of Golden Coast Mead, an opportunity to regenerate large landscapes with bees has opened up. High quality honey is needed for high quality mead, so beekeepers can now make a much more meaningful income with their honey if they can bring that higher quality honey in. By distilling honey's essence into mead, it reveals much of the place from where the nectar came in the flavor of the mead. It is much like how the grape variety determines the wine, yet mead is actually more versatile than wine or beer - in fact, it can taste like either! By focusing on mead made with regenerative honey in their alcohol consumption, consumers can drink and savor the regeneration with every sip. Mead can also be used to make medicinal ferments called *metheglins*.

The honey for the mead can come from areas that are being restored or are fully restored, or they can even be coming from restored farmlands where farmers are still working. Those areas need remediation as much if not more than most areas. If we could replace their biocides and petrochemical fertilizers with biology, their plows with harrows, their diesel with biodiesel, and their endless fields with a polyculture of species with native species for native pollinators mixed in, the bees would happily work for the farmer as pollinators and create amazing honey.

Restoring Landscapes with Holistically Managed Cattle

While meat in general has come under attack due to the way CAFO operations work, holistically managed cattle does not have the same environmental or health effects as their distant CAFO cousins. They can aid in carbon sequestration, emit enormously less methane, positively disturb the ground and plants, and produce nutrient-dense meats with healthy fats harvested from thriving ecosystems where they led rich lives connected with the cycles of nature. Not all cattle are same on the landscape - bison's hooves churn the topsoil in a unique way different from cows. Focusing on raising wild animals in situ is the best path though not always possible - holistic management allows us to mimic the wild in a safer and more controlled context.

Restoring the Landscape with Food Forests

As we restore landscapes, it provides an opportunity to mix in a higher proportion of edible natives and edible non-natives in the plant guilds we install. We can setup fruit and nut businesses that are rooted in the indigenous forest ecosystems. We can plant out the wild areas with the proper foods in the right proportions for the population densities that area can support. We can create animal food forests and keep animals destined to be harvested for meat in a near-wild environment where they can express their instincts to the fullest and enjoy a rich diet, catered to their needs.

Regenerative Land Flipping

Buying up large tracts of desertified land and regenerating them is an implied first step in the previous examples, but the logical next step is to sell that land to make a profit once it is viable for producing a holistically beneficial output - though some landscapes perform their highest benefits when left truly wild and uninhabited by human populations. That being said, a very lucrative business could be had in flipping desertified areas once inhabited and selling them to people looking for ecosystem integrated communities and businesses. As landscape restoration becomes more of a focus, it will become easier, cheaper, and more widely available, so we will see landscape flipping and selling as part of that. The number one fear of folks who spend time practicing permaculture is that when they leave that site or sell, it will all be ripped out, and sod will be placed over it by an ignorant real estate agency. This ignorance will be replaced with the market demand for restored landscapes as the work spreads.

Alternative Energy

Ending our reliance on fossil fuels and nuclear power is vital to our future survival - embracing alternative energy, using less electricity, and finding substitutions that don't require power is our future. We can heat our homes with the sun, the earth, and the seasons, and we can warm our homes with sticks instead of chopped wood and at a fraction of the volume. We can cool our homes by design as well - we can replace the heating and cooling of a home by design quite easily, but we cannot replace electricity as easily. We can let in more light, but for many of us, electricity is how we work, communicate, cook, travel, and heat our homes. While there is some research into harnessing plants for electricity, it doesn't generate the rates of electricity the average consumer uses - alternative energy technologies like wind, solar, geothermal, hydro, biomass, and gasification are substitutes that can fill the gap though each has drawbacks and advantages dependent on the context they are being used. Every site will utilize a blend of alternative technologies to support them that will change throughout the year and even evolve with time.

Site Analysis

What can your site offer? Is it windy? Is it sunny? Is there moving water? Falling water? Do you have tidal zones? Shoreline? Heavy rains? Flooding? The excessive site energies and forces can turn into electricity. There are also more than just one type of battery. Most folks think of storing energy in a battery, but water can easily be pumped uphill to a dam where it can be released to drive a turbine for electricity - making it an effective battery. Large weights can be used in this way as well. Regardless of what batteries you use, technology is rapidly changing, and it is hard to predict what the next iteration will be: scientists now are studying bacteria that consume electrons to explore ways of using biology to store energy in the future.

Solar

- *Solar Panels* - there are many types, options, and regulations around solar power. Research what's available in your area or order what you can online or locally to get started on getting off the grid with sun! Your area might even offer solar or alternative energy through your state-run energy programs as well, so your bill might come from the same people but be funding entirely different actions. Even if this is the case, seek to turn your site and home into a power generating space: include solar panels wherever possible.

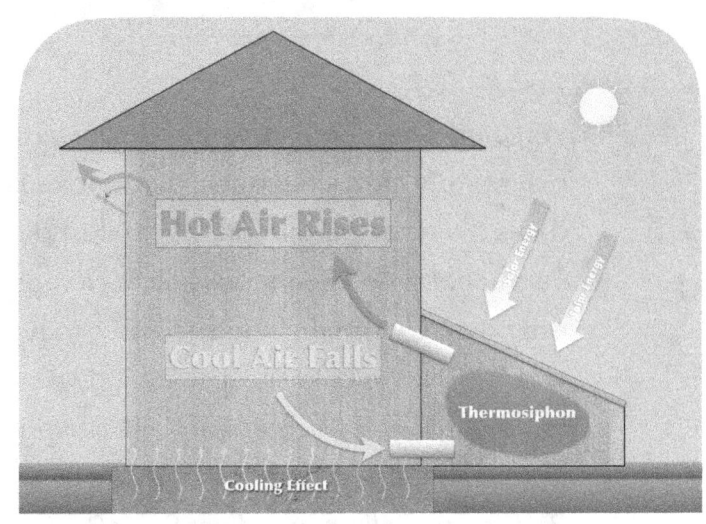

- *Thermosiphons* - using the sun and rising hot air, we can warm up a space and move the air inside it (refer to the picture), or we can use the moving air to cool down an area with a solar pump as well.
- *Solar Dehydrator* - these handy devices work just like a thermosiphon but they force the air through trays of food to dehydrate them with only solar heat. Wood, glass, and nails make this an easy and affordable project (refer to picture). You can also leave foods out in the summer sun in some areas and dry them that way too.
- *Solar Pump or Solar Chimney* - this is a tall black pipe that extends much higher than the building. It collects heat in the sunlight, drawing out heat from the house with the intensity of the heat at the top of the pipe. The hot air rising in the pipe near the hot top creates a suction that draws air out of the building.

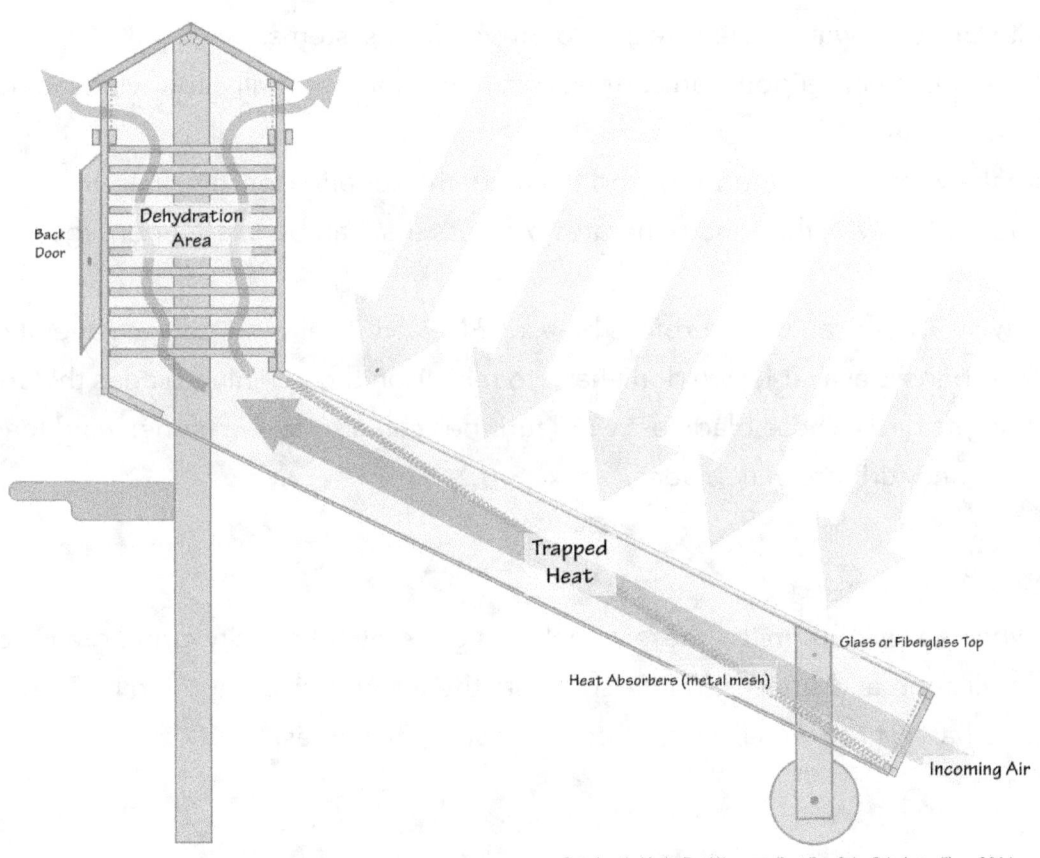

Based on the MotherEarthNews.com Best Ever Solar-Dehydrator Plans, 2014.

- *Walipini* - featured and pictured earlier, this is a growing area sunken into the earth with a glass or plastic roof aligned perpendicular to winter solstice's sun path and angle, so it gains the most warmth on the coldest day of the year.
- *Earth-Sheltered Greenhouses and Homes* - using an earthen back wall in a greenhouse can provide an enormous thermal mass to hold heat and radiate it back out during the night and far into the cold season. You could create an entire greenhouse back wall with an earth berm, and you can create entire buildings and homes with earth bag or rammed earth walls. The longest lasting manmade structures are made of earth.
- *Painting to Collect or Reflect Solar Radiation* - we can reflect away or focus the sun's energy with paint, mirrors, or polished metal.
- *Parabolic Mirrors* - these are mirrors that focus the sun's energy. They can be very powerful and have been used for thousands of years to create heat, warm water, and start fires. They can also be used to to run a sterling or steam engine.

"One hour of sunlight provides enough power to run a global economy for a full year"
- Jeremy Rifkin, <u>A Third Industrial Revolution</u> (2011).

Wind
- *Windmill* - used for thousands of years, windmills can grind grains into flour, generate electricity, or pump water - they are incredibly versatile systems.
- *Pond Aeration* - creating ponds in correlation to the wind path will allow winds to aerate them.
- *Windbreak* - trees growing in wind tend to create thicker and denser trunks to withstand the wind load - in this way, the wind generates biomass that can be used for energy like heating a home.
- *Wind Power* - where can wind turbines be used? New vertical wind power generation with no moving parts is available; we don't have to rely upon the spinning blades that many worry disrupts birds. These bladeless wind turbines can also take a higher wind load than traditional wind turbines with blades.

Water
- *Water Wheels and Watermills* - these wheels can generate electricity, grind grains, or pump water uphill at great distances. They also aerate the water they are turning in. They can even be used to harvest fish with fishing wheel harvesting machines.

- *Falling Water* - falling water both aerates water and provides an opportunity for generating energy with turbines and water wheels like the pelton wheel.
- *Water Turbines* - these are turbines to generate electricity that are used in a flowing body of water to generate electricity. They can be tethered like a kite in the wind, inside a pipe, multidirectional in tidal regions, or fixed in place.

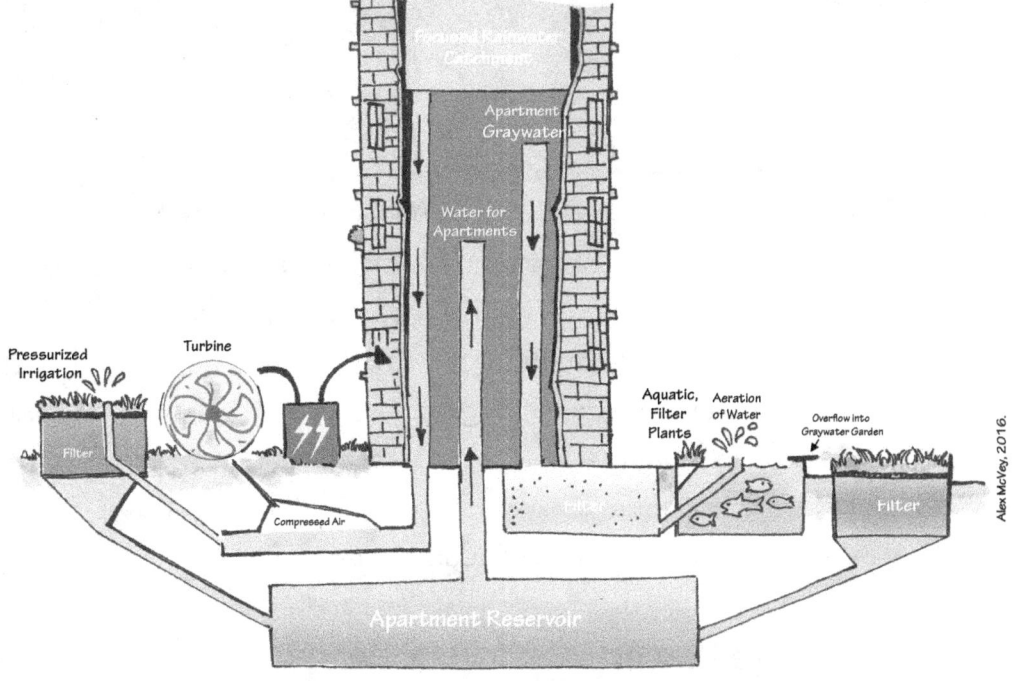

Rainwater catchment from larger buildings can be routed and focused into smaller building systems for energy generation, water pressure, or graywater usage. Some of these methods are already in use in some areas.

- *Hydraulic Ram Pumps* - these allow water to flow into them and build pressure, so they can release water at a higher pressure to create a water pump or to run a small hydropower system.
- *Trompes* - these use pressure from falling water like Peterhof's water fountains which are a dazzling dance of water that is all powered by pressure from diverted river water in an uphill pond. Ragged Chutes the power plant used the trapped air in falling water to generate compressed air to run turbines for pneumatic systems but could have been used to run turbines for electricity.
- *Tidal Turbines* - these can be simple or complicated - the basic concept is: the tide can lift huge heavy object like a floating dock several feet higher. Connected to a weight, this exchange can generate enormous amounts of energy. Many designs are being tested and piloted around the world currently.
- *Water Bubblers and Fountains* - aerating water keeps it clean. Fountains and bubblers help keep spring water fresh without chlorine.
- *Ring Water Feeder* - a Sepp Holzer concept where water is continuously cycled through a house system in a circle with the input at a higher level than the end of the ring, so pressure is maintained. The pressurized water is then returned to the start of the ring. There is an overflow valve for high water-volume time periods and to release pressure.
- *Refrigeration* - very cold water from mountain runoff can be routed through certain types of old refrigerators and freezers. These can create a very cool room or area if used wisely.

GeoThermal

- *Low-Grade Geothermal* - a newer concept where hot air is pumped into the ground and later released in the colder months to warm an area. The heat may well be coming from the sun originally, but it is held in the earth like a battery and then used throughout the cold season until it is used up and needs recharging.
- *Traditional Geothermal* - dating back to early human history, hot springs have been used for heating and bathing for thousands of years.

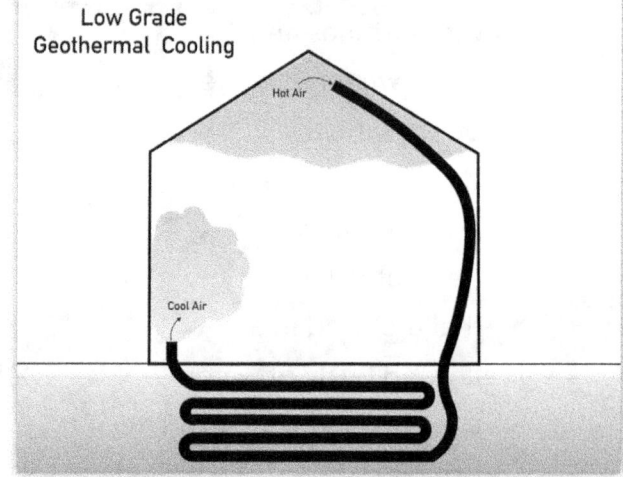

Bicycle-Power

There are bicycle powered generators being worked on to generate enough electricity in 45 minutes of biking to provide the electricity for your home and activities the rest of the day. Though individual usage ranges wildly the world over, it is clear that bicycles present a unique and amazing innovation that can truly take people power and magnify it using gears. We can run machines selectively and charge batteries with pedal power. While we may not be able to use it to do everything, it is a useful and healthy solution. It can also replace most of our fossil fueled transportation needs, saving us an enormous amount of energy in our travel.

RMH/Rocket Stove (Biomass)

Rocket Stoves and Rocket Mass Heaters

Rocket mass heaters are masonry heaters that use a J-tube to burn stick fires cleanly in a system that slowly radiates and conducts the fire's heat outward from a thermally charged mass. A rocket stove is a J-Tube without the mass; it has a focused point of heat that can be used for energy, cooking, or even blacksmithing. The intense heat and J-tube smokestack shape creates air-suction that pulls the fire sideways while gravity helps the sticks fall into the J. This prevents smoke from flowing back into the house if properly done. It's so hot that the smoke inside the J-tube becomes fuel for a secondary burn—making for a clean burn. Once the fuel is completely consumed, the exhaust that exits is comprised of sterile ash and CO_2. In very cold climates, the lack of sun makes solar panels and even greenhouse growing inefficient—wind energy may be used but wood is the most reliable and abundant heat source.

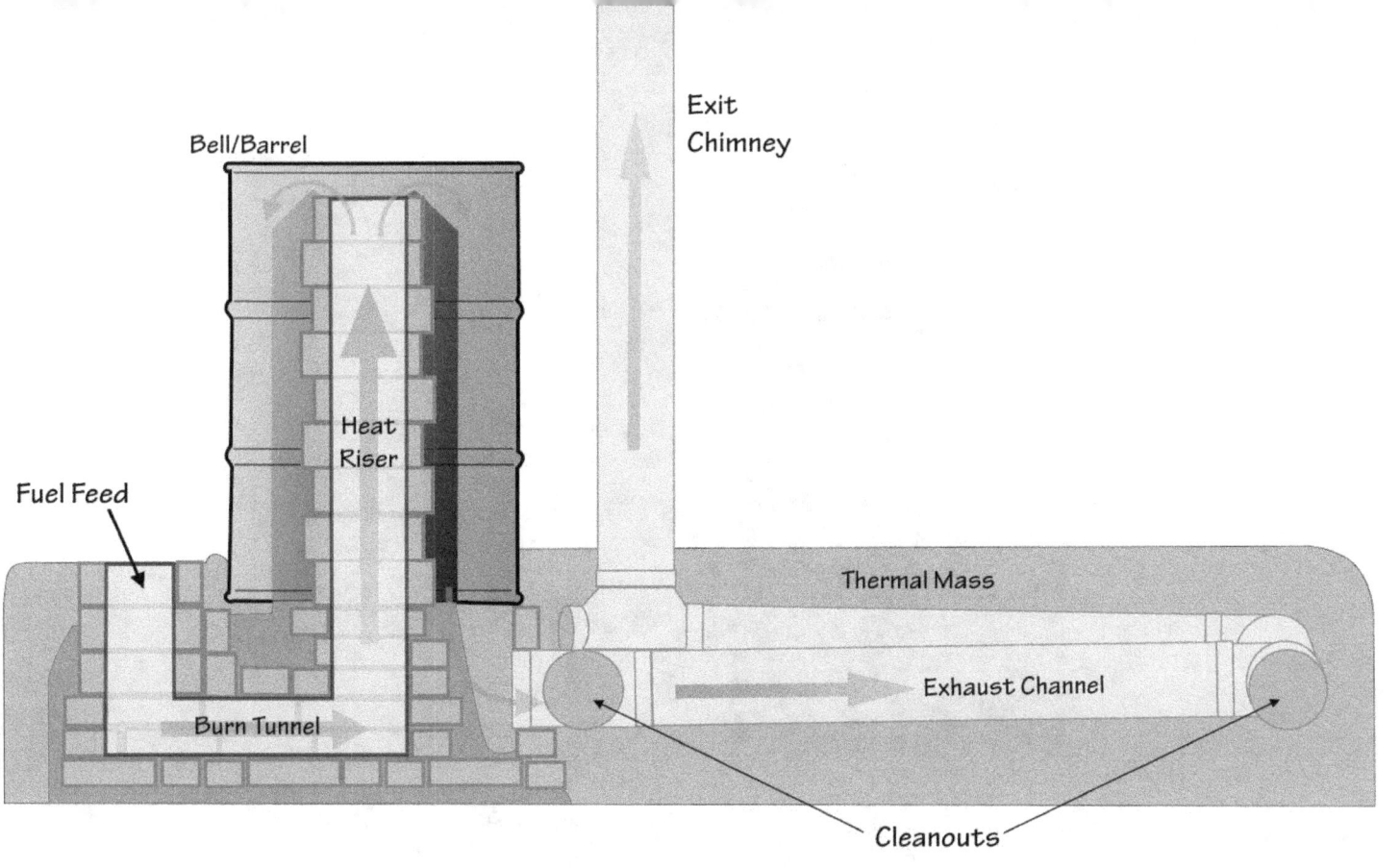

Based on diagrams from The Rocket Mass Heater Builder's Guide by Erica & Ernie Wisner.

Continue Learning
- _The Rocket Mass Heater Builder's Guide_ by Erica and Ernie Wisner (2017). Paperback.

Rocket Stoves for Hot Water, Electricity, and More

The extreme heat created by rocket stoves can be harnessed in many ways: heating a home, cooking food, heating water, metal smithing, glassblowing, or even making steam—even waste disposal plants are using J-tube-style designs to cleanly burn waste. Building steam is definitely the most dangerous application of rocket stove technology since it can explode and be fatal to anyone nearby. Water heaters need to have steam releases like a tempering valve, and they also need to mix the hot water with cold water to guarantee it is within tolerable temperature ranges.

The biggest hurdle for many who desire a RMH with uniform readouts is that every rocket stove layout, layout space, time of year, type of wood, and style of loading that wood will differ, and any metrics taken from different systems or even the same system with different wood, different times of year, or a different person lighting it, and you will get variable levels of heat which equates to varying levels of smoke in the exhaust. Rocket stoves and rocket mass heaters in general are each unique in their effectiveness at burning cleanly and heating

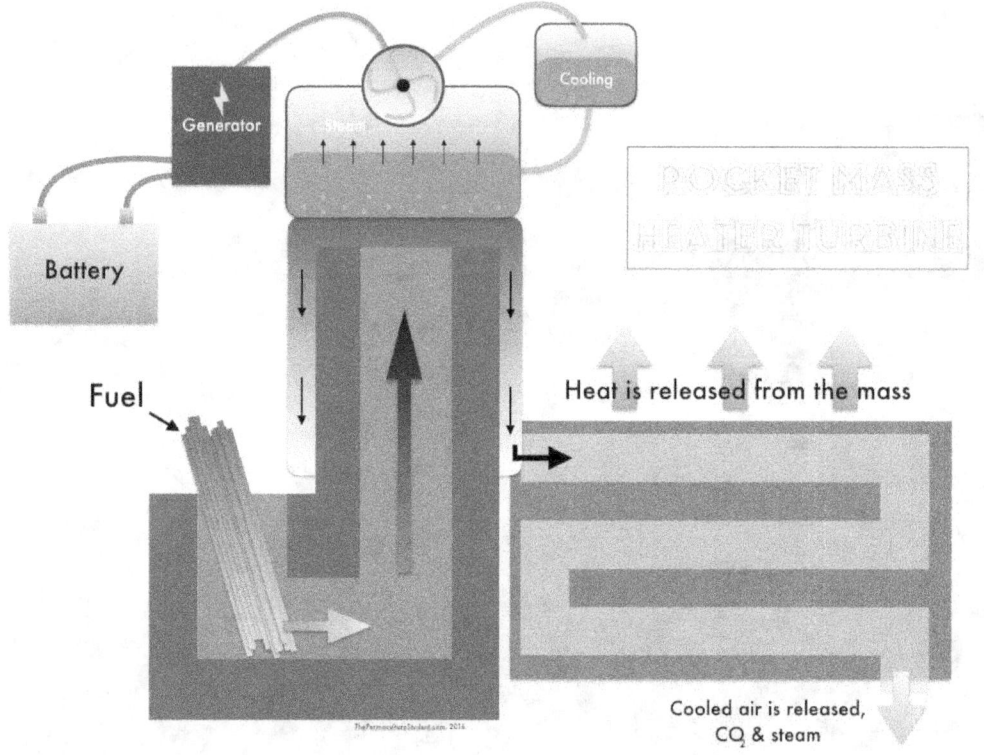

A concept map for a rocket mass heater steam generator. Notice the steam can vent off and return after cooling.

a space. Using a RMH or a rocket stove requires a person to be present and monitoring its operation carefully. It also takes knowledge of fire and the physics of the RMH itself. Rocket stoves have limitless potential—there are already miniature wood-burning stoves that charge cellphones. Once we embrace this technology ubiquitously, we will see innovation bloom as it did with the automobile and the internet.

"Wood burns clean at 1200°F degrees [648.8°C], but on average most fires probably burn around 900°F to 1000°F [482–537.7°C]. A RMH burns around 2000°F [1093.3°C] and can go as high as 4000°F [2204.4°C] but, around 2100F [1148.8°C], begins creating NO_X [Nitric Oxide]. We have a pretty narrow band to clean burning. We can do some real damage if we do not think this whole thing through. We really need as a society and global community to move in to the clean burning range because most things can be fabricated [to burn] in the clean combustion range rather than going over or under"
—Ernie Wisner, 2016.

Gasification (Biomass)

Gasification is the process of turning organic matter into synthetic gas (called syngas or producer gas) which works like regular fuel in a gas engine. Steam is combined with charred biomass to create carbon monoxide, hydrogen, and methane. The char can be made with coal (char-coal), peat, wood, walnut hulls, peanut hulls, and numerous other sources of carbonaceous biomass. While years of research still lie ahead, there are promising innovations surfacing for homesteaders that can be managed and fueled easily. Waste streams from farms and cities can easily turn into sources for reliable electricity, heat, and fuel. Most gasification systems are currently not carbon neutral, but designs can be adapted to sequester carbon if redesigned to capture all exhaust.

BioFuel

Biofuels themselves cover a spectrum that includes different processes and products—some of which could be regenerative and others which need to be redesigned to be carbon neutral or carbon-sequestering. It is imperative that all combustion engines capture all their exhaust before it enters the atmosphere, and it is also critical that they burn cleanly enough to only release carbon dioxide and water in that exhaust.

Alcohol is a biofuel that is being used worldwide. Alcohol can even be used to run an engine as has been done in Brazil with sugar cane biomass. Alcohol is a reliable fuel source that can be created easily and regeneratively from numerous biological sources and waste streams on a home-scale or even a citywide scale. Animal lard is a reliable source of biodiesel for Winfield Farms in California. Other areas rely upon used vegetable oil from fast food restaurants.

Biogas

Biogas is short for the biological gases released when decomposition occurs. When wood breaks down in a large quantity without any turning it begins to release CO_2 and methane (CH_4), both of which can be captured and used. Biogas can also be sourced from already partially broken-down wastes like human and animal manures or mixed sources of rotting biomass. The sewage, the kitchen scraps, and all the other organic wastes can be composted, and the gases can be captured from that event. Latrines can even be designed to do all the work passively. That gas can be used in numerous ways, and its CO_2 accompaniment and the resultant CO_2 from burning the CH_4 can also be sequestered if systems are properly designed. Biogas backpacks are being used to transport methane for cooking fuel to decentralized locations, spreading self-reliance and trade, in places like Ethiopia, Africa. Septic tanks could be redesigned to capture the biogas they generate.

A biodigester for biogas can be made on a small scale easily but offers only a modest amount of gas while a larger neighborhood or village-sized biodigester can easily generate more biological activity and therefore more gas. It should be noted that smaller size biodigesters are easier to manage. Transporting and storing the gas will always be a dangerous process, but if systems that generate the gas are built with extra capacity for high production or high-heat time periods and generally designed to provide the amount of gas regularly needed, then there will never be a build up of gas for that to become a problem. Additionally, containment vessels need to be double-chambered to withstand high pressure times. The waste product at the end is a fungal food or a soil amendment once it has been aerobically composted.

Professional Applications & Scaling Up
- Install Alternative Energy Services
- Teach Others How to Install or Work with Alternative Energy Systems
- Distribute Alternative Energy Solutions
- Work with community leaders and elected officials to adopt alternative energy on a larger scale.

Permatecture

The term "Permatecture" was coined by Stuart Muir Wilson, the grandson of Bill Mollison (the co-creator of permaculture), as a component of his Master of Architecture program. Permatecture's principles were created more recently in writing *The Permaculture Student 2*. How can we embrace permanent holistic and regenerative structures into our communities, designs, and sites? How can they honor the people and the environment? How can their construction and repair be easily done in the same fashion? How can our buildings become legacies that serve both future generations and biodiversity?

Permatecture Principles
- Durability and Longevity
- Natural and Non-Polluting Resources
- People-Powered
- Ethical Labor
- Fair Compensation
- Accessible to All, Affordable by All
- Repairability
- Stacking Functions

Site Analysis
What natural building materials does your site or bioregion offer? Clay? Wood? Stone? Hemp? Straw? Lime? What can you gather in quantity? How much can you make with what you can freely gather? How much do you need and what will it cost? Who can you get to help you build? Can you offer work-trade? Turn it into a workshop? What's your timeline for the build? What season will work best? What can go wrong? What permits do you need? What building codes need to be followed?

Natural Building
- *Cob* - a mixture of earth, straw, water, and sometimes gravel or sand to make a natural building material like adobe (but that sometimes has manure in it as well). This can be used to build structures, cover structures, and to finish structures. It is versatile and does not

have to obey the typical straight lines and geometry adopted by most conventional buildings: you can explore creatively all the curves and dimensions possible. Cob is fireproof, insect proof, and extremely affordable and easy to work with. Design whatever your dream's desire with cob!

- *Adobe* - adobe means mudbricks in Spanish, but it is more accurately mudbricks high in clay content. It is one of the earliest building materials known and similar to cob.
- *Hempcrete* - combining lime and properly cured and cut hemp creates incredibly strong and light hempcrete which overtime sequesters carbon from the atmosphere.
- *Mud and Lime Plaster* - walls can be artfully finished with a mud or lime plaster and easily repaired. Mud plaster floors have to be routinely redone. The mud again is high in clay content or nearly pure clay.
- *Straw Bale* - used in combination with other building methods, strawbales used in the main walls of a building provide incredible insulating power for the home. Very little heat or cooling is needed in a well designed strawbale house. A building frame of wood and/or metal is created before the straw bales are added and stacked. The bales are then sealed in with cob, hempcrete, or some other malleable earth building material high in clay.
- *Rammed Earth and Earthbagged* - earth can be contained and compressed to build structures as well. Earthbags are earth-filled sacks that are stacked and then have rebar driven through them and barbwire laid between the layers to hold them together. It may sound unstable, but it is actually a long-lasting and earthquake-resistant model - it really all depends on how well it's put together and the quality of the materials used. Rammed Earth Bricks are made by a machine that compresses dirt high in clay into durable and strong building bricks.
- *Thatch* - while it has been called a dying trade, creating thatch roofs is an art that needs a revival: making roofs out of straw, palms, reeds, and other biomass is a regenerative and sustainable practice that needs adoption everywhere possible, and these types of roofs are used from the tropics to the cold temperate.
- *Stone* - another ancient building material, stone is enduring, bold, and timeless. If you can move, shape, and safely build with stone, you can leave a legacy of beauty that shelters people or animals with a nontoxic sustainable building material.
- *Timber* - we have to be very careful with our standing carbon. The rocket mass heater allows us to avoid cutting down trees, using sticks instead and small branches for warmth each winter. Whatever we use in timber we must use wisely in the longest term use for the greatest benefit. Wood homes are seen all over the world and can be extremely beautiful while sequestering carbon for the longterm. Some timber like bamboo regrow quickly from a perennial root, making them ideal building sources and carbon sinks.

Professional Applications & Scaling Up

Natural builders are needed in all bioregions and for all sorts of projects big and small. In many areas, these skills are not being handed down, and now is the time to connect these craftsmen with students before these methods and skill sets are lost. You may have to travel to immerse yourself in a program to learn in-depth - natural building is, like many advanced permaculture niches, best experienced both hands-on and online in a self-paced setting, so find a program near you, online, or visit organizations like CalEarth.org that specialize in both in-person and online courses.

Continue Learning
- *The Hand-Sculpted House: a Practical and Philosophical Guide to Building a Cob Cottage* by Ianto Evans, Michael G. Smith, and Linda Smiley (). Paperback.
- CalEarth Online and On-Site Courses and Apprenticeships http://www.calearth.org

Social Permaculture

Rarely is social permaculture or care of people delved deeply into. Perhaps it is because it is often the most difficult area to design, manage, and predict. For everyone who dives into this arena, they quickly realize that the more work you get done on your own self (your zone zero), the greater influence you will have with others and the further your own work will go. There are many resources available to everyone today to better themselves, their communities, and the world at large - the hardest step is adopting those patterns and making them into intentional habits. That is the real challenge that social permaculture faces: to make people care an intrinsic part of our culture and not just lip service.

What is People Care?

Caring for people can come in as many varieties as there are people. It could be a kind word, a meal, a job, a place to sleep for the night, a gift, education, physical fitness training, medical care, mental health care, caring for children and the elderly, or just silent company. For some, cooking and making clothes or blankets for those in need or for those they care for is a deep expression of love. *The 5 Love Languages*, a book and concept by Gary Chapman describes the five ways people express care: Gift Receiving, Physical Touch, Words of Affirmation, Acts of Service, and Quality Time. He also points out in his work that not everyone has the same love language, so someone needing quality time doesn't value words of affirmation as a convincing expression of love - they do not communicate the care in the same way to that person. We must understand ourselves and others to properly care for both. Expressing care in this way is key to People Care, but it's not the full picture.

Beyond the personal 1:1 form of care we have a macro form of care that encompasses the autonomy, community support, and cultural legacy we as cultures facilitate in terms of access, equality, commons, mental and physical healthcare, and contribution. These systems can range from locally run, private groups providing these services, local governments, or state and federal. Human cultures vary in how they show macro care in a multitude of ways. Some governments are like an overbearing parent micromanaging, sometimes even spoon feeding their people, while others are like a distracted parent their people hardly see but may require strict obedience when they do appear. Others may never see a government representative their entire lives. How cultures care for their people is often how those people will care for themselves and each other because it generates an overarching cultural expectation. If the government leaves people to their own devices, the people become self-reliant and disconnected from government, mirroring the government. Our families, towns, cities, and countries can all focus on specific forms of care that support a permanent culture.

Autonomy and community are often seen as separate or in conflict, but they actually enrich each other in tandem as we provide more autonomy in terms of community involvement and influence as well as providing more choice by means of embracing local entrepreneurship, artists, craftsmen, health practitioners, and more! By giving more access to more voices, we build community as we allow for that individual to express themselves, exercise choice, influence their community, and get community feedback: it's a dialogue between the individual and the communal - not either/or.

That's really the crux of Jeremy Rifkin's *The Third Industrial Revolution* - the world's energy, communication, and transportation are going to be designed and operate like the internet where each component can be self-reliant but can also network with others. Rifkin describes the numerous way the internet has broken the story of the second industrial revolution. More like the mycelium in the soil, we will embody the currently appearing and decentralizing pillars of the new story: decentralized smart power grids where homes are the micro power generators in a huge network of generators, decentralized ownership of transportation like Uber, carpooling, and self-driving cars that work like the city bike share systems, and decentralized communication allowing anyone from anywhere to express an idea in the global community and be heard, and even more - the Gift Economy where we are bartering with abundance and sharing freely in a new economy that is about keeping the ball going for as long as possible with as many as possible - no longer is it a zero sum game of winners and losers. The scarcity economy has nearly destroyed our world and collective culture. The Gift economy won't replace all buying and selling, but it has already largely replaced entire industries with free services that are social capital-based (look at the music industry, Youtube, Facebook, etc.) Though much of our world will be automated in the next few years, we will never be able to replace the gift that the internet has given us with AI, automation, or robots: the social connection that people are making across cultures, borders, classes, and more. It's opening up and freeing minds everywhere from the old constructs of social order, class, race, and religion. We are adapting in all ways through the free flow of communication and learning. The internet will not replace face to face connections with people, local community, working or teaching with people in person, or working with animals or plants - humans are needed for that work. Though sensors and automation can improve the work people do with plants and animals, a person is needed to work with all the elements in an ecosystem on site hands-on in most cases. Our observation skills are superior to any machine's.

In the regenerative economy, all forms of capital are included - even the social capital economy that often leads the impetus for the Gift economy. It's this emerging economy that regenerates our cultural forms of care from the family to the local community to the bioregion to the government, promotes the gift economy by design, has people care built in, and regenerates the environment - it is a hybrid of many different paths, practices, and movements all striving for equality, access, autonomy, and contribution.

The 4 Modalities of People Care
- *Interpersonal* - commonly called Self Care, this is how we care for ourselves.
- *Intrapersonal* - caring for other people through personal service
- *Economic* - caring through providing a private service
- *Governmental* - caring through providing a community service

Principles for People Systems
- Treat Others Better than They Expect to be Treated
- Show Trust and Be Trustworthy
- Be Clear
- Set Clear Boundaries
- Educate by Example
- Share as much as you can
- Be Self-Reliant (Be Prepared)
- Be Patient
- Be Local
- Be Open
- Be Timely
- Solutions, Not Complaints
- Smile First
- Family First
- Work First on What Matters Now
- Always Innovate and Adapt

- Don't take Offense, be Better
- Look to Elders
- Celebrate Common Interests
- Listen to and Make Space for Children and Youth
- Include Everyone When Possible

Intrapersonal

Self Assessment

How are you doing? Are you consistently growing? How are you in a stressful situation? Do you like challenges? How do you view challenges? How are you doing with the Permaculture Principles for People Systems? How do you talk to yourself (in your mind)? Are you critical of yourself? Do you hear positive affirming thoughts more than negative ones? Is it easy to push the negative thoughts away? No matter who you are or what your answers are, we all can improve from whatever stage we are in now. Using reflection, goal setting (visualization), and daily growth habits, we can consistently progress and improve our inner zone like a garden over time. Regular assessments really help us face what we are avoiding taking on and clearly show us where we need to improve. This may also mean that you are constantly assessing too: daily measurements of how many pull-ups you do or miles you run will dramatically help you progress further.

Some practices like weekly and monthly assessments help us re-focus our attention on what's important to us. So, what is your purpose? Why are you interested in regenerative practices and permaculture? What do you want to give to the world? Are you living a life that will lead to that? Are you planning your days around the gift you'd like to give the world?

How we feel about ourselves and how we treat ourselves inside our own heads is the best indicator for how we will treat others. If we are plagued with negative thoughts, feelings, and doubts, we will likely project them onto others without being aware of it because they pervade our minds. The inverse is also blessedly true: the confidence and joy you feel will also leak into everything you say, do, and think. We can control how we feel by focusing on gratitude and our purpose. Discovering your purpose requires life planning.

Life Planning

Life planning is similar to a holistic goal for a site, but it is for your life, and just as with a site, it is constantly being adapted and changed. What do you want to accomplish in your life? What big dreams do you have? How do you want to FEEL on a daily basis? What's important NOW? How do you envision your ideal life, and what do you need to do to reach that vision? Write everything down, edit it, reflect on it, and build your dreams bigger each time you do - that will happen on its own as you develop your vision and encounter challenges.

Daily Practices

- *Affirmations* - incredibly powerful, saying positive things to ourselves, about ourselves, and about what we will do or be out-loud in the first five to ten minutes after waking in the morning has been proven to help people become the person they want to be. You can start out by saying things you've heard or read elsewhere, but try to write your own out. This will ultimately be more meaningful. Here's a few of my personal affirmations: *I will not be slowed down by those afraid to try, This is my day, and I will make it great!* and *I am resilient in the face of great adversity.* No matter what you say or do; make it something that makes you feel alive and rooted in who you are with joy.
- *Meditation* - visualizing the world we want to be in, a new product, site, or design, or just spending time releasing tension, setting our intentions, and clearing our mind, meditation can expand our capacity to handle stress and multiple variables in complex settings - most especially when times are challenging. Meditation allows us to slow down and listen to what's most important to us right now - which connects us to our purpose again and directs our attention to our goals.
- *Daily Physical Activity* - we are both physical and mental beings in tandem. We cannot get to our peak mental abilities without exercising and expanding our physical self. Taking walks, hikes, runs, or bike rides to get our heart rates up is critical. Daily yoga, tai-chi, pilates, and more core strength and flexibility training are all excellent at keeping our body limber and strong. Strength training like weight lifting, pull-ups, pushups, and exercises that focus on building muscle are also excellent to do throughout the week if not daily.
- *Daily Learning* - learning something new daily helps us to stay in a life learning mode of growth. Focus on reading, writing, watching videos, and listening to audiobooks, podcasts, or radio programs that can help you move forward on your life plan. The greater your purpose and enthusiasm, the easier the learning process it will be.

- *Daily Goal Setting* - keeping track of our goals, aligning our day's activities, and reflecting on the work to be done each day will help us stay focused, accomplish more, feel more satisfaction, and avoid complications that can slow your own progress.
- *Keeping a Gratitude Journal* - research has proven that our brains essentially take a picture of our minds at the end of the day before we sleep to create a template for our mindset for the next day. When we focus on gratitude as we reflect on the day we've just had, writing it down before bed, we train our minds to expect good things which in turn makes more good things appear simply because we are expecting them and ready for them to appear on our radar. We are also more confident and action oriented because we know good things can and will happen. Gratitude journals are a powerful best practice for cultivating a positive outlook.

Interpersonal
Social Climate Analysis

How is the community feeling? What do the neighbors think? What do your investors think? What does your spouse think? What do your parents think? What do the local farmers/ranchers/fisherman/hunters/politicians/etc. think? How do you feel about these opinions and insights? How can you respond in a way that improves your design and brings them into the pattern at the same time? What critiques can we source to improve our ideas and make them more understandable to our audiences? Often gathering advisors is critical to embodying a diverse lens to examine ourselves and others.

Sometimes opposition itself can be an indicator that you are on the right path - sometimes old patterns are much like a compacted field: it needs a keyline ripping to allow water or new ideas to infiltrate again. Teachers are in recent years have a saying: *Move Your Cheese* - it means if you leave the cheese in the same spot in the maze, there's no challenge for the mice, and there's not the same level of engagement and awareness. *Move Your Cheese* and watch the response: there's suddenly engagement and heightened awareness. What does it tell you? Change connects us to growth. Often opposition, obstacles, objections, change, critiques, and ideas not considered are our biggest breakthrough moments - just as they are often for the people providing those critiques and objections. How we respond to stress, opposition, and conflict can often indicate how well our ideas will be accepted as well - if we are open to consider, converse, explain, listen, and defend, we are more likely to treat each other with respect and honor each other's contribution by responding with our best selves. When we show we are willing to listen without judgement or negative emotions consistently, we create trust and allow space for continual improvement - it also lets that person know that we care more about them than any disagreement or potential conflict we might have. When our actions themselves, show care in our body language, patience, and ability to listen, we embody people care and can live it in our daily lives. It will also help us turn conflict into opportunities to bring people closer, dive deeper into our purpose, and practice compassionate communication.

Community Building

A critical missing ingredient in many areas is any sense of community. Community gatherings, religious attendance, youth sports, community groups of all kinds, and more are all in steady decline - what's going on? In many areas, we've lost the neighborhood connection that Fred Rogers, the children's public television educator, promoted, and it hasn't been through malice or an attack, but a withering away of an unused muscle. We've atrophied our leadership and community building skills in many ways, but we can rebuild and strengthen those muscles anew just like we can with our bodies. It just takes focus and commitment on key concepts.

Keys to Community Building

- *Find a Common Goal, Interest, Problem, or Solution in your Network*
- *Encourage Participation and Ownership in the Creative Process*
- *Be Open and Inclusive - Invite Everyone*
- *Use Permaculture Ethics and Principles to Solve Problems*
- *Create a Regular Schedule and Honor those that Participate*
- *Spread Awareness and Education*
- *Serve the Community and Environment in Meaningful Hands-On, Person to Person Ways*

Forming a Local Group

Whether a local self-reliance group that meets at the local library or a meet-up of unschooling moms at the park, people are forming community on the small scale all the time leveraging the internet. The old modalities of communicating are in decline but the new ones are having our children and adults reading, writing, connecting, and learning more than any of their ancestors ever did. We can form local groups by posting a monthly meeting place at popular local locations with flyers, we can create an online group to advertise and gather local people, and we can invite local leaders who can attract people to the event. If the group follows the keys to community building, it will find a growing group of loyal participants that will eventually influence the local area.

Land Trusts

Land trusts are generally legal contracts that grant rights of stewardship over a piece of land for a specific conservation or sustainable use, ideally, for a very long time. Led by an ethical mission statement and guided by any series of decision-making processes and governing structures, the community land trust, through its operation, protects the land and fulfills the community's mission statement, its holistic goals. These communities or families have to obey the laws of the county, state, province, territory, or country they are in, but they also follow their own by-laws. Methodologies of management and governance are stipulated as part of the mission statement or constitution. These land trusts can be managed by a caretaker, a single family, a group of relatives, a small village, or, conceivably, a town.

Co-Ops, Cooperatives, & Buying Clubs

When groups get together, form a new organization, and pool responsibility for the management for a communal benefit like lower prices or organic foods in an urban food desert, they are forming a cooperative organization. These range in their purpose and their actions, but they all involve people cooperatively owning and doing the work together to run the business or pooling their resources to get better products for lower prices. We can create these by identifying a need, creating a group, pooling resources and time, and committing to a regular schedule and place to host, distribute, and/or administrate the operation.

Intentional Communities

These are groups of people who choose to live near each other for a common purpose. Though many different organizations of intentional communities exist, there are several types commonly attempted. Some pool their income and resources but maintain separate lives, others share ownership of land and select community structures and patterns, and still others are based on a business that all are participating in collectively on-site. Each of these models has a different level of communalism that reflects that particular community's mission statement and values. Intentional communities called EcoVillages have a focus on ecology and living regeneratively as a group. Historically, Christian abbeys in the European Middle Ages qualify as intentional communities focused on their religion and providing for themselves bioregionally.

You can create your own permaculture-themed intentional community through pooling resources, creating a constitution or mission statement that all agree to, and finding an area suitable to supporting your group and future generations bioregionally.

Economic

Find Your Niche

What do you want to do for a living? What are you passionate about? What do you love to restore or regenerate? What do you like to design or install? Do you like soil? Animals? People? Teaching? Cooking? Foraging? Healing? Fermentation? Herbs? Fungi? What would you like to spend the majority of your time doing and thinking about? What service do you want to give? What need can you fulfill? What passion of yours can serve others and the environment?

Forming a Business or NPO

Once you know what you want to do, the next step is to figure out how to make money doing that. It requires a business plan which is very similar to a regenerative design: you want to harvest money in much the same way you would harvest water or solar energy. Neal Spackman once told me to make a *money swale* - this metaphor is a great one. You want a system that accumulates energy and grows in its ability to serve and scale over time. Design your business like a thriving and diverse food forest, and it will support itself. Rely upon polycultures, and it will improve the world around it as it feeds you and provides an abundance to creatively use in service to the greater economy or community. Forests have zero waste - they operate off solar, wind, and water power as well as biological power. They spend less above the ground as they do below the surface, depositing large percentages of their annual solar yields into longterm investments in the soil carbon with every exchange with the soil life (primarily fungi). Be like the forest - invest in the soil; invest in the future.

Some areas do not require a business license unless you cross a certain threshold of earnings or if you participate in certain business activities, but many areas do require a license and even a federal tax ID. Consult your local business regulations as well as your local support agencies - both can be very informative but sometimes discouraging. If the latter is the case, do not be discouraged, Bill Mollison was known to have said that restrictions only lead to more creative design responses, so drink in the complexity and find that solution, but be careful and be aware of laws, risks, and regulations always.

Further on that: consult doctors, lawyers, accountants, friends, family, and business consultants - get advice from everyone in your risky ventures! Take it all in with grains of salt - protect your heart and your dream by being objective and gathering the data without reacting until later. Use their feedback to fine tune your ideas and reach your goal faster and with their support even if they don't realize it at first. Turn the top three biggest objections into your best argument points. Try not to respond to them immediately online. Use them in the social marketplace at critical moments to deliver your best selling points and use them as times to share the reason why you want to be doing what you are doing. Once you have that feedback incorporated, you are ready to launch focused on showcasing how your business is the answer to a problem that many people are focused on, and you then use the objections to create a dialog that drives a narrative that leads to the reason for the existence of your business: the service it provides to the holistic picture.

Steps to a Regenerative Business Plan

- *Decide upon your Ecological Niche and Type of Regenerative Service* - what do you love in the regenerative spectrum, and how can you share that with the world?
- *Set Holistic Goals for your Business* - what are the big goals you want to achieve with this business? What larger beneficial currents or combined action are you contributing to?
- *Mission Statement* - what are the actions needed to achieve your holistic goal?
- *Structure and Systems of Operation* - how will it work? Will you have employees? What's the schedule?
- *Revenue Cycles* - how will money be earned, spent, saved, invested, and dispersed?
- *Products and Services* - what will you offer? How does it care for both people and the earth? How does it care for the future?
- *5 Steps Toward Success* - what five steps must you take to make your holistic goals happen? When you focus on these five steps in your daily, weekly, monthly, and annual goal setting, you will start moving much faster towards making your business a thriving reality.

Our Mission Statement:
- To Teach Regenerative Skills, Thinking, & Attitudes
- To Reverse the Damage to Ecosystems & Ourselves
- To Guarantee a Syntropic Future

Continue Learning
- *The Regenerative Entrepreneurs and Educators: Alignment, Crowdfunding, and Best Practices*, the online course http://www.thepermaculturestudent.com/course-signup/regenerative-entrepreneurs-educators-the-online-course-with-matt-powers

Governance

Sociocracy

Often called a deeper democracy, Sociocracy is a governance system that uses the self-organizing principles determined by members of a common-interest group to allow all the members to hear and speak to proposals in order to shape it until all members feel able to give their consent to a proposal. In this way rich inputs can be obtained and thorough understanding of issues reached by the members. This is very similar to holistic management in decision-making but has an organizational component added. All proposals and appointments are made with the participants' consent. Each group is organized around common interests, and each group manages itself. These groups work on projects and policies and seek out objections to improve the projects and policies from the people that those projects and policies affect. If it was inside a business, it would be the customers' objections informing the business' next product improvement. Instead of a board or an individual making decisions for all members, small groups or circles (whose members have been nominated by the members of the whole group) hold the power of decision-making in a prescribed area of concern. The decisions of such groups are the result of discussing exhaustively and amending proposals until every member of the group feels able to give their consent.

Sociocracy can be sourced for a business, a single event, a long-term project, or even a local or federal government; it can be added or overlaid onto any system. By seeking out objections, decisions are arrived upon that everyone recognizes as being holistically beneficial for the time being since later things may change, and the agreement can be adapted at that time; adaptability is key.

Continue Learning
- <u>We the People: Consenting to a Deeper Democracy</u> by John Jr. Buck. (2007) Paperback.

Holacracy

Holacracy is a trademarked, self-organizing government system for self-management based upon a constitution where all involved work towards an agreed set of common rules and mutually understood goals. This enables companies and organizations to behave and evolve in the way ecologies, organisms, and cities naturally do.

"Like Sociocracy, Holacracy is also organized into circles, groups of roles that work together for a common purpose (such as 'marketing') within the organization. Individuals act as the 'sensors' for the organization, taking action on behalf of their roles within the company, and channeling feedback back into the company to improve the way it works. Individuals who fill roles in the marketing circle may sense 'tensions' (opportunities for improvement) that impact the work of that circle. Any individual filling a role within the circle may make a proposal for a way to resolve a tension that he or she senses. Others may object if they see a reason, based on known information, that the proposal will cause harm to the organization. Using a special integrative process, these objections can then be addressed. The goal of the process is to allow the 'tension-sensor' to author a change that will address his or her tension without harming the work of others in the circle. Through these incremental changes, the structure of the organization evolves and improves"

–Tara Everhart, HolacracyOne, 2016

Continue Learning:
- Holacracy: A Radical New Approach to Management | Brian Robertson | TEDxGrandRapids, on Youtube (2015). https://www.youtube.com/watch?v=tJxfJGo-vkI&t=143s
- Holacracy: The New Management System for a Rapidly Changing World by Brian J. Roberston. (2015). Paperback.

NonViolent Communication

Created by Dr. Marshall Rosenberg, NonViolent Communication (NVC) is an empathic language technique that recognizes universal human needs and their communication as the key to unlocking conflict. Honesty, compassion, and empathy typify NVC's non-judgmental communication process. NVC is being used in businesses, schools, families, prisons, war zones, and more places to improve communications and resolve conflict. When both sides of a conflict can recognize the needs of each other without hearing judgment from the other side, the process for seeing how we can help each other can begin.

Practitioners focus on observations, feelings, needs, and requests. When we can observe or share an observation without judgement, we can also say how it makes us feel in relation to what our needs are, and then they can make a request. NVC can be used to develop self-empathy, find empathy for others, resolve conflicts, and to communicate honestly.

> **"Four Components of NVC**
> 1. Observations
> 2. Feelings
> 3. Needs
> 4. Requests
>
> **Two Parts of NVC**
> 1. Expressing Honestly through the Four Components
> 2. Receiving empathically through the four components"
>
> **NVC Process**
> The concrete actions we *observe* that affect our well-being
> How we *feel* in relation to what we observe
> The *needs*, values, desires, etc. that create our feelings
> The concrete actions we *request* in order to enrich our lives"*
>
> *from **Nonviolent Communication** 3rd Edition (2015).

Continue Learning:
- *Nonviolent Communication Training Course Marshall Rosenberg CNVC org (9 hrs approx.)*, on Youtube (2014).
  https://www.youtube.com/watch?v=O4tUVqsjQ2I
- *Nonviolent Communication Workshop - Marshall Rosenberg (3 hrs approx.)*, on Youtube (2014).
  https://www.youtube.com/watch?v=4LuPCAh9FCc
- Nonviolent Communication, 3rd edition by Marshall Rosenberg, Phd. (2015). Paperback.
- Nonviolent Communication Companion Workbook by Lucy Leu. (2003). Paperback.

Restorative Justice (Circles)

Much like a concentrated formula for NVC, this restorative justice method was pioneered by Dominic Barter of Rio de Janeiro in the mid-1990s. It is a holistic method that includes all voices that are involved with a conflict. Instead of punishment or judgement, it seeks restoration. The circles open and close with a reflective sharing process that allows everyone to have an initial and final say (refer to the diagram on the next page).

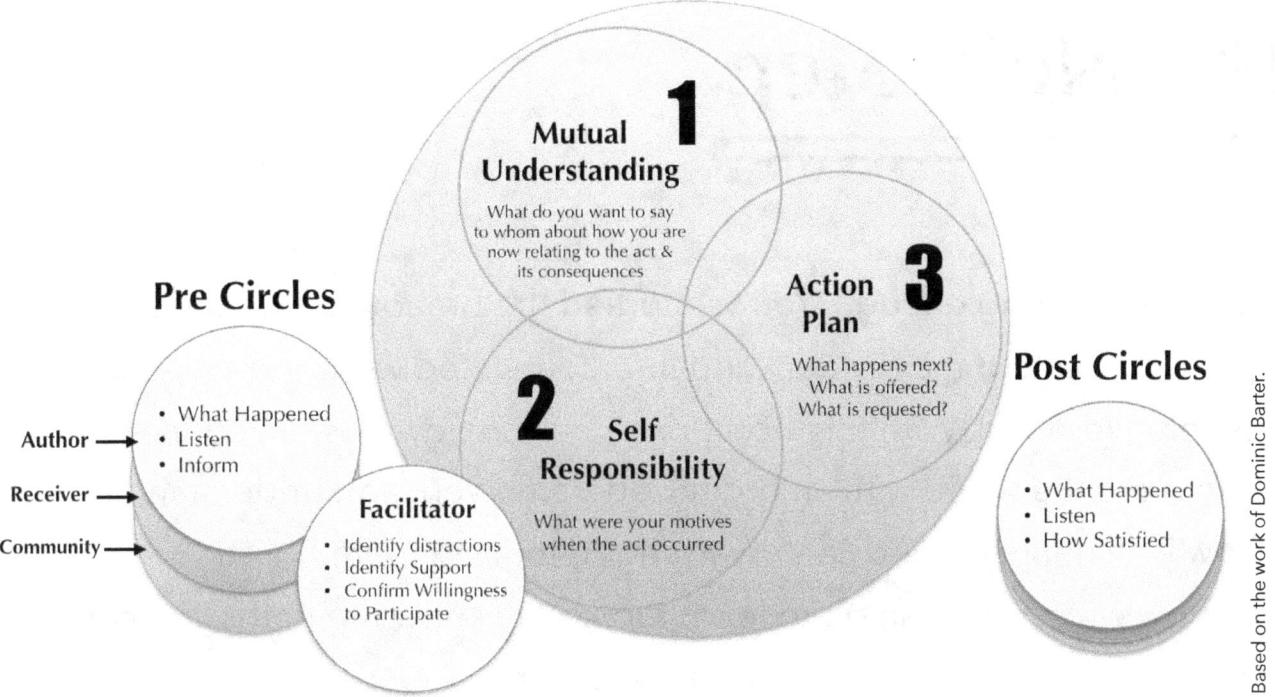

Professional Applications & Scaling Up

This truly is a wide open space. This section could be books long - we really need niche books in this area: socioeconomic permaculture, because positive unifying work in that area that gets beyond judgement and division is needed for the unification necessary for the regenerative economy to reach everyone and make the impact we all need to reverse climate instability. Our communities need all their people to be thriving regardless of yesterday's zero sum game's tally; once we are plugged into an energy grid that pays for itself after a few years, it will be a new ballgame economically, politically, and socially. Wars over limited resources won't make any sense since everyone will have access to the unlimited energy everywhere, and we'll all be in communication. Once food is growing everywhere and awareness of how to grow, prepare, and eat that abundance is too, then hunger is going to no longer be an issue anyone has to face. Once water harvesting is in place in our infrastructure and architecture everywhere, we won't have a lack of water either. The internet continues to grow in value, and internet access costs continue to plummet as online education from some of the best institutions in the world is increasingly more freely available. The amount of information available today online dwarfs the educational knowledge sets of every profession ever described. It is the greatest library of information ever collected and it continues to grow. If you can design your business to scale up and operate like the internet, like fungi, you will be successful in whatever you choose to regenerate.

The Next Step

You've waited long enough. You've studied the breadth and enough depth to see into the individual and interconnected worlds within our regenerative world. With this workbook you can now design, connect, and explore the world with an organized framework and understanding of how it all connects and can be arranged for maximum holistic benefit. You know where you can go to learn more. You know the paths you can follow to an abundant future. Now it's your turn…

Make It Your Lifestyle & Daily Practice
Make It Your Living & Life Study
Dive Deep Into Your Niche(s)
Share Your Joy & Passion With The World

If you haven't already, read *The Permaculture Student 2 the Textbook* and *The Regenerative Career Guide*, and if you already aren't enrolled, join *The Advanced Permaculture Student Online* with over 50 expert educators from around world. If it's past time to signup, new students can enroll in the spring. Learn how to turn these regenerative skills into a business, community, economy, and lifestyle with real experts doing it and thriving. Dive deeper with advanced permaculture and the niche experts this book series introduces!

About the Author

Matt Powers is a teacher, author, videographer, seed saver, plant breeder, researcher, gardener, and family guy. Matt and his family lived in the foothills of the Sierra Nevada mountains in the Central Valley California for almost a decade - before that Matt and Adriana lived in NYC where Matt was a professional musician. Matt and his family currently live in Issaquah, Washington.

Other books by Matt Powers
The Permaculture Student 1
The Permaculture Student the Workbook
The Permaculture Student 2 the Textbook
The Magic Beans
Permaculture for School Gardens
The Regenerative Career Guide
The Forgotten Food Forest
and Translations

Courses with Matt Powers
The Permaculture Student Online K-12
The Permaculture Student Online - for Adult Learners
The Advanced Permaculture Student Online
Permaculture Gardening with Matt Powers
Best Practices for Regenerative Entrepreneurs & Educators

References

A

- AgendaGotsch. *Films.* Documentary series with articles. Web. Accessed 2016. http://agendagotsch.com
- Alexandrina Council. *Environmental Health Fact Sheet: What is required with an application for a Reedbed (second-stage wastewater treatment) system?* Web. PDF. 2016. https://www.alexandrina.sa.gov.au/webdata/resources/files/Reedbeds.pdf
- aqysta.com *The Barsha Pump.* Web. Accessed 2016. http://www.aqysta.com
- Anderson, Jim, Beduhn, Rebecca, Current, Dean, Espeleta, Javier, Fissore, Cinzia, Gangeness, Bjorn, Harting, John, Hobbie, Sarah, Nater, Ed, and Reich, Peter. "Potential of Soils for Carbon Sequestration." A Report to the Department of Natural Resources from the Minnesota Terrestrial Carbon Sequestration Initiative (2008). The Potential for Terrestrial Carbon Sequestration in Minnesota. University of Minnesota, St. Paul, MN., Feb. 2008. Web. Oct. 2016. http://files.dnr.state.mn.us/aboutdnr/reports/carbon2008.pdf
- Asselin, Olivier. *The Permaculture Orchard: Beyond Organic.* Possible Media. Film. 2014.
- Aurovilleradio.org *Restorative Circles.* 2014. http://www.aurovilleradio.org/restorative-circles/

B

- Baird, A., Baird, G., Hill, G., Hoeppner, E., Payne, M., Seymour, M. *Manual of Composting Toilet and Greywater Practice.* BC Ministry of Health, Health Protection Branch. February 2016 Draft for Consultation. Accessed 2016. http://www2.gov.bc.ca/assets/gov/environment/waste-management/sewage/composting_toilet_manual.pdf
- BBC.com. *First UK homes heated with 'poo power' gas from sewage.* BBC.com Oct. 1 2014. Accessed 2016. http://www.bbc.co.uk/news/uk-england-29443622
- Benson Agriculture and Food Institute. *Walipini Construction (The Underground Greenhouse).* Brigham Young University. Utah, 2002. Open Source Ecology. Web. n.d. Accessed 2016. http://opensourceecology.org/w/images/1/1c/Walipini.pdf
- *Blue Vinyl.* Biography/Documentary Film. 2002.
- Bradley, Kirsten. *Why Pasture Cropping is such a Big Deal.* Milkwood. 2010. Accessed 2016. https://www.milkwood.net/2010/12/07/why-pasture-cropping-is-such-a-big-deal/
- Browne Trading Company. *Veta La Palma Seafood.* Web. Accessed 2016. https://www.brownetrading.com/veta-la-palma-seafood/
- Buck, John and Villines, Sharon. *We the People: Consenting to a Deeper Democracy.* Sociocracy.info, 2007.

C

- CompostGuy.com. *Bokashi - the fermentation of organic wastes.* The Compost Guy. 2012. Accessed 2016. http://www.compostguy.com/bokashi-resource-page/
- Cornell University. *Marine microalgae, a new sustainable food and fuel source.* Eureka Alert. Web. Accessed 2016. https://www.eurekalert.org/pub_releases/2016-11/cu-mma112116.php
- Coswell, Angel. *How to Calculate Stream Flow.* sciencing.com. Published 2018. Accessed 2018. https://sciencing.com/calculate-stream-flow-rate-6697587.html

D

- Davis, Tony. *Tucson's Rain-catching Revolution.* High Country News. High Country News, 27 Apr. 2015. Web. 28 Oct. 2016. http://www.hcn.org/issues/47.7/tucsons-rain-catching-revolution
- Deppe, Carol. *Breed your own Vegetable Varieties.* Little, Brown, and Company. Boston, 1993.
- Deppe, Carol. *The Resilient Gardener: Food Production and Self-reliance in Uncertain times.* White River Junction, VT: Chelsea Green Pub., 2010.
- Department of Environment and Primary Industries. *Trickle Flow Pipes for Farm Dams.* Agriculture Victoria. 2013. Web. Accessed 2016. http://agriculture.vic.gov.au/agriculture/farm-management/managing-dams/trickle-flow-pipes-for-farm-dams
- Design Coalition. *Measuring Sun Angles.* Web. n.d. Accessed 2016. http://designcoalition.org/kids/energyhouse/sunangles.htm
- *Determining Soil Texture by the Feel Method.* Baltimore Ecosystem Study. n.d. Accessed 2016. http://www.beslter.org/msp/institute.files/november/Determining%20Soil%20Texture%20by%20Feel%20Method.pdf
- Doherty, Darren J. and Jeeves, Andrew. *The Regrarians eHandbook.* Regrarians Limited, 2015.
- Doherty, Darren J. *Broad Acre Agroforestry Integration.* Permaculture Voices: PV3. March 2016. Conference.

E

- Evans, Ianto, Smith, Michael, G., and Smiley, Linda. *The Hand-Sculpted House: A Practical and Philosophical Guide to Building a Cob Cottage.* Chelsea Green. 2002.

F

- Farquhar, Brodie. *Wolf Reintroduction Changes Ecosystem.* YellowstonePark.com. 2016. National Park Trips Media. Web. Accesssed 2016. http://www.yellowstonepark.com/wolf-reintroduction-changes-ecosystem/
- fibershed.com. *About.* 2016. Accessed 2016. http://www.fibershed.com/about/
- Fiore, Corina. *How to Calculate Wind Speed.* Accessed 2018. https://www.ehow.com/how_5164972_calculate-wind-speed.html

- Footer, Diego. *PV3: Permaculture Voices 3*. Conference. San Diego. 2016.
- Footer, Diego. *PV2: Permaculture Voices 2*. Conference. San Diego. 2015.
- Fortier, Jean-Martin. <u>The Market Gardener</u>. New Society Publishers, 2014.
- Fortier, Jean-Martin. *The Market Gardener with Jean-Martin Fortier, Six Figure Farming*. Living Web Farms. web. Youtube Playlist. Accessed 2016. https://www.youtube.com/playlist?list=PLCeA6DzL9P4uRadXW0_hj5Ct3EAqWH1zl
- Fortier, Jean-Martin. *Profitable small-scale farming. How design sets the stage for success*. Permaculture Voices: PV3. San Diego. March 2016.
- Fukuoka, Masanobu. <u>Planting Seeds in the Desert</u>. Chelsea Green, Vermont. 2012.
- Fukuoka, Masanobu. <u>The One-Straw Revolution</u>. The New York Review of Books, 2009.

G

- *GoogleEarth Pro*. Free application by Google. https://www.google.com/earth/
- Greenman, Eliza. *A New Fruit Culture!* Permaculture Voices: PV3. March 2016. Conference.
- Gronbeck, Christopher. Web. 2009. Accessed 2016. http://www.susdesign.com/sunangle/
- *Growing Power - A Model for Urban Agriculture*. Documentary. Oct 2010. Web. Youtube.com. Accessed 2016. https://www.youtube.com/watch?v=vs7BG4lH3m4
- GrowingPower.org. *Will Allen*. Web. 2014. Accessed 2016. http://www.growingpower.org/about/leadership/will-allen/

H

- Hemenway, Toby. <u>The Permaculture City</u>. Chelsea Green, 2015.
- Holmgren, David. <u>Permaculture: Principles and Pathways beyond Sustainability</u>. Hepburn, Victoria: Holmgren Design Services, 2002.
- Holzer Permaculture. *The Krameterhof*. web. 2016. Accessed 2016. http://www.holzerpermaculture.us/krameterhof.html
- Holzer, Sepp. <u>Desert or Paradise</u>. Chelsea Green, 2012.
- Holzer, Sepp. <u>Sepp Holzer's Permaculture: A Practical Guide to Small-Scale, Integrative Farming and Gardening</u>. Chelsea Green, 2011.
- HydrateLife.org. *Eco-Latrine of the future: Tiger Toilets*. Web. 2012. Accessed 2016. http://www.hydratelife.org/?p=539
- *Homegrown Revolution (Award winning short-film 2009)- The Urban Homestead, Dervaes*. The Urban Homestead. Youtube. 2011. Documentary. Accessed 2016. https://www.youtube.com/watch?v=7IbODJiEM5A
- *How to Measures Stream Flow Rate*. appropedia.org Published 2017. Accessed 2018. http://www.appropedia.org/How_to_measure_stream_flow_rated

I

- Ingham, Elaine. *Biological Farming*. Permaculture Magazine North America. No. 3 Winter 2016. The Permaculture Bug, LLC. 2nd article in series.
- Ingham, Elaine. *Celebration Farm Tour*. Oroville, CA. 2016.
- Ingham, Elaine R., Moldenke, Andrew R., and Edwards, Clive A. <u>Soil Biology Primer</u>. Soil and Water Conservation Society in cooperation with the USDA Natural Resources Conservation Service. 2000.
- Ingham, Elaine. *Lecture Notes, Work in Beauty workshop, Gallup, NM -- November 7, 2015*. WorkInBeauty.org. 2015. Accessed 2016. http://bernalilloextension.nmsu.edu/mastercomposter/documents/2015-mc-project-mb.pdf
- Ingham, Elaine. *Email*. Message to Matt Powers. 22 March 2016. Email.
- Ingham, Elaine. *Restoring Your Soil Life, Increasing Yields, Lowering Costs*. Master Design Masterclass. Webinar. Sept 2016. http://www.sustainabledesignmasterclass.com
- *INHABIT: A Permaculture Perspective*. Director: Costa Boutsikaris. Producer: Emmett Brennan. Film. 2015.

J

- Jenkins, Joseph. <u>The Humanure Handbook</u>. 2nd Ed. Chelsea Green. Vermont, 1999. Accessed 2016. https://humanurehandbook.com/downloads/H2.pdf
- Jones, Christine and Frisch, Tracy. "*SOS: Save Our Soils.*" Acres U.S.A. Interview. March 2015. Vol 45, No. 3. Accessed 2016. http://www.amazingcarbon.com/PDF/Jones_ACRES_USA%20(March2015).pdf

K

- Kjellman, Mikael. *Podride a practical and fun bicycle-car*. indigogo.com. web. 2016. Accessed 2016. https://www.indiegogo.com/projects/podride-a-practical-and-fun-bicycle-car-bike-bicycle#/
- Kourik, Robert. <u>Understanding Roots</u>. Metamorphic Press, 2015.

L

- Lal, Rattan. *Managing Soils and Ecosystems for Mitigating Anthropogenic Carbon Emissions and Advancing Global Food Security*. BioScience, Vol 60 no 9, Oct 2010. Web. Accessed 2016. http://tinread.usarb.md:8888/tinread/fulltext/lal/managing.pdf
- Lancaster, Brad. <u>Rainwater Harvesting for Drylands and Beyond</u>. Rain source Press, 2013. Distributed by Chelsea Green.
- Lawton, Geoff. *The Geoff Lawton Online Permaculture Design Course*. Permaculture Research Institute of Australia. New South Wales, Australia. 2014. http://www.geofflawtononline.com
- Lennox, James. *Phone Conversation with Matt Powers*. Operator at TransAlta's Ragged Chutes Hydro Station. September 2016.
- Lewis, Wayne and Lowenfels, Jeff. <u>Teaming with Microbes</u>. Timber Press, Inc., 2006.
- Leu, Lucy. <u>Nonviolent Communication Companion Workbook</u> (2003). Paperback.
- Liu, John D. *Email*. Group discussion with Rhamis Kent. 2016.
- Liu, John D. *Green Gold*. Environmental Education Media Project. Web. 2012. Accessed 2016. https://www.youtube.com/watch?v=YBLZmwlPa8A
- Liu, John D. *Lesson from the Loess Plateau*. Environmental Education Media Project. Web. 2012. Accessed 2016. https://www.youtube.com/watch?v=8QUSIJ80n50

M

- McCoy, Peter. *Radical Mycology*. Chthaeus Press, 2016.
- McCoy, Peter. *Radical Mycology Webinar 1: Seeing Fungi*. web. Youtube. 2016. https://www.youtube.com/watch?v=aB9JSky8x6k
- Meisel, Ari. *A Resource Guide to Green Building*. Princeton Architectural Press, New York. 2010.
- Merton, Lisa, and Dater, Alan. *Taking Root: The Vision of Wangari Maathai*. Global Perspectives Collection. Film. 2009. http://itvs.org/films/taking-root
- Micropnics. *Black Soldier Fly Larvae*. May 2009. Accessed 2016. https://www.micropnics.net.au/diy-livestock-rations/black-soldier-fly-larvae/
- Mollison, Bill. *Permaculture: A Designer's Manual*. Tagari Publications, Tasmania. 1989.
- Morrow, Rosemary. *Earth User's Guide to Teaching Permaculture*. Permanent Publications, 2014.
- Morrow, Rosemary. *Permaculture and the Forgotten. Teaching Permaculture in Places That Absolutely Need It. A Message of Hope with Rosemary Morrow. (PVP068)*. Permaculture Voices. Podcast. http://www.permaculturevoices.com/permaculture-and-the-forgotten-teaching-permaculture-in-places-that-absolutety-need-it-a-message-of-hope-with-rosemary-morrow-pvp068/ Accessed 2015.
- Morrow, Rosemary. *Successful permaculture in Cambodia*. Email to Matt Powers. Aug 30 2016.
- *Mushroom Companion Plants*. The Medicine Garden. Accessed 2016. http://www.medicinegarden.co.za/about/companion-planting/mushroom-companion-plants/
- *Mycorrhizae-Compatible Plants*. Fungi.com. Accessed 2016. http://www.fungi.com/plant-list.html

N

- Natural Capital LLC. *Natural Capital Plant Database*. Web Database. 2014. Accessed 2016. http://www.permacultureplantdata.com/
- Nelson, K.D. *Design and Construction of Small Earth Dams*. Inkata Press. Melbourne, 1991. Accessed 2016 with nominal fee. https://soilandhealth.org

O

- OAEC.org. *Compost Toilet Research Project*. Occidental Arts and Ecology Center. 2016. Accessed 2016. https://oaec.org/our-work/projects-and-partnerships/compost-toilet-project/

P

- Permaculture Research Institute. *OVER 200 FOOD PLANTS ON JUST A TINY 1/10TH ACRE OF COLD CLIMATE URBAN LAND*. Web. PRI AU. 2014. Accessed 2016. http://permaculturenews.org/2014/01/18/perennial-abundance-200-food-plants-on-1-10th-acre-cold-climate-urban-land/
- Pickerell, John. *Oceans Found to Absorb Half of All Man-Made Carbon Dioxide*. National Geographic News. online. 2004. Accessed 2016. http://news.nationalgeographic.com/news/2004/07/0715_040715_oceancarbon.html
- Pineault, Jonathan, and Fortier, Jean-Martin. *Permaculture Meets Market Gardening*. Permaculture Voices: PV3. San Diego. March 2016.
- *Polyfaces*. Directors: Lisa Heenan and Isaebella Doherty. Producer: Lisa Heenan. Film. 2015.
- *Ponds: Planning, Design, Construction*. Natural Resource Conservation Service, United States Department of Agriculture. Agriculture Handbook 590. 1997. Web. Accessed 2016. http://soiltesting.tamu.edu/publications/USDAPONDS.pdf
- *PRI Zaytuna Farm, NSW, Australia*. PermacultureGlobal.org. web. 2011. Accessed 2016. https://permacultureglobal.org/projects/3-pri-zaytuna-farm-nsw-australia

Q-R

- *Regenerative Organic Certification*. The Rodale Institute. Accessed 2018. https://rodaleinstitute.org/regenerativeorganic/
- RestorativeCircles.org. *Restorative Circles*. 2014. web. Accessed 2016. https://www.restorativecircles.org
- *REX*, the online Regrarians Farming Planning Course with Darren Doherrty. http://rex.farm
- Rifkin, Jeremy. *A Third Industrial Revolution*. (2013). Paperback.
- Robertson, Brian. *Holacracy: The New Management System for a Rapidly Changing World*. Holacracy One LLC, 2015. Macmillan Audio, 2015.
- Rodale Press. *One Straw Revolution - by Masanobu Fukuoka*. Youtube. 2014. Accessed 2016. https://www.youtube.com/watch?v=8atbgaiekZI
- Rosenberg, Marshall. *Nonviolent Communication, 3rd edition* (2015). Paperback.
- Rosenberg, Marshall. *Nonviolent Communication Training Course Marshall Rosenberg CNVC org*. CNVC.org. Posted on Youtube.com. Aug 24 2014. Accessed 2015. https://www.youtube.com/watch?v=O4tUVqsjQ2I
- Rosgen, David. *Dave Rosgen PhD River Hydrologist on Buffalo Bayou & Braes Bayou*. Youtube.com. 2012. Accessed 2016. https://www.youtube.com/watch?v=Jz625ybka8U
- Rotheroe, Dom. *The Coconut Revolution*. Stampede Films. 2001. Hosted youtube.com. Accessed 2016. https://www.youtube.com/watch?v=mGUBuuUEC0s

S

- Savitz, Jackie. *Save the Oceans, Feed the World!* ted.com. TEDxMidAtlantic, 2013. Accessed 2016. http://www.ted.com/talks/jackie_savitz_save_the_oceans_feed_the_world
- Savory, Alan. *Holistic Management: A New Framework for Decision Making*. Island Press, 1999.
- Sawada, Kozue, and Koki, Toyota. *Effects of the Application of Digestates from Wet and Dry Anaerobic Fermentation to Japanese Paddy and Upland Soils on Short-Term Nitrification*. Microbes and Environments. The Japanese Society of Microbial Ecology (JSME)/The Japanese Society of Soil Microbiology (JSSM), 30 Mar. 2015. Web. 28 Oct. 2016. https://www.ncbi.nlm.nih.gov/pmc/articles/PMC4356462/
- Scanlin, Dennis. *Best-Ever Solar Food Dehydrator Plans*. MotherEarthNews.com, 2014. Accessed 2018. https://

- www.motherearthnews.com/diy/tools/solar-food-dehydrator-plans-zm0z14jjzmar
- *Sepp Holzer The Agro Rebel.* Documentary. Youtube. web. Accessed 2016. https://www.youtube.com/watch?v=Ekub958v7Ks
- Shepard, Mark. *Farming. It's Damn Hard. An interview with Mark Shepard. (PVP091).* Permaculture Voices. iTunes and Soundcloud Podcast. Accessed 2016. https://soundcloud.com/permaculturevoices/mark-shepard-restoration-agriculture-pvp091
- Shepard, Mark. *Restoration Agriculture: Real-World Permaculture for Farmers.* Acres U.S.A., 2013.
- Sheil, Douglas, and Murdiyarso, Daniel. *How Forests Attract Rain: An Examination of a New Hypothesis.* American Institute of Biological Sciences. Oxford Journal: BioScience. Vol. 50. Apr. 2009. Accessed 2016. http://bioscience.oxfordjournals.org/content/59/4/341.full
- Schultz, Grant. *Permaculture 2.0, Designing a Profitable Broadacre Perennial Farm with Grant Schultz. (PVP034).* Permaculture Voices. iTunes and Soundcloud Podcast. 2015. Accessed 2016.
- Sobkowiak, Stefan. *History - Miracle Farm.* Web. 2016. Accessed 2016. http://miracle.farm/en/history/
- Sobkowiak, Stefan. *Miracle Farm.* Facebook Message to Matt Powers. 2016.
- Spackman, Neal. *10 Keys for Greening Any Desert.* Sustainable Design Masterclass, LLC. 2016. Webinar. Accessed 2016. http://www.sustainabledesignmasterclass.com
- Spackman, Neal. *Facing Fear and Stepping into the Unknown - The Al Baydha Project.* Permaculture Voices: PV2. San Diego. March 2015.
- Spackman, Neal. *Email.* Message to Matt Powers. Ongoing 2015-2016.
- Spadaccini, Michael. *The Basics of Business Structure.* Entrepreneur.com. March 9 2009. Web. Accessed 2016. https://www.entrepreneur.com/article/200516
- Stamets, Paul. *How Mushrooms Can Clean Up Radioactive Contamination - An 8 Step Plan.* Permaculture Magazine UK. Web. 2011. Accessed 2016. http://www.permaculture.co.uk/articles/how-mushrooms-can-clean-radioactive-contamination-8-step-plan
- Stamets, Paul. Assisted by Yao, Dusty Wu. *MycoMedicinals: An Informational Treatise on Mushrooms.* 3rd Ed. Paul Stamets, 2002. MycoMedia Productions, Fungi Perfecti LLC.
- Stone, Curtis. *The Urban Farmer: Growing Food for Profit on Leased and Borrowed Land.* New Society Publishers, 2015.
- Stone, Curtis. *Re: Case Study on Green City Acres.* Email to Matt Powers. 2016.
- Stone, Curtis. *$75,000 on 1/3 acre. Profitable Urban Farm Tour. Green City Acres.* Urban Farmer Curtis Stone. Web. Sept 2015. Youtube. Accessed 2016. https://www.youtube.com/watch?v=adW3GCQGHug
- Stone, Curtis. *$80,000 on Half An Acre Farming Vegetables - Profitable Mini-Farming with Curtis Stone.* Permaculture Voices: PV1. Web. San Diego, 2014. Accessed 2016. https://www.youtube.com/watch?v=1MNhtcagNO0

- Stone, Nathan. *Renovating Leaky Ponds.* Southern Regional Aquaculture Center. 1999. Accessed 2016. http://aqua.ucdavis.edu/DatabaseRoot/pdf/105FS.PDF

T

- Teutsch, Betsy. *100 under $100: One Hundred Tools for Empowering Global Women.* She Writes Press. China, 2015.
- ThePermacultureOrchard.com. *The Farm.* 2016. Web. Accessed 2016. http://www.permacultureorchard.com/the-farm/
- The Corporation of the Town of Cobalt. *Ragged Chutes: A Modern Wonder.* 2016. Web. Accessed 2016. https://cobalt.ca/ragged-chutes/
- The Pennsylvania State University. *Inoculation of Legumes for Maximum Nitrogen Fixation.* Penn State College of Agricultural Sciences. 2016. Accessed 2016. http://extension.psu.edu/plants/crops/forages/successful-forage-establishment/inoculation-of-legumes-for-maximum-nitrogen-fixation
- *The Salatin Semester.* DVD Course & Book set. Verge Permaculture/Acres USA. 2016. http://salatinsemester.com
- The Urban Homestead. *By the Numbers.* UrbanHomestead.org. web. 2016. Accessed 2016. http://urbanhomestead.org/about/by-the-numbers/
- The World Bank. *Loess Plateau Watershed Rehabilitation Project.* 2011. Accessed 2016. http://projects.worldbank.org/P003540/loess-plateau-watershed-rehabilitation-project?lang=en
- Toensmeier, Eric. *Paradise Lot.* Chelsea Green, 2013.
- Toensmeier, Eric. *The Carbon Farming Solution.* Chelsea Green, 2016.
- Trump, Chris. *Chris Trump Youtube Channel* video archive. Accessed 2018.

U-V-W

- *Water Powered "Air Compressor and Water Pump". The "Trompe Hammer", Trompe and Water Ram.* Account: MrTeslonian. web. 2015. youtube.com. Accessed 2016. https://www.youtube.com/watch?v=xv1lQA-tnwo
- Weiss, Zachary. *Elemental Ecology.* Permaculture Voices: PV3. Conference. March 2016.
- Weiss, Zachary. *Email.* Email to Matt Powers. Oct 8 2016.
- *What is EM?* EMRO.com, Okinawa, Japan. Published 2016. Accessed 2018. https://emrojapan.com/what/
- Wisner, Erica and Ernie. *The Rocket Mass Heater Builder's Guide.* New Society Publishers, 2016.
- Wisner, Ernie. *Email.* Feb 13 2016.
- Wood, A.D., and Richardson, E.V. Design of Small Storage and Erosion Control Dams. Department of Civil Engineering. Colorado State University. 1975. Accessed 2016. https://dspace.library.colostate.edu/bitstream/handle/10217/52669/CER_Wood.pdf?sequence=1
- *Woody Agriculture - Breeding Trees, Restoring a Piece of America's Past and Establishing a Piece of Our Agricultural Future with Phil Rutter - Part 1 of 2 (PVP057).* Permaculture Voices. iTunes and Soundcloud Podcast. Posted 2015. Accessed 2015. http://www.permaculturevoices.com/woody-agriculture-breeding-trees-

restoring-a-piece-of-americas-past-and-establishing-a-piece-of-our-agricultural-future-with-phil-rutter-part-1-pvp057/
- Wright, Sara F; Nichols, Kristine A. *Glomalin: Hiding place for a third of the world's stored soil carbon.* Agricultural Research; Washington (Sep 2002). http://search.proquest.com/openview/32cd9540e48f8e2ace82786043736c1c/1?pq-origsite=gscholar&cbl=42132
- Wuerthner, George. *Climate Change and Livestock Grazing.* Counterpunch.org. Counter Punch, 04 Oct. 2015. Web. 28 Oct. 2016. http://www.counterpunch.org/2015/02/06/climate-change-and-livestock-grazing/#_edn3

X-Y

- Yeomans, Allan J. *Priority One: Together We Can Beat Global Warming.* Keyline Publishing Co., Australia. 2005.
- Yeomans, PA. *The Challenge of Landscape.* Keyline Publishing Pty. Limited. 1958. Soil and Health Library. Web. n.d. Accessed 2016. http://soilandhealth.org/wp-content/uploads/01aglibrary/010126yeomansII/010126ch4.html

Z

- Zeedyk, Bill. *2013 Quivira Conference, Bill Zeedyk.* Youtube.com. Web. Accessed 2016. https://www.youtube.com/watch?v=V3d85D4xlbA
- Zeedyk, Bill. *Understanding Slope Wetlands.* Slides from Quivira 2014 Conference. Zeedyk Ecological Consulting, LLC. Web. Accessed 2016. http://quiviracoalition.org/images/pdfs/5908-Zeedyk_1%2520and%25202.pdf

Index

A
aerobic **48, 57, 62, 82, 125, 147**
anaerobic **48, 57, 63, 64, 82**
artificial reefs **130-131**
aspect **16, 17, 23, 119**

B
biochar **31, 32, 47, 48, 54, 60-62, 64**
biodigester **146**
biofuel **131, 146**
biogas **146-147**
biological farming **118-119**
bokashi **54, 59, 64-66**
breeding, plant **109-110**
Brittleness Scale **6**
BRIX meter **104, 107**
Burlese Funnel **132**

C
carbon farming **125-126**
carbon sequestration **41, 61, 99, 119-120, 131, 137**
chinampas **82, 83, 88, 129**
chop and drop **120, 134, 135**
climate analog **6, 7, 27, 117**
coast **5, 15, 66, 119, 130, 131, 133**
cob **53, 148, 149**
compassion **163, 168**
compost (see thermophilic, mouldering, or vermicompost)
compost extract *(humic acid)* **59**
compost tea **57-61, 65, 82, 89, 95, 101**
compost toilet **54**
contour **11, 12, 18-21, 35, 37-42, 49, 82, 88, 91, 93**
cooperatives/co-ops **158**
cover crop **60**
crop rotation **60, 103-105, 111**

D
dams **9, 12, 13, 15, 29, 30, 32, 35, 41-46, 52, 53**
desert **5, 6, 15, 38, 54, 61, 133-135**
desertification **6, 38, 61, 95, 113, 133, 137**
diversion banks and drains **35, 39, 80, 81, 89**
dry farming **94-95, 101-102**

E
earthbagging **141, 149**
earth-sheltered greenhouses and homes **83, 141**
earthworm **30, 56, 57**
espalier **90–91**
erosion **11, 34, 36, 37, 39, 45, 46, 49-51, 75, 78, 79, 81, 88, 121, 135**
ethics **2, 22, 34, 157**

evaporation **13, 42**

F
fence/fencing **17, 24, 41, 55, 60, 79, 81, 82, 90, 91, 113, 116**
freeboard **15, 42, 46**

G
gasification **139, 145, 146**
geothermal **139, 143**
grafting **88, 91-93**
graywater **24, 34, 35, 47, 48, 67, 142**
graze/grazing **17, 37, 59, 79, 81, 90, 113-116, 134**
greenhouse **24, 83, 85, 93, 96, 103, 111, 141, 143**
green manure **105, 111**

H
Hawaiian aquaculture **129**
holacracy **161, 162**
holistic management **23, 113, 114, 117, 137, 160**
hugelkultur **39, 58, 78, 100**
humid **38, 80, 85, 135**
humanure **48, 49, 61**

I
induce meandering **50, 51, 131**
irrigation **35, 38, 40, 47, 80, 81, 95, 103, 128, 142**

J
Jar Soil Test **28**

K
keyhole garden **100**

keyline **36, 39, 40, 41, 78, 82, 88, 94, 134, 135, 156**
keyway **49**
keypoint **40, 42, 134**
Koppen-Geiger **6-7**

L
land trust **158**
layers of a forest **91–93**
legumes **60, 73, 79, 85, 91, 105**
liquid culture **68, 70, 71, 76**

M
medicine/medicinal **7, 24, 67, 68, 71, 75-77, 85, 106, 136**
mediterranean **5, 14**
microclimate **6, 15, 53, 127**
mouldering compost **49, 57**
mudbrick **149**
mulch **27, 54, 60, 85, 87, 99–102, 109, 111, 125, 127**
mycelium **59, 65-68, 70, 71, 73-76, 122, 152**
mycoremediation **49, 50, 103**
mycorrhizae **54, 65, 73**

N
natural farming **54, 59, 65, 66, 97, 120, 121**
net and pan **39, 89**
NonViolent Communication **162, 163**
nursery **85, 93, 96, 99**

O
ocean **15, 119, 130, 135**
orientation **7, 16, 122, 126**

P
pasture cropping **105**
pH **32, 58, 62, 63, 101, 124**
pitfall trap **36–37**

plant guild **87, 137**
polyculture **79, 87, 88, 119, 121, 134, 135, 137, 159**
precipitation **3, 4, 8, 9, 12, 13, 15, 35, 42, 45**
pruning **85, 90–92, 120**

Q-R
rammed earth **141, 149**
refractometer **101**
restorative circles **163–164**
rewilding **6, 50**
riparian **50, 130**
ripping **36, 37, 39, 78, 79, 82, 156**
rocket mass heater **143-145, 149**
rocket stove **143-145**
rooting plants **85**
runoff, calculating annual **11, 15**

S
Salatin, Joel **24, 59, 113, 115–117, 132**
savanna **89, 121**
scarification **93**
seed balls **103–104**
seed saving **112-114**
sewage **47, 146**
slope **16, 17, 19, 24, 35, 37, 42, 45, 46, 78–81, 89, 129**
sociocracy **167–168**
soil food web **28, 31, 60, 65, 66, 93, 95, 119, 121, 135**
solar pump **146**
solar **17, 24, 83, 139-141, 143, 159**
spillway **15, 39, 42, 44-46, 80, 81**

spillway pipe **44**
stocking, fish **122, 127**
stratification **93, 108**
STUN method **100**
succession **23, 59, 85, 103, 114-116, 129, 135**
sun angle **7, 8**
swales **11, 35, 37, 39, 41, 57, 78–80, 88, 91, 133**
swimming pool, natural **134**

T
temperate climate **5, 61, 87, 123, 135, 149**
thermophilic (hot) compost **54–56, 58, 60, 67**
thermosiphon **146**
throw sow **97, 106, 120**
transplanting **93, 94, 99**
trickle pipe **44**
trompe **142**
tropics/tropical **5, 54, 61, 80, 121, 135, 149**

U-V
vermicompost **30, 62-63**
Veta La Palma **121, 132**

W
walipini **83, 141**
water harvesting **27, 332, 35, 36, 39, 79, 82, 102, 134, 135, 164**
water tanks **46–47**
water wheel **141-142**
watersheds **19, 24, 45, 134**
wetland **50, 82, 130–132, 135**
windbreak **14, 17, 24, 25, 80, 141**
wind power **14, 141**

XY
Yeomans **23, 36, 39, 40, 82**

Z
zones **24, 25, 27, 94, 124, 151, 154**

www.ingramcontent.com/pod-product-compliance
Lightning Source LLC
Chambersburg PA
CBHW080849020526
44118CB00037B/2321